LEARN TO
Drive

First published in 2003
Reprinted in 2004

A catalogue record for this book is available from the British Library

ISBN 1 85960 994 5

Published by Haynes Publishing, Sparkford,
Yeovil, Somerset BA22 7JJ, England

Tel: 01963 442030 Fax: 01963 440001
Int. tel: +44 1963 442030 Fax: +44 1963 440001
E-mail: sales@haynes-manuals.co.uk
Web site: www.haynes.co.uk

Haynes North America, Inc.,
861 Lawrence Drive, Newbury Park,
California 91320, USA

Printed and bound in England by J. H. Haynes & Co. Ltd, Sparkford

LEARN TO
Drive

Haynes

EVERYTHING YOU NEED TO PASS YOUR DRIVING TEST

- Theory Test
- Practical Test
- Official DSA Questions

ALL IN **ONE** BOOK

CONTENTS

INTRODUCTION

A driving licence is the most useful practical qualification you can have. It brings independence and social and career opportunities. It gives you the freedom to go where you want when you want, without relying on train or bus timetables or cadging lifts from friends or parents. It lets you experience things you could never see without having your own transport. But a driving licence also brings responsibilities, and that's why first of all you have to earn your licence by taking and passing a driving test.

Driving isn't so difficult – around half a million people pass their driving test each year. But it's a fact that over half of those who take their driving test fail. In most cases the reason is simply lack of preparation.

That's where this book comes in. *Learn To Drive* brings together all the information you need to pass your theory and practical driving tests. It's important to prepare for the two tests side by side. Despite their titles, you can't pass the practical driving test without a thorough knowledge of driving theory, and you'll struggle to succeed in the theory test without getting some practical driving experience under your belt first.

Learning to drive is a great adventure and it can be a lot of fun too. We hope this book helps to put you on the road towards a long and safe driving career.

01
FIRST STEPS

There's more to starting to drive than reaching your 17th birthday and jumping behind the wheel. You need to make sure you're licensed and insured to drive, and that you are legally supervised while on the road. You also need to think about your own fitness to drive, so get your eyesight checked and make sure you are physically and mentally prepared for the challenge of getting behind the wheel. As a first step, it's best to arrange some driving lessons to get you started. Even if you have access to the family car (and this is a good way to build up extra experience) you'll benefit from professional tuition too.

PREPARING FOR THE TEST

Being able to drive brings independence, freedom and exciting new work and social opportunities. Getting the driving licence that brings these benefits involves hard work, determination, and inevitably, money. Don't try to rush the process. Driving examiners complain that the main reason test candidates fail is lack of practice. Put in the time and effort to prepare really thoroughly for your test, and your investment will certainly be worthwhile.

learners and the law

As a learner driver using a car on public roads you must:

- be at least 17 years old (except if you receive the highest rate of mobility allowance when you may start learning at 16)
- hold a provisional driving licence
- have at least minimum insurance cover
- be accompanied by a supervising driver
- ensure that your car is roadworthy, taxed and if it is over three years old has a current MOT certificate
- display L-plates on your car front and rear
- not drive on motorways.

As a learner driver you are not allowed to use a motorway or drive without proper supervision

getting a driving licence

Driving licences are issued by the Driver and Vehicle Licensing Agency (DVLA). Apply using form D1 obtainable from the post office. The fee for a provisional licence is currently £38. (In Northern Ireland the licensing authority is Driver and Vehicle Licensing Northern Ireland.)

L-plates

The size, shape and colour of L-plates is laid down by law, so don't try to economise by making your own. Make sure the plates are positioned on the front and rear of the vehicle so they are clearly visible. Fix the plates to the car bodywork, not on the front or rear screen where they could obscure the driver's vision. Remove or cover the plates when someone who is not a learner is driving the car. In Wales a D-plate can take the place of an L-plate.

You must have a signed provisional driving licence before you can get behind the wheel as a learner

insurance

If you drive a friend's or relative's car make sure they check with their insurance company that you are insured to drive it. You must have at least the legal minimum of third party insurance cover. For more information about arranging insurance cover, as well as tax and MOT requirements, see p200.

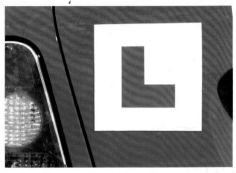

Fix L-plates where they can be clearly seen, but not where they might impair your own vision

You must pass your theory test before you are allowed to take the practical driving test

preparing for the test

There are two parts to the driving test – theory and practical.

The theory test is itself split into two elements. First is a touch-screen multiple-choice exam which takes 40 minutes. This is followed after a three-minute break by a video-clip based hazard perception test, which takes up to half an hour.

The practical test consists of a 40-minute drive accompanied by a driving examiner.

You must pass the theory test before you can take your practical test. Despite this, it's not a good idea to put off starting to drive until you've passed your theory test. The theory element of the test will make much more sense – and be a lot easier to master – if you can relate it to the real experience of driving on the road.

Driving test procedure is covered in detail in chapter 14.

driving lessons

Driving lessons may seem expensive but there is no substitute for expert one-to-one tuition. If you have access to a family or friend's car, this can be a useful way of getting extra experience behind the wheel. But it makes sense to start out under the expert supervision of an Approved Driving Instructor (ADI). Once your instructor is happy that you've mastered the basics of car control, then you can think about getting extra practice sessions with a friend or relative supervising. Practice is the key to passing the driving test: the more miles you cover before taking your test, the greater the variety of driving situations you'll encounter and the less likely it is that you will be caught out by an unfamiliar situation during your test.

choosing an instructor

Only an Approved Driving Instructor (ADI) registered with the Driving Standards Agency (DSA) can accept money in return for giving driving lessons. All ADIs have to pass a strict driving test and they undergo regular assessments. However, as with all teachers, some are better than others.

The DSA grades driving instructors. A grade 4 ADI is classed as competent, grade 5 is good and grade 6 is a very high standard. All ADIs must display a green certificate on the windscreen. Trainee driving instructors are permitted to give driving lessons, in which case the certificate they display is pink instead of green.

As well as looking at your instructor's qualifications, it's just as important to choose one who you get along with and have confidence in. Ask friends who have been preparing for the test if they know an instructor who they would recommend.

practice makes perfect

Get in as much practice as you can in the run up to your driving test. Try to experience as many different driving situations as possible: drive in the country as well as in town, on dual carriageways, at night and in wet weather. Thoroughly practise the reversing manoeuvres required in the driving test (but don't spend too much time reversing round the same quiet back streets or you may irritate local residents).

Fully-qualified Approved Driving Instructors are allowed to display a green certificate in their car windscreen (top); Trainee Driving Instructors are also authorised to give tuition to learners, and they display a pink certificate (bottom)

You may find it helpful to use a Driver's Record. Fill it in to keep track of the topics you've covered in your lessons, and it will give you an idea of your progress towards the test. Driver's Records are available from your ADI or local practical driving test centre

Most test failures are caused by lack of practice, so get in as much driving as you can before your test

IT'S THE LAW

SUPERVISORS

By law the person who supervises you when you are learning to drive must:

- be at least 21 years old
- hold a full driving licence for the type of car being driven (a licence valid for cars with automatic transmissions isn't adequate if the car being driven is a manual)
- have held their driving licence for at least three years.

01 FIT TO DRIVE

Driving a car demands a high degree of alertness, concentration, quick reactions and a sober, safety-conscious state of mind. Many forms of illness or disability, alcohol or drug use, or simply tiredness can affect your ability to the point where you are not safe to be on the road. Remember: it doesn't matter how important it seems to get to a job appointment or friend's party – if you're not fit to drive, stay off the road.

You must by law contact the DVLA if you develop a serious illness which may affect your driving

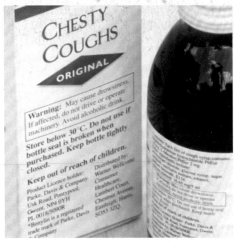

Even everyday medicines can impair your ability to drive, so always check the packet for warnings

health and safety

How you feel affects how you drive. If you develop a serious illness (see *It's the law* overleaf) then you must inform the DVLA. This won't necessarily mean you'll lose your licence, but the DVLA may ask you to undergo a medical check-up to ensure you are still fit to drive.

Less serious medical problems can also affect your safety behind the wheel. Even a severe cold or flu can lower your concentration and reactions and make you unfit to drive. If you're feeling unwell enough to need medication, then ask yourself if you are really fit enough to drive.

medicines

Many medicines can affect your ability to drive. Some of these are available without a prescription across the counter at a chemists.

Certain drugs prescribed to treat depression cause drowsiness and impair concentration. Driving should be avoided while taking these and for some months afterwards. Some tranquillisers and sleeping pills have similar side-effects.

Drugs available at a chemists without a prescription which impair driving include certain hayfever treatments and cold remedies. These can reduce concentration, slow reaction times and promote drowsiness, and they make driving particularly dangerous when taken with any amount of alcohol.

Whenever you take a medicine, carefully check the label for a warning – sometimes not as prominent as it might be – that you should not drive while using it. If prescribed a drug by your doctor, always ask if it will affect your driving.

If you drive to the pub, either don't drink any alcohol at all, or arrange to go home by taxi

alcohol

Drinking and driving don't mix. It's a message that has been rammed home by endless publicity campaigns in the last 25 years, but still around one in five drivers killed on the road is under the influence of alcohol.

When a driver has been drinking alcohol it makes them less in control of their vehicle, slows their reactions and impairs their ability to concentrate and judge speed accurately. It also gives them a false sense of confidence which can lead them to take dangerous risks.

The police treat drink-driving very seriously. Drivers involved in an accident are now routinely breathalysed; if convicted they face at least a one-year driving ban, as well as higher insurance premiums when they get back on the road.

Remember:

- you must not drive if your breath alcohol level is higher than 35µg per 100ml (equivalent to a blood-alcohol level of 80mg per 100ml)
- alcohol takes time to be broken down by the body and if you have had a heavy night's drinking session the chances are that you will still be over the limit the next morning
- any amount of alcohol impairs your ability to drive safely, even if you're still under the legal limit. So if you plan to drink anything at all, the safest option is to leave your car at home.

Don't mix driving with drugs or alcohol: it's dangerous, illegal and the penalties are severe

Pay a visit to an optician and get your eyesight checked before you start learning to drive

illegal drugs

Outlawed drugs such as cannabis, ecstasy, cocaine and heroin have the potential to impair your driving and it is an offence to drive under their influence. The police are cracking down on drug-driving and introducing roadside tests to identify drivers who are under the influence of drugs.

eyesight

You must be able to read the current style of numberplate (introduced in September 2001) at a distance of 20 metres (66 feet). If you need to wear contact lenses or spectacles to do this then you must wear them at all times when driving (it makes sense to keep spares in the car too, in case you lose or damage your usual pair). Other eye defects such as tunnel vision can also affect your driving so it's a good idea to take a full eye test before you start to learn, and again at regular intervals throughout your driving career.

IT'S THE LAW

FIT TO DRIVE?

You must by law inform the DVLA if you suffer any of the following:

- epilepsy
- giddiness, fainting or blackouts
- a severe mental handicap
- diabetes
- heart pain while driving
- Parkinson's disease
- any chronic neurological condition
- a serious memory problem

- a stroke
- brain surgery, a brain tumour or a severe head injury
- severe psychiatric illness or mental disorder
- long-term problems with your arms or legs
- dependence on alcohol or drugs or chemical substances in the past three years
- any visual disability which affects both eyes (not short/long sightedness or colour blindness)
- have a pacemaker, defibrillator or anti-ventricular tachycardia device fitted.

02
BEHIND THE WHEEL

You've signed your provisional licence, you're sitting in a roadworthy car with a lawful supervisor beside you, you've checked your eyesight and health and you can't wait to start the engine and head off down the road. But try to be patient. You're in a complex piece of machinery and before you go anywhere you need to take a good look around and make sure you know exactly what all those switches do, how the controls work and what the warning lights mean. Remember, you could run into a patch of fog for the first time in the middle of your driving test – and the examiner won't be impressed if you have to search high and low to locate the switch that works the foglights.

speedometer

On British cars the speedometer shows both miles per hour (mph) and kilometres per hour (km/h). The kilometre scale is marked in smaller figures on the inner ring of the dial and should be ignored unless the car is driven overseas. A few cars have digital speedometers, which are actually less convenient to read. It is a legal requirement to have a working speedometer and it must not show a reading lower than the actual speed. If you ever fit a different size of wheel or tyre, you should get the speedometer checked as doing so may affect its accuracy.

fuel gauge

The fuel gauge gives a rough indication of how much fuel remains in the fuel tank. As this reaches the lower limit a fuel warning light may illuminate, indicating that only a few litres (check the car handbook for the exact amount) of fuel remains.

water temperature gauge

Until it is thoroughly warm the engine does not operate efficiently. Avoid working the engine hard until the dial reaches its normal working temperature, or you will waste fuel and cause extra engine wear.

The instrument panel is fitted with dials and warning lights which give you visual information while you drive. Only a few dials – such as the speedometer and fuel gauge – are truly essential. Some car makers deliberately keep the instrument panel simple to minimise distraction, and rely on warning lights to alert the driver if something goes wrong. Others take the view that the more information the driver has the better, and add a profusion of extra dials. Whatever is fitted to the car you're driving, you must make sure you know what all the dials and warning lights mean before driving off.

rev counter

Many cars are fitted with a rev counter (or tachometer) which shows the engine speed in revolutions per minute (rpm). Most engines tick over at around 1000rpm. The maximum engine speed permitted is usually indicated by a red line, marked on the dial at around 6000–7000rpm on a petrol engine. (Most cars also have a rev limiter which prevents the engine running too fast.)

other gauges

Additional gauges may be fitted to indicate oil temperature, oil pressure and battery charge. In some cars a trip computer gives a digital read-out of information including fuel consumption, journey time and average speed, and the distance the car will be able to cover on the fuel remaining (bear in mind that if fuel consumption increases, for instance by joining a motorway, this figure may drop alarmingly). Before driving, consult the car handbook for a full explanation of all the gauges fitted.

warning lights

Warning lights are fitted to alert you to serious faults and remind you about items which are switched on.

Lights monitoring your car's systems (such as the ignition, oil and ABS lights) should come on when you turn on the ignition, then extinguish. If they come on while you are driving, stop the car and investigate.

Reminder lights (such fog lamps, heated rear window, headlight main beam) will illuminate when these items are in use.

other lights

Depending on the make or model of car there may be extra warning lights in addition to those explained here. These include low windscreen washer fluid level, service needed, clogged fuel filter, immobiliser fault and fasten seat belt reminder. Make sure that you know what all the warning lights in your car mean. If a light comes on that you don't recognise, stop at the first safe opportunity and consult your car handbook to see if it is safe to continue.

oil pressure
If this light comes on when driving it means the oil pressure is low. Stop as soon as possible to avoid serious engine damage. Check the oil level and top up if necessary, but do not drive if the light stays on.

ignition
If lit when the engine is running this indicates there is a problem with the battery charging system.

water (coolant) temperature/level
If lit when the engine is running the engine is overheating or water level is low. Stop as soon as possible and investigate.

ABS
If this lights up when driving it indicates a problem with the anti-lock brakes (see p46). Stop and consult the handbook to see if the car is still safe to drive, and get the braking system checked immediately.

handbrake/ brake warning
Make sure the parking brake is fully disengaged when the car is in motion. If this light comes on while driving, it may indicate low brake fluid or a serious brake fault: stop and consult the handbook.

door/boot open
Warns if one of the doors or the boot is not shut properly.

left/right indicator
The warning light is accompanied by an audible ticking when the indicators are activated.

air bag
If this lights up when driving it indicates a fault with the airbag. Get the car professionally checked as soon as possible.

diesel pre-heating
Some diesel engines require pre-heating and will not start after turning on the ignition until this light goes out.

heated rear window
Lights while the heated rear window element is active.

hazard warning
There is an audible ticking as well as an in-car flashing light when the hazard warning lights are operating (see p58 for advice on when to use them).

side/headlamp on
Reminds that these lights are switched on.

headlamp main beam
Warns that headlamps are on main beam setting which may dazzle other road users.

fog light
Reminds that the rear fog lamp is switched on. There may be a separate warning light for front fog lamps if fitted (see p190 for advice on using fog lights).

choke warning
In older cars only, this reminds that the manual choke is out (see p27 for how to use the choke).

All cars have lights, wipers, a horn and a heater. But the switches which operate them may be located in different places depending on the model of car. There may be a confusing variety of extra switchgear too. Some cars now have wipers and headlamps which work automatically, radar to help you park and even an electronic voice to guide you to your destination using satellite navigation. Your driving instructor's car may not feature such refinements, but you must be prepared to cope with unusual switches whenever you get into an unfamiliar car. Before driving off you must know where each switch is, so when you need to sound the horn, flash the headlamps or flick on your windscreen wipers, you can do so instantly without having to take your eyes off the road.

windscreen wipers

These are usually activated by the right-hand stalk. Most offer a choice of intermittent, slow and fast settings. It is often possible to change the wiping frequency on the intermittent setting. Some cars have an automatic setting for rain-sensing windscreen wipers, but you should be prepared to override this if necessary.

windscreen washers

The windscreen washer jets are activated by pulling the stalk or pressing the end of it. Use them to clean mud or spray off the windscreen. Using the washers should automatically trigger several passes of the wipers to clear the windscreen.

rear wiper/washer

Most hatchback and estate cars have a rear wiper and washer which should be used whenever rear visibility becomes obscured by dust or spray on the back window. Usually the switch for the rear wiper and washer is on the same stalk that operates the front windscreen wipers.

lights

In most cars the lights are switched on by rotating the left-hand stalk. The first setting switches on the rear lights, number plate lights, and side lights (or dim-dip headlights if fitted). In the second position the dipped headlights come on. For main beam, move the stalk either backwards or forwards.

direction indicators

Press the left-hand stalk up to activate the right indicators, down for the left indicators. The indicators are self-cancelling, and should stop automatically when you have turned a corner. In a few models the indicator stalk is on the right of the steering wheel and the wiper stalk on the left.

25

heating and ventilation

Basic heating/ventilation systems have a fan, a dial to control the temperature and another to direct the airflow onto the feet, face, or windscreen.

If fitted, air conditioning is useful for providing cooling air in hot weather (the windows must be kept shut to allow it to work effectively). Air conditioning also helps keep the windows free of mist in wet weather. Run the system regularly to keep it working properly.

Where fitted, climate control allows you to select a temperature at which the interior of the car will be automatically maintained whatever the weather outside.

Air recirculation shuts off air entering from outside and recirculates the air already in the car. This is useful when starting in icy conditions, as the inside of the car heats up more quickly with no cold air coming in. You can also use it to prevent unpleasant smells and exhaust fumes entering the cabin. But don't leave air recirculation on for too long: it makes the windows more prone to misting up, and the lack of fresh air can make you sleepy.

The heated rear window keeps the rear screen clear of mist and ice. Do not leave the rear screen heater on once the screen is clear as it drains a lot of power from the battery. Some models also have a front screen heating element.

For maximum demisting, select the highest temperature and fan setting, direct the airflow to the windscreen, and switch the screen heaters on.

Make sure you know how to set the heating to its maximum setting for demisting the windscreen

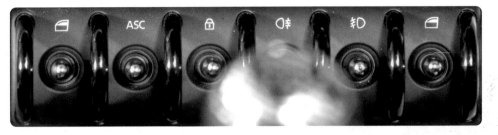

headlamp adjustment

This adjusts the angle of the dipped headlamp beam to prevent it dazzling other road users when the car is heavily laden (see p211).

fog lights

Cars must by law have at least one rear fog lamp. Front fog lamps are optional (see p190 for advice on using fog lights).

electric windows

Use this switch to lower or raise the windows. Some feature one-touch operation. Where rear windows are electric, there may be a switch which you can use to deactivate them when young children are in the rear seats. Some cars have an electrically operated sunroof with switches usually located above the mirror.

horn

Usually sounded by pressing part of the centre of the steering wheel. Make sure you know where the horn is before you have to use it in an emergency.

central locking

Locks and unlocks the doors independently of the keyfob.

traction/skid control

Abbreviations such as TSC, ASC or ESP refer to traction/skid control systems (see p195). Where fitted, it may be possible to switch off traction/skid control, but it is safer to leave it permanently engaged.

cruise control

This allows the driver to set a constant speed at which the car cruises automatically. If fitted, use cruise control only in light traffic and read the manual to make sure you fully understand how it works.

choke

Many older cars (from the mid-1980s or earlier) have a manual choke lever which needs to be pulled out before starting the car and for the first few miles of driving. Once the engine is warm make sure the choke is pushed all the way back in or fuel is wasted and engine damage may result.

other switches

Depending on the model, various other switches may be fitted. Always consult the car handbook for a full explanation of all the switches before driving.

Unlike the minor switchgear, the major controls are laid out in a similar fashion whatever the make of car. The pedals, from left to right, are the clutch, brake and accelerator, and they are in this order whether the car is right-hand drive (like a British car) or left-hand drive like those from mainland Europe. Operate the accelerator and brake with your right foot and the clutch with your left. In a right-hand drive car the gear lever is operated with the left hand, as is the parking brake which usually sits between the front seats.

steering wheel

Most cars have power-assisted steering which means less effort is needed to turn the wheel. A lever beneath the steering column may allow the position of the steering wheel to be adjusted up or down, and in or out. Most cars have a steering lock fitted as an anti-theft precaution. This means the steering locks into place if the wheel is turned without the key in the ignition. It may be necessary to jiggle the wheel to allow the key to be turned in the ignition to release it.

parking brake

The parking or handbrake is a lever, usually located between the front seats, which activates the rear brakes. Press the button in and pull it up to engage it: hold in the button and let it down to release it. If you pull the handbrake on without pressing the button the ratchet slips, causing a harsh noise and unnecessary wear. A few cars have foot-operated parking brakes which are engaged by pressing a pedal and released by a separate handle or button.

gear lever

Most cars have a gear lever next to the driver's left thigh, although in some the gear stick sprouts from the dashboard.

There will be five or six forward gears in addition to a reverse gear. The gears are laid out in an H pattern. The central bar of the H represents the neutral position, and when the lever is in this position no gear is selected. This means the engine can tick over without power being transmitted to the wheels.

Reverse gear is normally on a dog leg to the left or right. Often there's a device fitted to prevent reverse being selected by accident: depending on the model of car, you may have to lift a ring beneath the gear lever, or press the gear lever downwards, before reverse will engage.

Always fully depress the clutch pedal before engaging any gear.

You may need to lift the gear knob upwards or press it downwards to engage reverse gear

accelerator pedal

Pressing your right foot on the accelerator pedal (also called the gas pedal or throttle) increases the flow of fuel to the engine, giving extra power when you need to increase the speed of the car or climb hills. Light and gentle use of the accelerator improves fuel economy and ensures a smooth driving style.

brake pedal

Use your right foot to operate the brake pedal, which applies the brakes on all four wheels. On most cars the brakes are servo-assisted, which means no more than a gentle pressure is needed to slow the car. Pressing the brake pedal also operates the rear brake lights, giving a warning to following traffic that you are slowing.

how the clutch works

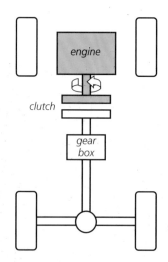

Clutch pedal fully depressed: the gear box is separated from the engine, no power is being transmitted to the wheels and the car is stationary

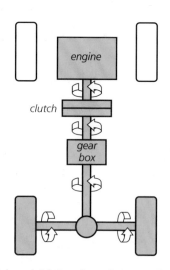

Clutch pedal fully released: the gear box is joined to the engine, power is being transmitted, to the wheels and the car is now in motion

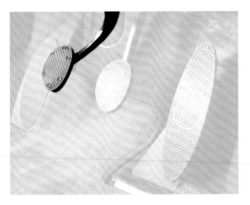

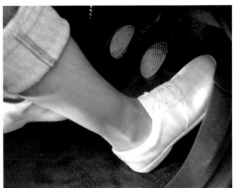

Wear sensible, flat-soled shoes when driving to prevent your feet slipping off the pedals

clutch pedal

The left-hand pedal in a manual car operates the clutch. When the clutch pedal is pressed down, it disconnects the engine from the wheels. This allows the car to stop without stalling the engine.

The clutch consists of a pair of friction plates which are pulled apart when the clutch pedal is pressed down.

As you let the clutch pedal up, the two plates touch and power starts to be transmitted to the wheels. This is termed the 'biting point'. The further you release the clutch pedal, the more power is transmitted. Once the clutch pedal is fully released the clutch plates lock together and all the power from the engine is delivered to the wheels. When you hold the pedal so the clutch is only half engaged, it is called 'slipping the clutch' or 'clutch control'. Clutch control is useful when you want to drive very slowly – for instance when carrying out low-speed manoeuvres – but you should take care not to slip the clutch for too long or premature wear to the clutch plates will result.

Never:
- rest your foot on the clutch pedal while you are driving as this causes unnecessary wear to the clutch mechanism
- hold the clutch at the biting point to prevent the car from rolling back on a slope. Always apply the handbrake when you come to a halt on a hill.

KNOW THE CODE

HIGHWAY CODE RULE 102

Coasting. This term describes a vehicle travelling in neutral or with the clutch pressed down. Do not coast, whatever the driving conditions. It reduces driver control because:
- engine braking is eliminated
- vehicle speed downhill will increase quickly
- increased use of the footbrake can reduce its effectiveness
- steering response will be affected particularly on bends and corners
- it may be more difficult to select the appropriate gear when needed.

SAFETY CHECKS

Airline pilots carry out a detailed routine of instrument checks before they even think of heading for the runway. Driving a car doesn't involve quite such a complex cockpit drill, but it is essential that you always run through a short series of checks to ensure that you are sitting comfortably and safely before driving off. Get in the habit of carrying out these checks every time you get into the car.

cockpit drill

Before turning the key in the ignition, you must always:

- check that the doors and boot are fully closed
- adjust your seat and steering wheel to give you the correct driving position
- check that your head restraint is in the right position
- put on your seatbelt
- check your mirrors are properly adjusted
- check the handbrake is on
- ensure the gear lever is in neutral (or in Park [P] or Neutral [N] in an automatic).

sitting comfortably

Finding a comfortable driving position is vital. You need to be able to reach all the controls without stretching. At the same time you don't want to sit too close to the wheel – which could be dangerous in a crash – or adopt an awkward posture which will put a stain on your back. Follow these steps to achieve a comfortable driving position:

- raise the seat as high as possible without your head making contact with the roof
- move the seat forwards until you can easily depress the clutch pedal and accelerator fully
- tilt the base of the seat so that it provides support along the length of your thighs
- recline the seat back to the point where your shoulders and upper back are resting comfortably on the seat and your arms are slightly bent when you hold the steering wheel in the 'ten-to-two' position. Avoid sitting too upright, as this can put a strain on your wrists and shoulders as you lean forward to grip the wheel, or reclining too far back, as this means your neck muscles have to work harder to support your head

Adjust the seat and steering wheel to give yourself a comfortable driving position

- adjust the height and reach of the steering column so your hands are resting comfortably a little lower than your shoulders, and you can see the instrument panel clearly
- if fitted, lumbar support can give extra support for the lower part of your back and help prevent backache on a long journey. But too much lumbar support does more harm than good. Only if you feel a lack of support should you slowly turn the knob on the side of the seat back until you feel a slight, even pressure.

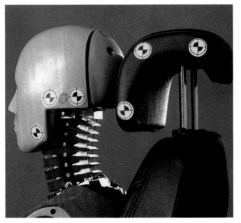

A correctly adjusted head restraint can significantly reduce the risk of neck injury in a crash

Adjust the door mirrors so that the side of your car can just be seen in the edge of the mirror

seatbelt

You must by law wear your seatbelt at all times while driving a car, except:

- when carrying out reversing manoeuvres
- if you have a medical exemption certificate.

Most cars have a seatbelt height adjuster on the door pillar by your right shoulder. Move this down until the belt gives a firm but not excessive pressure over the top of your right shoulder, with no gap between the belt and the front of your shoulder. Do not position the adjuster any lower than shoulder height.

head restraint

It's sometimes called a head rest, but it's not there to rest your head on. The head restraint performs an important safety function. If a vehicle collides with the rear of your car, your head may be jerked abruptly backwards, causing your neck to suffer whiplash injuries. The head restraint helps prevent this, but only if it is correctly adjusted, so check it before driving off. The base of the head restraint should be level with the base of your skull where it meets the top of the neck, and the restraint should be about an inch away from the back of your head while driving.

mirrors

Your mirrors should be positioned so that you can see what is happening behind you at a glance, without moving your head unnecessarily. Adjust the interior rear view mirror while you are in your normal driving position with your seatbelt fastened. A lever beneath the mirror shifts the angle of the mirror at night to reduce the glare from following headlamps (some cars have mirrors which react automatically to reduce glare at night). Side mirrors are adjustable from inside the car, either manually or by an electric switch. Adjust them so just a sliver of the side of the car is showing in the mirror, and there is a roughly equal proportion of road and sky visible.

handbrake

Check this is securely engaged by pulling the lever upwards slightly.

gears in neutral

Always check the gear lever is in neutral before starting the engine. If it is in gear then the engine will not start when you turn the key in the ignition. Instead, the car will lurch forwards (or backwards if it is in reverse gear), causing a potential hazard.

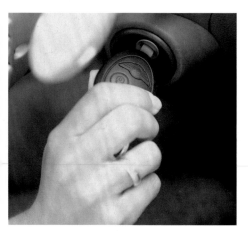

Twist the key all the way to start the engine but remember to release it the instant the engine fires

A growing number of cars now have keyless ignition with a separate starter button

starting the engine

The ignition switch usually has four positions:

0: the ignition is switched off
I: disengages the steering lock and operates some electrical systems, such as the radio
II: turns on the ignition and activates the warning lights and dials
III: activates the starter motor.

To start the engine, turn the key all the way to position III. You will hear a whirr as the starter motor activates and turns the engine. Release the key as soon as the engine fires or the starter motor may be damaged. The switch is spring loaded so the key returns to position II automatically.

Some cars have an ignition card instead of a key; in this case a push button activates the starter motor.

In a modern car fitted with fuel-injection you do not need to touch the accelerator pedal while starting the engine (though this may be necessary with older vehicles).

When the engine starts, let it settle to a steady tickover. Make sure the ignition and oil pressure lights have gone out.

Once started the engine should settle to a steady tickover at around 1000rpm (revs per minute)

03
CAR CONTROL

Mastering the car's main controls is the first step in learning to drive. It's a lot easier than it used to be because today's cars have light, smooth controls designed for ease of use. Power steering is fitted to just about all new cars, taking the effort out of turning the wheel even in tight parking spaces. Brakes are servo-assisted and need only a light pressure to bring the car to a swift halt. It can take a bit longer to get the knack of clutch control and smooth gearchanging, but this too should soon become second nature.

03

MOVING OFF

Turning a stationary car into a moving one demands careful co-ordination of clutch and accelerator pedals. Everyone takes a bit of time to master this, and you can expect your fair share of jerky starts and the occasional stall. Don't despair – keep practising and you'll soon get the hang of it. In these early days of driving you can't expect to be in full control of the car, so it's best to start out on a quiet, clear piece of road, with an experienced driving instructor sitting beside you.

moving off on the level

- push the clutch pedal to the floor
- engage first gear
- press the accelerator pedal gently until the engine revs rise
- let the clutch up gradually until you can feel the biting point
- release the handbrake
- bring the clutch pedal smoothly upwards while gradually increasing the pressure on the accelerator.

Extra power is needed to prevent the engine stalling when you are moving off uphill

stalling

If you bring up the clutch too quickly or don't apply enough power, the engine may cut out. This is called stalling. A common reason for stalling is trying to start in third gear instead of first by mistake – so check that you're in the right gear before you try again to move off after stalling.

moving off at an angle

Often you need to move off and at the same time steer round an obstacle such as a parked car. This means moving off very slowly to give yourself time to check all around your car while you pull out. To do this you need to use clutch control: lift the clutch pedal just past the biting point and press on the accelerator until the car starts to creep forward. Keep looking all around for other vehicles, pedestrians or cyclists as you pull out.

hill starts

Uphill Moving off uphill needs more power to prevent the engine stalling. It's vital not to let the car roll backwards, which could be dangerous. To hold the car steady, press more firmly on the accelerator and hold the clutch a little further past the biting point than you would on the level. After releasing the handbrake, apply a little more power to move off while releasing the clutch fully.

Downhill Keep your right foot on the brake, not the accelerator. Find the clutch biting point, release the handbrake, then ease off the brake pedal. As the car rolls forward, release the clutch fully and apply some power. On a steep downhill slope, moving off in second gear instead of first can give a smoother start.

TEST TIPS

DO

- remember to carry out the cockpit drill (p32-5) before moving off at the start of your test
- stay cool if you stall the engine. This isn't normally considered a serious fault – but if you panic, restart the engine and drive off without rechecking your mirrors and blind spot, it will be

DON'T

- let the car roll back on a hill start
- block the path of oncoming traffic when pulling out from behind a parked car on a narrow road.

CHANGING GEAR

If you've ridden a bicycle fitted with gears you'll understand the effect that choice of gear has on speed, as well as on the amount of work the rider has to do. Try to move off in too high a gear and you'll struggle to turn the pedals. Stay in a low gear on a level stretch of road and you'll find yourself pedalling furiously for no extra forward velocity. It's the same in a car, except that the engine does the work instead of the rider. The low gears provide lots of acceleration but run out of steam before the car is travelling very quickly. Higher gears provide plenty of road speed, but not much acceleration. Your job is to match the gears to the speed of the car, moving up the gearbox as your speed rises, and to select a lower gear when more power is needed, for instance when overtaking or approaching a steep hill.

It can be easier to select the right gear if you cup your palm round the gear knob on the opposite side to the gear you want, rather than placing your hand directly on top of the gear knob

how to change gear

- release the accelerator pedal and at the same time press down the clutch to disengage the engine from the gearbox
- cup your hand around the gearknob and move the lever gently but positively from one position to another
- re-engage the clutch and simultaneously apply the power.

Although it sounds straightforward, changing gear requires careful co-ordination of foot and hand movements, so don't be surprised if your gear changes feel clumsy at first. Practice makes perfect, and by the time you are ready for your test you should not be having to concentrate to make smooth gear changes.

Don't use unnecessary force when changing gear. Ease the lever from one position to another, and try not to rush your changes.

To make even smoother changes down the gearbox, keep your foot slightly on the accelerator as you shift the gear lever. The engine revs rise to match the gear selected – which means that with practice you can make your changes down the gearbox almost seamless.

selecting the right gear

You don't have to use the gears in exact sequence. Where appropriate, you can skip a gear, which is called 'block changing'. For instance, when overtaking a slower vehicle you might accelerate in third gear from 40mph to 60mph, then change directly from third into fifth once you are safely past.

When approaching a hazard such as a road junction or roundabout, you should first reduce your speed, then select the appropriate gear to negotiate the hazard. This may mean changing directly from fifth gear into second gear. Changing sequentially down through the gear box in this situation would be pointless, making your progress less smooth and causing unnecessary clutch wear.

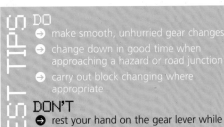

TEST TIPS

DO
- make smooth, unhurried gear changes
- change down in good time when approaching a hazard or road junction
- carry out block changing where appropriate

DON'T
- rest your hand on the gear lever while not changing gear
- look at the gear lever while changing gear: keep your eyes on the road
- race the engine unnecessarily, especially in the lower gears
- coast when approaching a hazard (see *Know the Code* p31).

03
AUTOMATICS

Don't ignore this section just because you're preparing for the test in a manual car – you are sure to find yourself behind the wheel of an automatic at some stage in your driving career. Automatic transmissions have always been less popular than manuals for three reasons: they give less precise control over gear selection, they are thirstier on fuel and they add extra cost to a new car. But automatics are getting increasingly sophisticated and economical. Don't be surprised if in 20 years time a manual gearbox has become an unusual option and automatics are the norm.

taking your test

It makes a lot of sense to take your test in a manual even if you intend to drive an automatic, because passing in a manual qualifies you to drive both manual and automatic cars. If you pass in a car which isn't fitted with a clutch pedal, your licence won't cover driving a manual.

how an auto works

In an automatic there are just two pedals – the accelerator and brake. When the transmission is put into Drive (D) the car changes gears automatically according to the load on the engine and the road speed. Most autos have four or five gears. A CVT automatic uses pulleys and belts to change the gearing continuously, giving a smoother drive and better economy.

Semi-automatic transmissions are becoming more common. The simplest have a manual gear shift but no clutch pedal – the clutch is operated automatically as you engage a gear. More sophisticated paddle-operated systems are available on high-performance cars. Consult the handbook carefully before driving one of these.

Semi-automatic transmissions are becoming more popular; they give all the control of a manual without the effort of operating a clutch pedal

driving an automatic

Automatic transmissions vary from car to car, so it's important to read the handbook to get the best out of each system. In general, follow this advice:

- check the gear shift is in Park (P) and your foot firmly on the brake pedal before trying to start the ignition. Most autos are designed not to start unless these precautions are taken

- when you are ready to drive away, move the lever out of Park and into Drive (D). To do this you will need to push in the security button mounted on the gear lever. Hold down the footbrake as the car will try to creep forward as soon as Drive is engaged

- do not use your left foot for braking. You could confuse which foot you should be using if you have to brake in an emergency

- when coming to a brief halt, for instance at traffic lights, there is no need to move the gear shift out of Drive, but you must always use the parking brake to ensure the car is safely immobilised

- if you need to accelerate quickly while the gearbox is in Drive, for instance to overtake another vehicle, press down firmly on the accelerator. This causes the gearbox to kick down automatically to a lower gear

- on steep downhill sections engage a lower gear manually to give extra engine braking. The lower gears are marked with numbers equivalent to the intermediate gears on a manual (first gear is sometimes marked L for Low). You should also select these positions to give extra control over the gears when overtaking or cornering, in heavy traffic, or to stop the gearbox changing gear unnecessarily when climbing uphill

- on stopping the car at the end of the journey, put the gear shift into Park and engage the parking brake before switching off the ignition.

Turning the steering wheel causes the front wheels to change direction, which makes the car alter course. But because only the front wheels do the steering, you must remember to leave extra room on tight turns to stop the rear wheels clipping the kerb. Just about every car on sale nowadays has power-assisted steering, which is light and easy to use. If you drive a car without power assistance you will find it needs much more effort to turn the wheel at low speeds and when parking.

holding the wheel

Imagine the steering wheel is a clock face and keep your hands in the 'ten-to-two' or 'quarter-to-three' position, whichever you find more comfortable. Grasp the wheel firmly but not tightly and keep both hands on the wheel except when you have to take one hand off to operate another control. Never take both hands off the wheel while you are driving.

turning the wheel

For small steering movements you can keep your hands in the ten-to-two position. However, when turning a sharp corner you will need to feed the wheel smoothly through your hands. You should also do this as you straighten the wheel after a turn – allowing the wheel to spin back can lead to loss of control.

When turning the wheel, it's important to look in the direction that you want the car to turn. Looking where you want the car to go helps your brain to send the right messages to your arms and hands about just how much to turn the wheel and when to start straightening up.

TEST TIPS

DO
- keep both hands on the wheel
- steer smoothly, avoiding abrupt changes in direction

DON'T
- dry steer by turning the wheel when the car is stationary
- cut corners: remember to leave extra room when emerging from tight junctions to avoid the rear wheels touching the kerb.

dry steering

Turning the steering wheel when the car isn't moving is called dry steering. It's not a good idea because it puts unnecessary strain on the steering mechanism, and causes premature wear to the front tyres. When carrying out a low-speed manoeuvre, get the car moving before you start to steer.

steering lock

When you turn the steering wheel as far as it will go it is at full steering lock. This is the maximum angle the front wheels will reach, and on full lock the car's turning circle – the space it needs to turn around in the road – is at its smallest.

Avoid crossing your hands on the wheel – this could prevent you keeping control of the steering

The greater the steering lock, the easier it is to manoeuvre the car in and out of tight spaces

03

BRAKING

Modern cars have extremely effective brakes and you may be surprised when you carry out your first emergency stop just how powerful the brakes can be. But in everyday driving you should aim to use the brakes as little as possible by anticipating the need to slow down well in advance. Harsh, late braking is a sign of poor driving and it will not impress the examiner on your driving test.

using the brakes

Apply the brakes gently at first, then progressively increase the pressure. Never brake harshly, or you risk making the wheels 'lock up' – stop rotating – and the car will skid. Once the front wheels start skidding you lose the ability to steer the car and will not be able to avoid obstacles in the road ahead. Special care is needed when the roads are wet or icy as the risk of skidding becomes much higher.

Try to brake only when the car is travelling in a straight line. Tyres have a limited amount of grip. They can use this grip to help the car go around a corner, or to help it stop. If you ask your tyres to do both these things at once there may not be enough grip to go round, causing a skid.

anti-lock brakes

An anti-lock braking system (ABS) works electronically to prevent the wheels from locking up and skidding under emergency braking. This means that you can still steer the car, which you would not be able to do with the wheels locked.

ABS works by sensing when the wheels are on the point of locking up. At this point it releases the brakes momentarily and reapplies them, then repeats this cycle several times a second.

Even with ABS fitted it still takes longer to stop on a wet or slippery surface, and ABS may not prevent skidding on a loose surface or where there is standing water on the road.

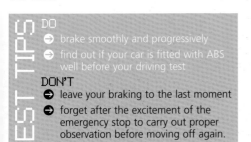

TEST TIPS

DO
- ➔ brake smoothly and progressively
- ➔ find out if your car is fitted with ABS well before your driving test

DON'T
- ➔ leave your braking to the last moment
- ➔ forget after the excitement of the emergency stop to carry out proper observation before moving off again.

emergency stop

You may be required to carry out an emergency stop during your driving test. The technique depends on whether or not your car is fitted with ABS.

Without ABS: Keep both hands firmly grasping the steering wheel. Brake firmly, but not so hard that the wheels lock up and you start to skid. If the wheels do lock, ease off the brake until they start to rotate again then reapply the brake less harshly. Press the clutch down just before you come to a halt to prevent the engine stalling.

With ABS: Keep both hands firmly grasping the steering wheel. Press as hard as you can on the brake pedal and keep full pressure applied until you come to a stop. Don't be put off by any noise or pulsating sensation you feel through the brake pedal – this is a normal feature of ABS. Press the clutch down just before you come to a halt to prevent the engine stalling.

brake fade

Overuse of the brakes can cause them to overheat and lose efficiency – known as brake fade. This is most likely when driving down a steep hill, when heavily laden or towing, or if the brakes are worn. If brake fade occurs, stop and let the brakes cool before continuing, and get the braking system checked as soon as possible.

engine braking

When you lift off the accelerator the engine slows the car even if you don't put your foot on the brake pedal. Engine braking is hardly noticeable in top gear, but in the lower ratios it is much more effective. Make use of engine braking by selecting a lower gear to give more control when descending a steep hill.

handbrake

Apply the handbrake to secure the car whenever you are stationary for more than a few seconds. The handbrake should never be used while the car is moving.

STOPPING

There's more to stopping than just pressing the brake pedal and bringing the car to a halt. First you have to select a suitable place to stop, where you won't be endangering or inconveniencing any other road users.

stopping

When stopping at the side of the road, you should aim to pull up close and parallel to the side of the road.

To do this, lift off the power and gently steer towards the kerb, braking smoothly and progressively as you do so. As you get near to the kerb, steer away from it and then straighten the steering wheel. Just before the car stops, press the clutch pedal down to prevent the engine stalling. Easing off the brake pedal as you come to a halt will prevent the car stopping with a jerk.

Avoid letting the wheels touch the kerb as this might damage the wheels and tyres.

where to stop

During your test your examiner will ask you to pull up at a convenient place on the left to carry out a manoeuvre. This doesn't necessarily mean you are expected to pull immediately to the side of the road. You must use your judgement to select an appropriate place to stop where you will not be endangering, inconveniencing or obstructing anyone.

Don't stop or park:

- near a school entrance
- where you would prevent emergency access
- at or near a bus stop or taxi rank
- on the approach to a level crossing
- opposite or within ten metres of a junction
- near the brow of a hill or hump bridge
- opposite a traffic island
- opposite another parked vehicle if it would cause an obstruction
- where you would force other traffic to enter a tram lane
- where the kerb has been lowered to help wheelchair users
- in front of an entrance to a property
- on a bend.

Places where you must not stop include level crossings (left) and school entrances (right)

04
READING THE ROAD

When you start to drive you may be surprised by
how much information there is on the road to
help you drive safely. Road markings and signs
warn of a whole range of hazards as well as
giving you instructions and information. Then
there are the signals coming from other drivers.
Their indicators, brake lights and even how they
position themselves on the road tell you a lot
about what they are going to do. And at the
same time you need to communicate to
everyone else what you intend to do by giving
clear and accurate signals yourself.

MIRRORS

You need to use your mirrors to observe what is happening all around your car. Modern cars have three mirrors – an interior mirror and two exterior or door mirrors. Use all three to stay aware of what traffic around you is doing, and be sure to always check your mirrors before changing your speed or position on the road.

adjusting mirrors

Always make sure your mirrors are correctly adjusted and clean before starting the engine (see p34). Check again after going through a car wash in case the door mirrors have been knocked out of position.

On frosty mornings make sure you de-ice your door mirrors along with all the windows before driving off. If your car has heated door mirrors, switching them on will help stop condensation forming on the mirrors.

Don't hang anything from your interior mirror. It will restrict your view and distract your attention

image distortion

Compare the images in your interior and exterior mirrors. You may find the image on the exterior mirrors is smaller because these mirrors use convex curved glass. This means you get a greater field of view, but it will also make following vehicles look like they are further away than they really are.

blind spot

Even with your mirrors perfectly adjusted there are areas around the car which do not appear in any of your mirrors. The most dangerous of these blind spots is the one behind your right shoulder. If you check your mirrors frequently you can reduce the chance of a vehicle creeping unseen into this blind spot but there are times – such as before pulling out from the kerb or joining a motorway or dual carriageway from a slip road – when it is essential to glance over your right shoulder to make sure there is nothing hidden in your blind spot.

Some door mirrors have curved glass which makes vehicles seem further away than they really are

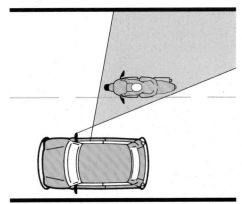

nearside and offside

These terms are sometimes used when referring to door mirrors. The nearside mirror is the one nearest the kerb (that is, on the left-hand side of the car); the offside door mirror is the one on the right-hand side.

Always remember the blind spot between your mirrors where a vehicle may be hidden from view

using your mirrors

You need to keep alert to what is happening behind you at all times when you are driving. Get into the habit of glancing frequently in your interior mirror to monitor what following traffic is doing. That way you will never be caught out by a car or motorbike overtaking unexpectedly.

You must always check your mirrors before carrying out any manoeuvre that affects your speed or position on the road. This includes:

Use your door mirrors to check for vehicles which are alongside you or about to overtake

- **moving off**
  Check your mirrors, and back this up with a glance over your right shoulder to confirm that nothing is in your blind spot
- **changing lanes**
  Use your mirrors plus a shoulder glance to check the blind spot
- **overtaking**
  Use your mirrors, especially your right door mirror, to check no one is about to overtake you before you begin the manoeuvre
- **turning right or left**
  Check the appropriate door mirror before turning. Never forget to check the left hand mirror when turning left in town – a cyclist may be passing on the inside

It's vital to glance over your shoulder before pulling out to make sure your blind spot is clear

- **slowing down or stopping**
  A vehicle following too closely may not be able to stop in time when you brake. Check your mirror in good time so you can lose speed more gently if necessary
- **increasing speed**
  Check your mirrors before accelerating, for instance when leaving a lower speed limit, in case a following vehicle is about to overtake you
- **leaving the car**
  Always check your mirrors and blind spot before opening the door in case a vehicle is passing.

Check your nearside door mirror before turning left in case a cyclist is passing on the inside

mirror-signal-manoeuvre

The mirror-signal-manoeuvre routine is fundamental to safe driving. Every time you intend to change your speed or position you must first check your mirrors. Next give a signal if it might help other road users. Only then can you start to carry out the manoeuvre.

The mirror-signal-manoeuvre routine must become an automatic part of your driving. But be careful not to let yourself fall into the trap of doing it without considering *why* you are doing it.

You must start the sequence sufficiently in advance of your planned manoeuvre to allow yourself plenty of time to act on what you see in the mirror.

For instance, suppose you are planning to move from the left to the right-hand lane of a dual carriageway. A mirror check shows a car about to overtake you in that lane. You need to act on this information and delay giving a signal until the car has gone past – if you signal too early the message you are sending to the overtaking car is that you haven't noticed it's there.

1 mirror

2 signal

3 manoeuvre

55

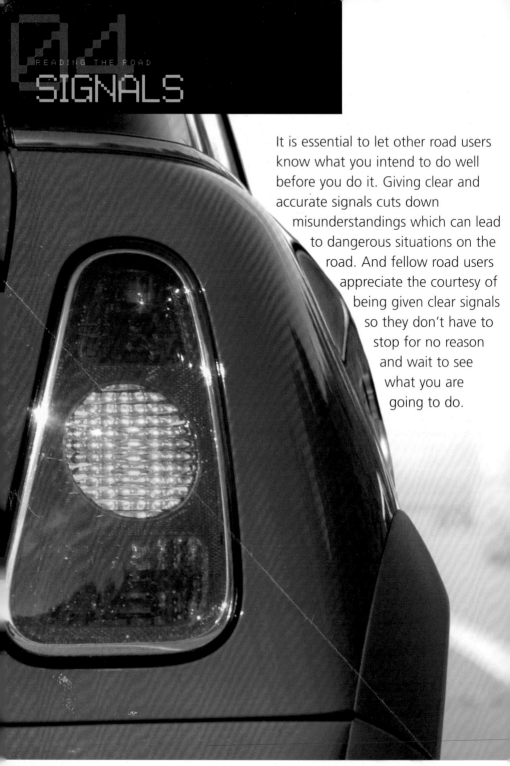

It is essential to let other road users know what you intend to do well before you do it. Giving clear and accurate signals cuts down misunderstandings which can lead to dangerous situations on the road. And fellow road users appreciate the courtesy of being given clear signals so they don't have to stop for no reason and wait to see what you are going to do.

Give a signal well in advance when you have to change lanes so that other road users have plenty of time to see and react to your signal

indicators

Use your indicators – the flashing amber lights situated at each corner of the car – to signal that you intend to move out or change direction. Always:

- give a signal in good time so other road users have time to react to it before you start changing your speed or position. If a road user shows no sign of reacting to your signal, don't carry out the manoeuvre until you're sure they have seen you
- think before using your indicators. Identify who may benefit from a signal and make that signal as clear as possible. There's no point indicating if there is no one in the vicinity to see your signals
- avoid making ambiguous signals. For instance, if you want to pull into the kerb just after a left turn, don't indicate until you are past the turning, or other drivers may think you're turning left
- make sure your indicator is cancelled after carrying out a manoeuvre, or you could mislead other road users.

Don't signal where it might confuse other road users. For instance, if you want to turn left into a driveway immediately after this junction, you should wait until you are past the junction before signalling. If you signal too early, the driver waiting to emerge might pull out in front of you, thinking you intend to turn into the side road

Brake signals give a useful advanced warning that traffic ahead is slowing down or stopping

Engaging reverse gear activates your reversing light which helps indicate your intentions to others

brake signal

Each time you press the brake pedal the rear warning lights come on, giving a signal to traffic behind that you are slowing down. You can also press gently on the brake pedal to warn following drivers that you intend to slow for a hazard which they may not yet have noticed.

There are other situations where the brake lights can give a useful warning. For instance, pressing the brake pedal as well as engaging the handbrake while you are stopped at roadworks or traffic lights can help alert approaching drivers that you are stationary. But remember to release the brake pedal once a vehicle has pulled up behind you or your brake lights may dazzle and irritate the driver.

hazard warning lights

Use these:

- when you have broken down
- when your car is temporarily obstructing traffic
- while driving on a dual carriageway or motorway to warn other road users of a hazard ahead.

Do not use them:

- as an excuse for dangerous or illegal parking
- while towing or being towed.

reversing signal

White reversing lights come on at the back of the car when you engage reverse gear. This can be useful to signal to other road users or pedestrians that you intend to reverse into a parking space or around a corner. But avoid engaging reverse where it could worry approaching drivers, who might think you're about to back out in front of them without giving way.

headlamp flash

This signal has only one meaning, which is to alert another road user to your presence. A headlamp flash is useful in situations where a horn may not be heard, such as at high speed on a motorway, or at night when horn use is not permitted.

Don't flash your headlamps for the wrong reason. It must never be done to intimidate a slower driver or to give instructions to another driver – you might know what *you* mean when you flash your lights, but the other driver may not, with potentially dangerous consequences.

The same reasoning applies if another car flashes its headlights at you. Don't assume this is an invitation to drive on – the driver may intend it to mean 'stop, I'm coming through'. Always wait until you are certain what the other driver is doing before proceeding.

Treat signals from other drivers with caution: they may not necessarily mean what you think they do

Make sure you know where the horn button is so that you can find it instantly in an emergency

acting on signals

Imagine you are waiting to emerge from a T-junction. The road is clear to the left, and a car is approaching from the right with its left-hand indicator flashing. Does it mean that the driver is about to turn into your junction so it's safe for you to pull out ahead of it? Or does it mean that the driver:

- is hard of hearing and has forgotten to cancel the indicator since their last manoeuvre
- has knocked on the indicators by mistake while reaching for the radio
- intends to pull left into a driveway immediately past your junction
- has a faulty indicator switch?

The answer, of course, is any of the above. Never assume another driver is about to do something simply because they are indicating. Always wait for them to confirm the signal, for instance by slowing down or starting to turn, before making any manoeuvre in front of them.

Be cautious if you see another driver signalling for no apparent reason. Never overtake a vehicle that is indicating right, even if you think that the driver has left on their indicator by mistake.

horn

The horn is one of the most misused items on the car. Never sound the horn to tick off another driver who you think has driven badly. This achieves nothing, and it may provoke an aggressive response. Use the horn only to alert another road user who you think may not have noticed that you are there. Give a short toot and consider raising your hand to show there was no aggressive intent on your part.

It is illegal to sound the horn when you are stationary, or in a built-up area between 11.30pm and 7.00am except when another moving vehicle poses a danger to you.

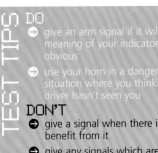

TEST TIPS

DO
- give an arm signal if it will make the meaning of your indicators more obvious
- use your horn in a dangerous situation where you think another driver hasn't seen you

DON'T
- give a signal when there is nobody to benefit from it
- give any signals which are not in the Highway Code
- use your horn or lights to reprimand other road users.

Never wave pedestrians across the road. You could put them in danger if they walk out without checking for themselves that the road is clear

arm signals

Although arm signals are rarely used nowadays, there are certain situations when an arm signal can be really useful to confirm a signal given by your indicator. For instance:

- a right turn arm signal emphasises that you are turning right and not just passing a parked car
- a slowing down arm signal makes your intention clear when you want to show you are pulling in to the kerb, not turning left
- a slowing down arm signal is clearly visible when your indicators are hard to see because of strong sunlight
- pedestrians waiting at a crossing can't see your brake lights. Giving the slowing down arm signal tells them you are about to stop.

I intend to move to the left or turn left

I intend to move to the right or turn right

I intend to slow down or stop

You will not be asked to give arm signals in your test but you must be able to recognise what the different arm signals mean.

police directing traffic

When traffic lights fail or when traffic is unusually heavy, a police officer may use arm signals to direct the traffic flow.

Familiarise yourself with these signals, and also the signals you should give to tell the officer which way you want to go. You must by law obey arm signals given by authorised persons – police officers and traffic wardens – as well as signs displayed by school crossing patrols.

Consider making an arm signal where it would be helpful, for example to show waiting pedestrians you are slowing as you approach a zebra crossing

You must by law stop and wait whenever a school crossing patrol signals you to do so

arm signals given by authorised persons

Traffic coming from the front must stop	*Traffic approaching from behind must stop*	*Traffic from both front and behind must stop*
Traffic from the side may proceed	*Traffic from the front may proceed*	*Traffic from behind may proceed*

arm signals to persons controlling traffic

I want to go straight on	*I want to turn left*	*I want to turn right*

ROAD SIGNS

Road signs give drivers vital information and you must obey them to stay safe and within the law. Many signs show simplified pictures instead of written instructions, which makes it easier to take in the message at a glance. You must be able to recognise and understand the meaning of all road signs. More importantly, you must act on the information given by signs. If there's a sign warning of a hazard ahead – such as an uneven road surface, no footway, slippery road or traffic queues – you should consider adjusting your speed and position on the road so that you are ready to deal safely with the hazard when you encounter it.

shapes and colours

You'll know that some signs are round, some square and some triangular, and that they come in different colours, but you may not realise why. In fact, all these various shapes and colours have distinct meanings.

Circular signs give orders.

Those with a red border tell you what you must not do. For example:

Triangular signs warn of a hazard on the road ahead.

For example:

Blue rectangular signs give information.

For example:

no motorcycles   *no overtaking*   *children crossing*   *low bridge*   *no through road*   *end of motorway*

Blue circular signs tell you what you must do. For example:

minimum speed 30 mph   *turn left ahead*

unique shapes

Two particularly important traffic signs have unique shapes: the give way sign is an upside down triangle, and the stop sign is an octagon.

The reason? So that even if these signs are obscured by snow and can't be read, drivers can still recognise them by their shape alone.

give way sign is an inverted triangle   *stop sign is octagonal*

Direction signs use different colours depending on what sort of road they are on. Signs on motorways are blue, those on primary routes are green, those on other roads are white with a black border, diversion signs are yellow and signs showing local attractions are brown.

route finding

Despite the high quality of direction signing in this country, it's not a good idea to rely on signs alone, so always keep a road atlas in your car. If you do lose your way, find somewhere safe to stop before consulting it.

Generally, the more important the road, the more warning you get of the turning. Minor roads often have no advance warning sign at all, so you need to be alert to spot a small finger sign post showing where to turn off. Major roads provide more warning, with an advanced sign and also a sign to confirm which route you're on after the junction. On the motorway, junctions are signposted at one mile and half-mile intervals before the exit, and each junction is numbered.

motorways (blue signs)

left hand lane leads to a different destination (the arrows pointing downwards mean 'get in lane')

inclined arrow indicates the destinations that can be reached by leaving motorway at next junction

sign placed at a junction leading onto a motorway

on approach to motorway junction ('25' is the junction number)

route confirmed after the junction

diversions (yellow signs)

when you encounter a diversion, follow the signs or the symbols that indicate the alternative route

non-primary and local routes (white signs)

signs on the approach to the junction. Route numbers on a blue background show the way to a motorway; those on green show the way to a primary road

sign at the junction

primary routes (green signs)

on the approach to the junction

at the junction (symbol warns of a hazard on this route)

blue panel indicates that the motorway starts at the next junction; motorways in brackets can also be reached along the route indicated

bilingual sign in Wales

route confirmed after junction

local attractions (brown signs)

tourist attraction *camp site* *picnic site*

other direction signs

 R HR

ring road (by-passes town)

ring road (non-primary road)

holiday route

ROAD MARKINGS

Road markings are a vital source of information for drivers. They are often placed alongside road signs, and have the advantage of being visible when the signs are hidden by traffic. Or they may be used without other signs to give a continuous message as you drive along the road. Remember the general rule that the more paint there is on the road, the greater the danger. When you approach an area criss-crossed with white lines and warnings, take note, slow down and prepare to negotiate a serious hazard ahead.

types of road marking

There are a number of different types of road marking which each have distinct meanings. The main types are (with specific examples):

Lane arrows tell you in advance which lane you need to get into, and are often accompanied by road numbers or place names marked on the road.

traffic lane directions

Lines across the road separate traffic at road junctions, telling you where you must stop or give way to other vehicles.

give way

Written warnings on the roads give specific commands or warnings of hazards ahead.

do not block entrance to side road

Lines along the road divide lanes of traffic, give information about hazards on the road ahead and tell you when you are not permitted to overtake.

no overtaking

Parking restrictions are shown by yellow lines running alongside the kerb. They indicate that waiting restrictions are in force.

no waiting

Speed reduction lines are raised yellow lines across the road at the approach to a hazard such as a lower speed limit. They make drivers aware of their speed so they will slow down well in time. Rumble strips are red and give an audible warning too.

slow down for hazard ahead

KNOW THE CODE — HIGHWAY CODE RULE 111

Reflective road studs may be used with white lines.

➜ White studs mark the lanes or the middle of the road
➜ Red studs mark the left edge of the road
➜ Amber studs mark the central reservation of a dual carriageway or motorway
➜ Green studs mark the edge of the main carriageway at lay-bys, side roads and slip roads.

TRAFFIC LIGHTS

Traffic lights automatically control busy junctions. They ease traffic flow by switching priorities in sequence, allowing vehicles from one direction to flow freely while vehicles from another direction are held back to wait their turn. Approach junctions controlled by traffic lights with caution and be prepared for the lights to change.

approaching traffic lights

Use the mirror-signal-manoeuvre routine as you approach a junction controlled by traffic lights. Slow down and be prepared to stop. Never speed up to try and get through while the lights are still green.

Remember that green means go only if the road is clear and it is safe to do so. Always check the road is clear before you proceed when the lights go green. Serious collisions occur at junctions controlled by traffic lights when one car moves off through a green light at the same time that a driver from the other direction has left it too late to stop after the lights have changed.

When a green filter arrow is illuminated you may proceed only in the direction it indicates

traffic light sequence

1 RED means stop. Wait at the stop line.

2 RED AND **AMBER** also means stop. Do not start to move off until the lights change to green.

3 GREEN means go if it is clear and safe to do so. Give way to pedestrians who are crossing.

4 AMBER means stop. You may only continue if the amber light appears after you have crossed the stop line or if you are so close to it that it might be dangerous to pull up. (Red then follows amber and the sequence repeats itself.)

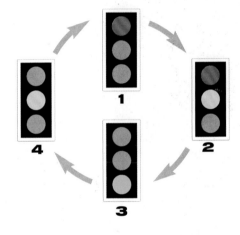

traffic light failure

If a set of traffic lights is not working, you should treat the intersection as an uncontrolled one where no one has priority. Be prepared to stop as traffic from other directions may assume they have right of way. If a police officer is controlling the junction, follow the signals you are given (see p61). When signalled to stop by a police officer, wait at the stop line.

Proceed with great care when traffic lights are out of order

HIGHWAY CODE RULE 154

Advanced stop lines Some junctions have advanced stop lines or bus advance areas to allow cycles and buses to be positioned ahead of other traffic. Motorists MUST wait behind the first white line reached, and not encroach on the marked area. Allow cyclists and buses time and space to move off when the green signal shows.

You may find this hard to believe at first, but controlling the car – making it start and stop, and go round corners and up hills – is the easy bit. On today's busy roads, the real driving skill is interacting with other road users. Good drivers blend in with the traffic flow, watch what other drivers are doing, communicate their own intentions clearly, make good progress without needing to brake or accelerate harshly, and arrive at their destination relaxed and unruffled. Bad drivers fail to observe what other drivers are doing, get into misunderstandings, drive too close and too fast on congested roads, and arrive feeling angry and tired and blaming everyone but themselves. Learning to cope with traffic requires concentration and self-discipline, but it's a skill you must master to pass your test.

POSITIONING

There's a lot more to positioning your car than just keeping it on the correct side of the road. By always being in the right place you will make your intentions clearer to other road users, facilitate the free flow of traffic and increase your margin of safety when approaching hazardous situations.

lane discipline

Always keep within the road markings indicating your lane unless you are changing lane or direction. Try to anticipate when lanes will have to split, and get ready to move across into the correct lane. Don't change lanes at the last moment if you find you have got into the wrong lane: instead carry on and find another way back onto your route. Never straddle lanes or weave in and out of lanes.

Get into the correct lane in good time when arrows indicate that lanes are changing direction

IT'S THE LAW

CROSSING WHITE LINES

You are permitted to cross a central solid white line only if it is safe and necessary to do so in order to:

- ➔ enter or leave a side turning or driveway
- ➔ pass a stationary vehicle
- ➔ avoid an accident
- ➔ pass a working road maintenance vehicle displaying a keep left/right arrow and moving no faster than 10mph
- ➔ pass a pedal cycle or horse moving no faster than 10mph
- ➔ comply with the direction of a police constable or traffic warden.

lane markings

A broken white line marks the centre of the road

Longer broken white lines indicate a hazard ahead. Never cross a hazard warning line unless you are sure it is safe

Lane lines divide the lanes on dual carriageways and motorways: keep between them except when changing lane

You may overtake if it is safe to do on double white lines where the line nearest to you is broken

You must not overtake on double white lines where the line nearest to you is solid. You also must not park on a road with double white lines whether broken or solid

Double solid white lines mean that overtaking is prohibited in either direction

An edge line marks the left-hand side of the carriageway

Diagonal hatching is used to separate lanes of traffic and to protect vehicles waiting to turn off the road. If the area is bordered by a broken white line you can enter it, but only if it is necessary and safe to do so; if it is bounded by a solid white line then you must not enter it except in an emergency

If it is safe to do so, position the car towards the middle of the road when turning right

Leave enough room for a door to open unexpectedly when passing parked cars

road position

Normally you should position your car in the centre of your half of the road. Avoid getting too close to the kerb: the road surface is more uneven near the gutter and if you accidentally clip the kerb you may lose control of the car. However, there are times when it is useful to move a little nearer to the kerb. For instance to:

- make space for oncoming traffic through a narrow gap
- let a vehicle overtake
- let motorbikes pass in congested traffic
- increase your vision and safety when approaching a right-hand bend.

Conversely, you should move out towards the centre of the road, if it is safe to do so, when:

- making a right-hand turn; this confirms your intentions to other road users and gives following vehicles space to overtake you on the left
- the pavement is busy with pedestrians.

passing parked vehicles

When passing parked vehicles, leave plenty of space in case a car starts pulling out, or a car door opens unexpectedly. Making more space also helps you to see children coming out from between parked cars to cross the road. If you have to pass closer to parked cars, then reduce your speed and be ready to stop.

When passing a series of parked cars, don't weave in and out between them: maintain a straight course which clearly indicates your intentions to other road users.

Take care to observe lane markings in one-way streets, and beware of vehicles passing on your left

Bus lanes are marked by a solid white line. You must not use them except when signs say you can

one-way systems

In a one-way street select the most appropriate lane in good time before you have to turn at the end of the street.

It is legal to overtake on either the left or the right on a one-way street, so take particular care when changing lanes. If you drive down a one-way street by mistake, you must continue to the end of the road – don't try to turn round or reverse out again.

One-way streets may have contra-flow bus or cycle lanes, allowing these vehicles to proceed against the direction of traffic flow.

keep out

Remember that you must not drive in a bus lane, cycle lane or tram lane unless signs state otherwise. You must also not drive on the pavement except to cross it when using a driveway into a property, or where signs specifically permit parking on the pavement.

turn left *turn right* *vehicles may pass either side* *two-way traffic crosses one-way road* *two-way traffic ahead*

one-way traffic *ahead only* *turn left* *turn right* *keep left* *keep right*

On our busy roads much of your driving time will be spent following the vehicle in front. You'll find that many drivers commit the serious error of following too closely. They get away with this until one day the vehicle ahead brakes unexpectedly and they end up careering into the back of it. Most serious collisions – such as motorway pile-ups – could be avoided if drivers left more space between their vehicles.

how close?

When you are following another vehicle, ask yourself: 'if it suddenly slams on its brakes, have I left myself enough space to be able to react and stop without hitting it?'

If the answer is no, pull back until you have created a safe gap. A useful way to ensure you are keeping a safe distance in dry, bright conditions is to use the two-second rule. Watch as the vehicle in front goes by a lamp post or driveway, then count how long it takes for your car to pass the same point. If you can slowly count 'one thousand – two thousand' (or repeat the apt phrase 'only a fool breaks the two-second rule') before your car reaches the marker then you are keeping a safe distance.

wet roads

On wet, greasy or icy roads you will take much longer to stop in an emergency. When it rains, double the two-second rule and leave a four-second gap. If the road is slippery or icy you should leave up to ten times the distance in which to stop.

Wet roads mean you will need further to stop in an emergency, so leave at least a four-second gap

large vehicles

Another time you should leave extra space is when you're following a large truck or bus. If you are too close to it your view past will be obscured and you won't be able to anticipate what is happening on the road ahead. Keeping well back also means you don't have to breathe in the truck's diesel exhaust fumes, or get your windscreen smeared by spray thrown up from its rear wheels on a wet road.

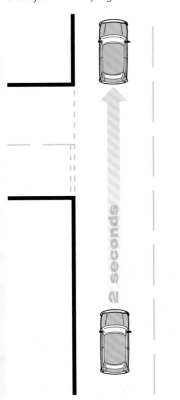

Use a fixed point on the road side to help you measure a two-second gap from the car in front

Keep well back when following a bus or you won't be able to see past to overtake it when it stops

Many drivers cause unnecessary risk by tailgating on the motorway – don't become one of them

Leave enough space from the vehicle ahead to give following drivers room to overtake you safely

tailgating

This is the dangerous habit of following too closely behind the vehicle in front. When someone is tailgating you, it means that if you have to stop in an emergency they may not be able to avoid running into the back of your car. Reduce this risk by easing off the accelerator and increasing your following distance from the vehicle in front. Because you have created more space in front of you, you won't have to slow so abruptly in an emergency, which in turn gives the driver behind extra time to react.

Often drivers tailgate because they are impatient to get past. If this is the case, let the driver overtake at the first opportunity. Never try to retaliate to a tailgating driver by putting on your brakes or driving obstructively. The fact that they are driving dangerously means that you have to take even more care to drive responsibly to ensure everyone's safety.

queues

When in a slow-moving traffic queue, hold back if keeping up with the queue would mean obstructing the exit of a junction or straddling a pedestrian crossing or level crossing. Wait till the traffic in front has moved forward far enough for you to be able to clear the junction or crossing before proceeding.

being overtaken

When you're in a line of traffic on the open road, remember that even if you don't intend to overtake, drivers behind may want to overtake you. Leave enough space for them to do so safely.

If another driver is trying to overtake, you should help them get past quickly and safely. Keep a steady course, slow down if necessary and leave plenty of space from the vehicle in front for the overtaking car to move into. But leave the decision to overtake to the other driver – don't beckon them to pass, or indicate left, as there may be hazards which you haven't spotted.

Don't ever try to obstruct or prevent someone from overtaking, even if you are already driving at the speed limit. Let the other driver get by and concentrate on ensuring your own safety. Slow down if someone overtakes where there is not enough forward vision for them to carry out the manoeuvre safely, or to assist a large vehicle which is taking a long time to pull past you.

Never be the cause of a tailback of traffic. If you are driving a slow-moving vehicle on a narrow road with little opportunity for overtaking, pull over as soon as it is safe and let the traffic pass before resuming your journey.

Leave a gap when approaching side turnings in queuing traffic so you don't obstruct access to them

If you don't leave enough space when stopping in traffic you could get stuck behind the car in front

When leaving a safe gap you may find that other drivers pull in front of you, especially when you are driving on a dual carriageway or motorway. Don't think of this as a problem – simply ease off the power and pull back until you open up a safe gap again. Even if ten vehicles pull in front of you during the course of a journey you'll still get where you're going only a few seconds later – and more importantly, you'll get there safely.

stopping in traffic

Avoid getting too close to the vehicle in front when it stops at traffic lights or a junction. Leave enough space so you can see where its rear tyres touch the tarmac. That way, if it stalls or breaks down you have enough room to manoeuvre safely past without getting stuck behind it. On a slope leaving this gap also gives room for the car in front to roll back if the driver performs a bad hill start.

KNOW THE CODE

HIGHWAY CODE RULE 129

In slow moving traffic you should:

➡ reduce the distance between you and the vehicle ahead to maintain traffic flow

➡ never get so close to the vehicle in front that you cannot stop safely

➡ leave enough space to be able to manoeuvre if the vehicle in front breaks down or an emergency vehicle needs to get past

➡ not change lanes to the left to overtake

➡ allow access into and from side roads, as blocking these will add to congestion.

If you meet an oncoming vehicle where an obstruction such as a parked car reduces the width of the road so there is only room for one vehicle to pass, one of you has to give way. Forward thinking and anticipation make all the difference when dealing with this sort of situation. You need to anticipate, and adjust your speed and position well in advance so that if it is necessary for you to give way you can do so smoothly and safely.

Where a parked car causes an obstruction ahead, stop and give way to oncoming traffic

A hump bridge is a potentially dangerous meeting place because the brow of the bridge restricts your forward view. Hump bridges are often narrow so you may encounter oncoming vehicles or pedestrians in the middle of the road. Slow right down and consider sounding your horn to give a warning of your approach

giving way

Where the obstruction is on your side of the road you should be prepared to stop and give way to oncoming traffic. But don't assume you necessarily have priority if the obstruction is on the other side of the road. If an oncoming car carries straight on through, you must be able to stop safely and give way to it. Thinking in terms of 'right of way' in this sort of situation isn't helpful: drivers who insist on always taking what they see as their 'right of way' end up in a collision sooner or later.

judging the gap

As you approach a meeting situation use the mirror-signal-manoeuvre routine. The oncoming vehicle may pull nearer to the kerb to create enough space for you to continue through the gap. But if you are not absolutely certain there is enough room, hold back until the other vehicle is through. Never pull past an obstruction expecting the oncoming vehicle to move over to make space for you.

hills

It's courteous to stop and give way to vehicles, particularly large lorries and buses, which are coming towards you up a steep hill. If a heavily-laden truck loses momentum on a hill it has to work hard to regain it.

Hold back and give way where vehicles or pedestrians make a meeting situation hazardous

Use passing places to pull in and give way to oncoming vehicles on single track roads

VITAL SIGNS

give way to vehicles from other direction

you have priority over oncoming vehicles

road narrows on both sides

road narrows on right (left if symbol reversed)

HIGHWAY CODE RULE 133

KNOW THE CODE

Single-track roads These are only wide enough for one vehicle. They may have special passing places. If you see a vehicle coming towards you, or the driver behind wants to overtake, pull into a passing place on your left, or wait opposite a passing place on your right. Give way to vehicles coming uphill whenever you can. If necessary, reverse until you reach a passing place to let the other vehicle pass.

Overtaking is a vital driving skill. When drivers lack the confidence to overtake where it would be safe to do so, long queues of slow traffic can build up, causing congestion and frustration among following drivers. But overtaking is also one of the most potentially dangerous driving manoeuvres, and it demands careful judgement and a full assessment of the risks involved. Remember the golden rule: if you're not sure it is safe to overtake, don't.

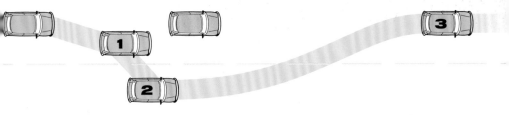

how to overtake

1 Maximise your observation of the road ahead before overtaking. Don't get too close or you will reduce your view past the vehicle you want to overtake. Position yourself towards the centre of the road so you can see past. (When following a large vehicle it can also be useful to move towards the kerb to get a view along its nearside.) Check your mirrors and give a signal before pulling out. Make sure you are in a lower gear that gives enough power to get past quickly, but try to avoid having to change gear in the middle of an overtaking manoeuvre.

2 Move to the other side of the road to make a final check of the road ahead. If it is clear then apply full power and drive past as swiftly as possible.

3 Don't cut in too early after overtaking. Check your mirrors to ensure that it is safe to pull back in.

when to overtake

The only reason to overtake is when it will help you to make progress. There's no point overtaking when you are approaching a built-up area or if you intend to turn off the road soon. Don't try to overtake when you are in heavy traffic and overtaking will achieve nothing but putting you a couple of places up the traffic queue. If there are signs indicating the distance to a stretch of dual carriageway, take note of them and wait till you get there before overtaking.

Keep back and move towards the centre line to maximise your field of view past a slow vehicle

IT'S THE LAW

NO OVERTAKING

It is illegal to overtake:

- ➜ if you would have to cross or straddle double white lines with a solid line nearest to you (apart from the exceptions mentioned on p73)

- ➜ if you would have to enter an area surrounded by a solid white line that is designed to divide traffic streams

- ➜ the nearest vehicle to a pedestrian crossing

- ➜ if you would have to enter a lane reserved for buses, trams or cycles during its hours of operation

- ➜ after a 'no overtaking' sign until you pass the sign cancelling it.

A white arrow in the middle of the road is warning you to move back to the left when overtaking. Never overtake where you see this marking

Don't try to squeeze past a cyclist: hold back and wait until it is safe to pass, and leave as much room as you would to overtake a car

dangers from other vehicles

If you overtake at 60mph while an oncoming car approaches the same speed, it means you are closing at a combined speed of 120mph. This leaves little margin for error. Make sure you spend the minimum amount of time exposed to danger on the wrong side of the road when overtaking. Select a gear that will give you plenty of power and use the full acceleration of your car to get past quickly. Never overtake where you may force another vehicle to swerve or slow down.

While you are deciding whether to overtake, be aware that the driver behind may be thinking about overtaking you. Check your mirrors, and give a signal to indicate your intentions both to following traffic and to the vehicle being overtaken.

Make sure there is no possibility that the vehicle you intend to overtake is about to make a right turn or swerve across the road to overtake a cyclist or pedestrian you haven't seen. Take care before overtaking at the start of a downhill stretch or when leaving a lower speed restriction in case the vehicle in front speeds up. If you are unsure that the vehicle you want to overtake is aware of your presence consider sounding your horn or flashing your headlamps briefly to warn that you are about to overtake.

If the driver in front waves or indicates left to encourage you to overtake, don't rely on their judgement: overtake only if you can see to your own satisfaction that it is safe to do so.

It is very dangerous to follow straight after another overtaking vehicle as your view ahead will be obscured and oncoming vehicles may not be able to see you. Hold back and make sure the road is clear before overtaking.

overtaking hazards

Overtaking is potentially dangerous because there are so many different hazards to assess before making the manoeuvre. Never overtake:

- where there are road junctions or driveways from which a vehicle may emerge in front of you
- where the road narrows
- where you cannot see the road ahead to be clear, such as on the approach to a bend, a hump bridge, the brow of a hill or a dip in the road
- when approaching a school crossing patrol
- between the kerb and a bus or tram when it is at a stop
- where traffic is queuing at junctions or road works
- at a level crossing.

Caution is required when overtaking on three-lane roads, especially where traffic from either direction is allowed to overtake on the same stretch

Overtaking on the left is permitted in certain situations, but take extra care as other drivers may not be expecting you to do so

three-lane roads

Take special care when overtaking on a road which is divided into three lanes so that traffic from either direction may use the middle lane to overtake. Don't pull out unless you are completely certain there is no risk of an oncoming vehicle trying to overtake at the same time.

overtaking on the left

You must normally overtake on the right only. However, there are a few situations where you are permitted to pass slower moving vehicles on the left-hand side:

- ⊜ where a vehicle is signalling to turn right
- ⊜ where traffic is moving slowly in queues on a multi-lane road
- ⊜ in a one-way street
- ⊜ in a lane turning left at a junction.

KNOW THE CODE

HIGHWAY CODE RULE 140

Large vehicles Overtaking these is more difficult. You should

- ⊜ drop back to increase your ability to see ahead. Getting too close to large vehicles will obscure your view of the road ahead and there may be another slow moving vehicle in front
- ⊜ make sure that you have enough room to complete your overtaking manoeuvre before committing yourself. It takes longer to pass a large vehicle. If in doubt do not overtake
- ⊜ not assume you can follow a vehicle ahead which is overtaking a long vehicle. If a problem develops, they may abort overtaking and pull back in.

VITAL SIGNS

side winds: take special care when overtaking cyclists, motorbikes or high-sided vehicles

Hidden dip

hidden dip in road: don't overtake as oncoming traffic may be obscured

no overtaking

06

JUNCTIONS

A road junction is where two or more roads meet. Traffic has to merge and with this comes the risk that mistakes may lead to collisions. At junctions you need to signal clearly and position your car accurately to give a clear indication to other road users of what you intend to do. Good all-round observation is needed to make sure that when you pull out at a junction, you do so without endangering or inconveniencing other road users. However, in today's busy traffic you can't afford to wait until the road is clear as far as the eye can see before moving out. Judging when to cross a junction takes skill and confidence which can only be acquired by getting in lots of experience at all types of road junction.

If no one knew who had priority where two roads meet the result would be chaos. To promote a smooth traffic flow, most junctions are organised so that traffic on the major road has priority and traffic on the minor road must wait until it is clear to proceed. Although there are few basic types of junctions, individual circumstances make each junction unique and they need to be negotiated with care. Assess each junction as you approach it by looking at such things as bends, visibility, obscured sightlines, the amount of traffic, road markings and signs.

types of junction

There are five main types of junction:
- T-junctions
- Y-junctions
- staggered junctions
- crossroads
- roundabouts

priorities at junctions

Priorities at junctions are indicated by give way signs and markings, stop signs and markings, and traffic lights – or there may be no priority marked. Remember that even if you are on the road that has priority, you need to be ready to slow down or stop for vehicles which pull out in front of you, or for vulnerable road users such as cyclists or pedestrians who you may need to give priority to whatever the road signs say.

give way sign

A give way sign means you must stop at the line to give priority to traffic on the road you are joining. You do not need to stop if the road is clear and it is safe to proceed. A give way junction is indicated by double broken white lines across your half of the road, or a single broken white line at the entrance to a roundabout.

HIGHWAY CODE RULE 146

Take extra care at junctions. You should:

- watch out for cyclists, motorcyclists and pedestrians as they are not always easy to see
- watch out for pedestrians crossing a road into which you are turning. If they have started to cross they have priority, so give way
- watch out for long vehicles which may be turning at a junction ahead; they may have to use the whole width of the road to make the turn
- not assume, when waiting at a junction, that a vehicle coming from the right and signalling left will actually turn. Wait and make sure
- not cross or join a road until there is a gap large enough for you to do so safely.

STOP
100 yds

distance to stop line ahead

GIVE WAY
50 yds

distance to give way line ahead

GIVE WAY

give way to traffic on major road

side turning

T-junction (the road with priority is shown by the broader line)

STOP

stop and give way

roundabout

mini-roundabout

crossroads

staggered junction

stop sign

A stop sign is used instead of a give way sign where reduced visibility means it would be dangerous to proceed through a junction without stopping. You must come to a complete halt at the line and check that the road is clear before proceeding. A stop junction is indicated by a single continuous white line across your side of the road. This type of line also shows where you should stop at traffic lights, level crossings, swing bridges and ferries.

box junctions

Box junctions are designed to prevent the junction being blocked by queuing traffic. It is illegal to enter the area of yellow criss-cross lines marked on the road at a box junction unless your exit road is clear. But remember the important exception to this rule: you *can* enter a box junction when you want to turn right and your exit road is clear but you are prevented from proceeding by oncoming traffic or right-turning vehicles in front of you.

traffic lights

At junctions controlled by traffic lights the priorities change with the lights. See p69 to remind yourself of the sequence and meaning of traffic lights.

uncontrolled junctions

On minor roads some junctions may not have road signs or markings. This means all vehicles approaching the junction have equal priority. Slow down, look for traffic coming from all directions and be prepared to stop and give way if necessary.

road markings at junctions

This marking appears on the road just before a give way sign

Give way to traffic on a major road

Stop line at stop sign

Give way to traffic from the right at a roundabout

Give way to traffic from the right at a mini-roundabout

Stop line at signals or police control

Stop line for pedestrians at a level crossing

KNOW THE CODE — HIGHWAY CODE RULE 150

Box junctions. These have criss-cross yellow lines painted on the road. You MUST NOT enter the box until your exit road or lane is clear. However, you may enter the box and wait when you want to turn right, and are only stopped from doing so by oncoming traffic, or by other vehicles waiting to turn right.

approaching junctions

You are already familiar with the mirror-signal-manoeuvre routine. When approaching a road hazard such as a junction you need to take this procedure a step further by developing a structured approach to carrying out the manoeuvre.

After checking your mirror and signalling, you need to:

- ⊙ check your position on the road and adjust it if necessary
- ⊙ check your speed and adjust to suit
- ⊙ select the appropriate gear
- ⊙ take one last good look all around to check it is safe to proceed
- ⊙ make the manoeuvre if it is safe to do so.

The diagram opposite shows how this procedure works when making a right turn.

1    *check mirror*

2   *signal if necessary*

3   *change position towards the centre of the road*

4   *slow progressively to the required speed*

5   *select the appropriate gear*

6   *check all round including your mirrors*

7   *make the right turn if it is safe to do so*

TEST TIPS

DO

- ⊙ scan each junction as you approach to get as much information as possible about approaching traffic and the junction layout
- ⊙ make progress by proceeding straight through a give way junction without coming to a complete stop when it is safe to do so

DON'T

- ⊙ assume that because you are on the major road you will not have to give way to other road users
- ⊙ creep across a stop line, however slowly. Make sure you always come to a complete halt.

06

EMERGING FROM JUNCTIONS

When you emerge from a junction you may have to join traffic which is heavy or fast-moving. If making a right turn there is the additional hazard of crossing the path of oncoming vehicles. This is a potentially dangerous situation and you must exercise careful judgement and continually monitor what is happening all around your car.

Careful all round observation is essential when you are emerging from a road junction

emerging left from a junction

- check your mirrors
- if other road users would benefit from a signal give it in good time
- position your car to the left of the road, about one metre from the kerb
- slow down and be prepared to give way or stop at the junction
- look in all directions before pulling out. Check your left door mirror for bicycles or motorbikes passing on your nearside
- pull onto the main road, then check your mirrors again, make sure your indicator is cancelled and accelerate to a safe speed for the road you have joined.

emerging right from a junction

Carry out the same procedure, but position your car as near to the centre of the road as possible (although if the road is narrow, you must leave enough space for other vehicles to turn into the junction). Take extra care when pulling out as you have to give way to traffic coming from both directions.

When stopping at a junction make sure that you pull right up to the give way or stop line (above). Do not stop short of the line (below) or you will restrict your view out of the junction

maximising vision

Sometimes you will find that your view out of a junction is obscured, for instance by parked vehicles. If this is the case, stop at the junction and then edge carefully forward until you can get a good view down the road in both directions.

Large vehicles may also obscure your view. Before pulling out in front of a bus or lorry, ask yourself if there might be a hidden motorcycle overtaking it. Remember that motorcyclists and cyclists are particularly vulnerable at junctions because they are smaller and harder to see, and can easily be hidden behind your windscreen pillars.

judging traffic speed

Judging when to emerge from a junction requires great care: on the one hand, you must be able to emerge from the junction without forcing other vehicles to slow down or change position; on the other, you should not be over-cautious so that you fail to take advantage of safe opportunities while a queue of frustrated drivers forms behind you. As a rough guide, if you would feel happy about walking across the road in front of an oncoming vehicle, then there should be space for you to emerge. Once you have joined the main road accelerate briskly to match your speed to that of other traffic.

staggered junctions

This is where two minor roads join a major road not quite opposite each other. When you are on a minor road and wish to pass across the major road you should usually treat this as two manoeuvres: first join the major road, then make a second turn into the minor road. If the junctions are very close together you may proceed across the major road in one manoeuvre, but check carefully that the road is clear in both directions.

When approaching a staggered junction on the major road you should treat it with caution. Be prepared to slow down and give way to vehicles emerging.

When parked cars obstruct your view out of a junction, edge cautiously forward until you can see if the road is clear for you to pull out

Y-junctions

At a Y-junction the minor road meets the major road at an angle. When turning right at a Y-junction you may need to pull up at a right angle to the major road to prevent your view to your left being obscured.

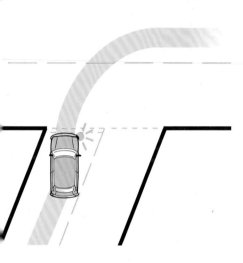

Pulling up at a right angle to the major road at a Y-junction means that you can get a clear view in both directions through your side windows

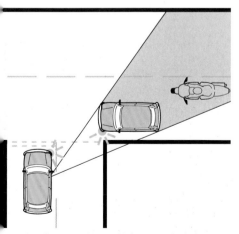

Be alert for overtaking vehicles – particularly motorbikes – which can easily be hidden from view behind other vehicles at junctions

turning right across a dual carriageway

Crossing a dual carriageway needs extra care because of the high speed of traffic. There are two types of right turn across a dual carriageway:

➡ **where there is a waiting area within the central reservation**

You should cross the road in two stages. First, check that the road to your right is clear of oncoming traffic and drive into the waiting area. Stop here and check if the road is clear to the left before joining the carriageway. You must not not join the right-hand lane and expect approaching traffic to pass you on the left. Wait until both lanes are clear so you are able to cross safely to the left-hand lane.

Take care if you are driving a longer vehicle or pulling a trailer. Check before emerging that there is enough space for your whole vehicle to fit into the central reservation without obstructing traffic already on the dual carriageway.

➡ **where there is no waiting area within the central reservation**

You must cross the dual carriageway in a single manoeuvre. This calls for careful observation in both directions before pulling out.

Where there is a central reservation wide enough to wait in, split a right turn across a dual carriageway into two separate manoeuvres

96

JUNCTIONS

TURNING INTO SIDE ROADS

Careful observation is needed when turning into a minor road. Try not to concentrate your attention on the danger from just one direction – for instance, oncoming traffic when you are turning right – as you may overlook other hazards, such as motorbikes overtaking you, or pedestrians crossing the road you are turning into.

turning left

- first check your mirrors
- if other road users would benefit from a signal give it in good time
- position your car to the left of the road, about one metre from the kerb. Don't move too far to the left or following drivers may think you are pulling up, not turning left
- slow down, then select the appropriate gear. Your speed must reflect how sharp the corner is and how clearly you can see round it. Remember that a vehicle could be parked just round the corner out of sight, or an oncoming vehicle may be in the middle of the road passing parked cars
- check your mirrors again, especially your nearside mirror in case a cyclist or motorcyclist is passing on your nearside. Look all round, and check that the road you are turning into is clear. You must stop and give way to any pedestrians crossing the road
- turn the corner, making sure you stay well on your side of the road, and that your rear wheel does not clip the kerb. Remember the rear wheels don't exactly follow the front wheels, but take a short cut which brings them closer to the kerb.
- check your mirrors again, make sure your indicator is cancelled and build up speed if it is safe to do so.

Keep close in when turning left, but don't cut round so tightly that your rear wheel hits the kerb

KNOW THE CODE

HIGHWAY CODE RULE 158

Turning left. Use your mirrors and give a left-turn signal well before you turn left. Do not overtake just before you turn left and watch out for traffic coming up on your left before you make the turn, especially if driving a large vehicle. Cyclists and motorcyclists in particular may be hidden from your view. Do not cut in on cyclists. When turning:

- keep as close to the left as is safe and practical
- give way to any vehicles using a bus lane, cycle lane or tramway from either direction.

Do not cut in on cyclists

TEST TIPS

DO

- take care to check that the road you are driving into is clear before starting to turn
- judge your positioning carefully when turning right on a road which has no centre line

DON'T

- swing back to the left before turning right, or swing out to the right before making a left turn
- cut the corner on a left turn so your rear wheel hits the kerb.

Continuous observation is vital when turning right. As well as checking for oncoming traffic, look for vehicles overtaking you and hazards – such as pedestrians – in the road you are turning into

turning right

- first check your mirrors
- if other road users would benefit from a signal give it in good time
- position your car towards the centre of the road, keeping as close as you can to the white line. This helps other road users see what you are intending to do, and also lets following traffic pass on your nearside while you are waiting to turn. If there is a waiting area marked on the road for traffic turning right, follow the road markings into this
- slow down and be prepared to stop if you need to give way to oncoming traffic or if the entrance of the road you are turning into is blocked
- look out for vehicles waiting to turn right from the road you are driving into – they may try to pull out ahead of you. If there is not enough space for you to manoeuvre around them and enter the road then hold back and wait for them to emerge. But don't beckon or flash them to come out
- check your mirrors before turning, especially your right-hand mirror in case a vehicle is overtaking you. Be particularly alert for motorbikes
- do not start to turn unless you are sure you can enter the side road and will not be forced to stop in a dangerous position halfway across the main road
- take care not to cut the corner as you make the turn
- check your mirrors after completing the turn, make sure your indicator is cancelled and build up speed if it is safe to do so.

Never cut a corner like this. Steer so that you stay on your own side of the road when turning right or you risk colliding with an emerging vehicle

stopping at junctions

Whenever you have to halt at a junction for more than a few seconds, always apply your handbrake. This is a safety measure which will help stop your car being pushed into the path of other traffic if it is hit from behind while you are stationary at the junction. The impact could easily knock your foot off the brake pedal if you were holding the car on the footbrake alone.

When waiting to make a right turn, do not turn the steering wheel before you are ready to move off. If you were hit from behind while waiting in the middle of the road with your front wheels already turned, the impact could push you across the road into the path of oncoming traffic

VITAL SIGNS

no motor vehicles
except motorcycles
without sidecars

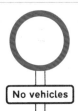

no vehicles
except bicycles
being pushed

no entry for
vehicular traffic

no left turn

no motor vehicles

no right turn

These signs all mean that you must not drive into a road. Sometimes there will be a plate giving exceptions – for instance, you may be able to enter outside certain hours, or if you need to gain access to a property in the road

06 CROSSROADS

At a crossroads there are two T-junctions opposite each other. Serious collisions can occur at crossroads when one vehicle pulls out in front of another travelling at high speed. Take special care when you are on a major road and see a crossroads ahead. Slow down and be prepared to give way in case another driver proceeds straight across without seeing you.

turning right

When turning right at the same time as another vehicle wants to turn across you, you have two choices:

➡ **turn right side to right side**
This is the safer option. It has the advantage of giving you a clear view of approaching traffic.

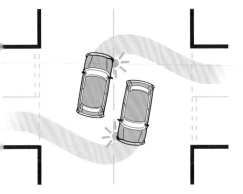

➡ **turn left side to left side**
This method can be useful when turning against a long vehicle, or where the side roads are slightly offset. But because the other vehicle is passing in front of you, it blocks your view of oncoming traffic, so take extra care.

Sometimes there are road markings which direct which course you should take. Where there are no markings, watching the course of the other vehicle and establishing eye contact with its driver may help you decide.

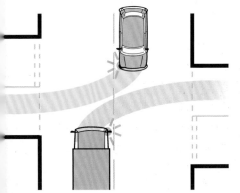

emerging

When you are emerging from one minor road at a crossroads and another vehicle is waiting to emerge from the minor road opposite, what you should do depends on the circumstances:

➡ if you are turning right and the other vehicle is turning left or going ahead, you should wait for the other vehicle to proceed before you emerge, otherwise you would be cutting across its path

➡ if you are turning left or going ahead you should proceed with caution in case the other vehicle emerges and cuts across your path

➡ if you are turning right and the other driver is turning right, neither of you has priority and you should proceed with extra care.

In practice you will find that many drivers are unfamiliar with the priorities described above. It is usually helpful to establish eye contact with the other driver to help determine what they intend to do. The other driver may gesture you to come out first – but do so only if you are completely certain that their meaning is clear and it is safe to do so. You should not wave or flash at another driver across a crossroads – it could be dangerous if they pull out without checking for themselves that the road is clear.

Extra caution is needed when you are emerging from a crossroads at the same time as another car

Roundabouts are designed to allow vehicles to merge smoothly and so keep the overall traffic stream flowing. A driver who is looking well ahead and anticipating traffic movements may be able to traverse a string of roundabouts safely and smoothly without once having to come to a complete halt. But negotiating roundabouts correctly does demand a high degree of concentration, anticipation and accurate signalling.

Signal clearly at roundabouts to let other road users know which direction you intend to take

roundabout safety

Fewer serious crashes occur on roundabouts than at crossroads. Yet paradoxically there are more collisions in total at roundabouts. That's because roundabouts slow down the traffic flow so when accidents happen they tend to be less severe. But the give and take nature of roundabouts means that minor shunts are more common. Careful observation, anticipation and signalling are needed to stay out of trouble.

Take care when anticipating what other road users intend to do on roundabouts. Some drivers have strange ideas about the correct lane or signalling to use, others don't bother signalling at all and some may simply be lost and unsure of which exit to take. So look out for vehicles:

- ⊜ turning right without indicating
- ⊜ indicating right but going straight on
- ⊜ using the right-hand lane to go straight ahead even if the left lane is clear
- ⊜ making a U-turn at the roundabout.

Beware also of cyclists, horse riders and long vehicles, all of which may take an unusual course at roundabouts.

negotiating a roundabout

As you approach the roundabout, scan all the approach roads to spot vehicles which may arrive at the same time as you do. Aim to make progress by adjusting your speed so you can join the traffic flow, but be prepared to stop and give way if necessary. Use the mirror-signal-manoeuvre routine on the approach to a roundabout, and always check your nearside mirror before taking your exit road in case someone – especially a cyclist or motorcyclist – is trying to pass on your left.

lanes and signalling

On some roundabouts, particularly larger roundabouts with multiple exits, white arrows painted on the approach road indicate which lane you should get into for the exit you intend to take. Where there are no arrows or signs indicating which lane to take, follow these guidelines:

Turning left:
- indicate left as you approach
- take the left-hand lane
- keep left on the roundabout
- continue to indicate left until you have exited the roundabout.

Turning right:
- indicate right as you approach
- take the right-hand lane
- keep right on the roundabout
- after passing the exit before the one you intend to take, indicate left
- check your nearside mirror before taking your exit road.

Going straight ahead:
- do not indicate on approach
- take the left-hand lane
- keep left on the roundabout
- after passing the exit before the one you intend to take, indicate left
- check your nearside mirror before taking your exit road.

It is also acceptable to use the right-hand lane when going straight ahead if the left-hand lane of the roundabout is blocked, for instance by vehicles turning left. In this case you should stay in the right-hand lane as you drive through the roundabout. You will need to check your nearside mirror carefully before taking your exit, in case a vehicle is moving up on your inside.

It is perfectly legal to carry out a U-turn by going all the way round a roundabout, but other drivers may not be expecting you to do this so take special care and signal clearly.

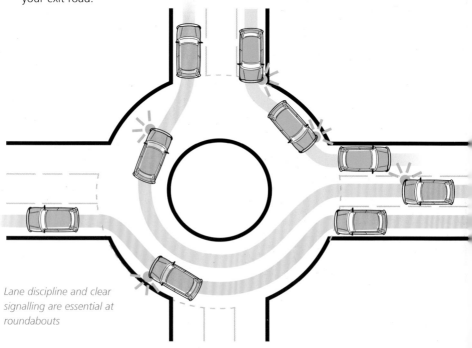

Lane discipline and clear signalling are essential at roundabouts

Where there are mini-roundabouts close together, you must treat them as separate junctions

mini-roundabouts

Treat mini-roundabouts in the same way as larger roundabouts. You must by law pass around the white central circle (but watch out for other drivers who may cut straight across without slowing down).

When turning right at a mini-roundabout you should indicate right as you approach but the small size of the roundabout means it is usually not practical to indicate left before exiting.

Some junctions consist of a series of mini-roundabouts. Treat each separately and give way if necessary as you approach each one in turn.

If there are lanes marked on the approach, get into the correct lane as soon as possible

Avoid driving alongside large vehicles on roundabouts as they may need to take up more than one lane to make their turn

TEST TIPS

DO

➜ give special caution to cyclists: they can find it difficult to pull across the traffic stream and may stay in the left-hand lane even when they want to turn right

➜ take extra care in the wet, as the road surface on roundabouts can become polished and slippery, causing your wheels to spin if you try to move off in a hurry

DON'T

➜ creep forward when waiting to join the roundabout. Drivers on the roundabout may think you are about to pull out in front of them. It could also lead to someone driving into the back of your car because they assume you are pulling onto the roundabout

➜ drive alongside a long vehicle – it may need more than one lane when negotiating a roundabout, so hold back and leave it room.

As a driver you have to deal with constantly changing situations on the road. In a single day you could find yourself negotiating busy city back streets, cruising on an empty motorway, tackling a twisting country lane and queuing in head to tail traffic at roadworks. You need to be ready to adapt your driving style to meet these changing conditions, and be aware of the specific hazards you are likely to encounter in different driving situations.

A car weighing around a tonne and a half and travelling at 50mph has a lot of momentum. This means that when you want to change course, you have to persuade the car to turn even though the forces acting on it are trying to make it carry straight on. Because of their sophisticated suspension systems, modern cars are reassuringly surefooted. But never forget that ultimately all that gets your car round a bend is the contact of four patches of tyre tread – each no bigger than a handprint – on the tarmac.

cornering

Road signs and markings give advance warning when you approach some bends ahead, but not all sharp bends have warnings. Remember that the bend sign not only warns you of a corner ahead, it also tells you which direction the road turns.

Carry out the mirror-signal-manoeuvre routine on the approach to a bend. Take care nothing is hidden from view behind your windscreen pillars. On a right-hand bend, move a little nearer to the kerb to improve your view through the bend. But don't move towards the centre of the road at the start of a left-hand bend: this could put you in danger from oncoming traffic, particularly if an oncoming vehicle cuts the corner.

If you need to change down a gear do this before you enter the bend. Steer gently into the bend, and apply some power to help balance the car. Once you see the bend start to open out, progressively apply more power and build up to the appropriate speed.

speed and grip

The golden rule when driving through a bend is that you must be able to stop, on your side of the road, in the distance you can see to be clear. Most bends are blind – your view through them is obscured by hedges or walls. At every bend ask yourself what might be hidden from your view halfway round. A horse rider? Stationary traffic? A fallen branch? Some drivers get into the habit of cornering a little too fast because experience tells them that most of the time there is nothing hidden round a bend. Until one day their luck runs out and they cause a serious accident.

Corner at a speed that keeps you well within the limit of grip of your tyres on the road. On a damp or greasy road the amount of grip you have is greatly reduced. If you try to take a corner too fast, the tyres will start to slide, putting you in danger of skidding off the road or into the path of another vehicle.

Another factor which influences how quickly a car can corner is the camber – the

way the road slopes to one side to allow rainwater to drain off. On an adverse camber a car will start to slide at a lower speed.

Remember that if you have to carry out an emergency stop while cornering, your car will not stop as quickly or smoothly as if you were travelling in a straight line, and if you brake too harshly it may skid.

Never stop or park on a bend. If you are forced to stop on a bend, for instance by meeting stationary traffic, put on your hazard warning lights to warn other vehicles.

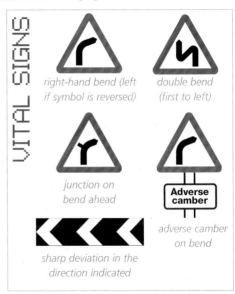

VITAL SIGNS

right-hand bend (left
if symbol is reversed)

double bend
(first to left)

junction on
bend ahead

Adverse
camber

adverse camber
on bend

sharp deviation in the
direction indicated

*Slow down when approaching a bend and be ready
to stop in the distance you can see to be clear*

On hills you have to take into account the force of gravity. Going uphill, the car needs more power to maintain its speed, so you may have to change down the gearbox. Downhill, the car will pick up speed and you may need to use the brakes and gearbox to restrain it. Hills affect the feel of the controls: harder braking is needed to slow a car when it is going downhill, and in a high gear the car may lose speed up a steep hill even with the accelerator pedal flat to the floor.

hill warnings

Steep hills often have warning signs shown as a percentage: 25% indicates a steep one-in-four gradient, where the road rises one metre for every four metres travelled horizontally; 10% means a less severe one-in-ten slope.

driving uphill

You will need to apply more power when climbing a hill, and your car will slow more quickly than when driving on the level. When approaching an uphill gradient don't wait until the engine starts to labour before changing down. Anticipate the need for more power and select the appropriate gear before the car starts losing momentum.

Look out for slow-moving heavy vehicles going uphill. If you want to overtake, remember that your car will feel more sluggish than on the level, and you will need more space to get past safely.

Slow vehicles may be directed to use a special crawler lane on uphill sections of motorway.

driving downhill

You need to prevent your car picking up unwanted speed when going downhill. Doing this with the brakes alone isn't a good idea as they may overheat and lose effectiveness. Use engine braking as well by engaging a lower gear to help slow the car. The steeper the hill, the lower the gear: as a rule of thumb, you should use the same gear to go down a hill as you would to come up it.

Always apply the brakes carefully when driving downhill as harsh use may provoke a skid, especially if the road is wet or slippery.

Leave extra space between your car and the vehicle in front when going downhill, as you will need a greater distance to stop in an emergency. On very steep hills an escape lane is sometimes provided, filled with loose gravel which will bring a vehicle to a halt if its brakes fail.

When parking on a hill extra precautions are needed to make sure your car cannot run away. Check the handbrake is firmly engaged. Then, if facing uphill, turn the front wheels so they are pointing away from the kerb (above) and leave the car in first gear; if facing downhill, turn the front wheels into the kerb and leave the car in reverse

VITAL SIGNS

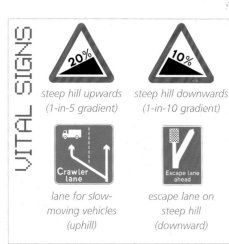

steep hill upwards
(1-in-5 gradient)

steep hill downwards
(1-in-10 gradient)

lane for slow-
moving vehicles
(uphill)

escape lane on
steep hill
(downward)

Driving in a built-up area poses an extra challenge because of the sheer number of hazards. You are sharing the road with vulnerable road users such as cyclists, pedestrians and children, there are numerous traffic signs and speed limits to observe, and your view of the road ahead is often obscured by parked vehicles. It means that extra concentration, anticipation and observation is required to stay safe in town.

speed

Because they are so hazardous, town streets have low speed limits – usually 30mph. Remember that there is no requirement for 30mph repeater signs to be displayed on roads with street lighting. Where buildings are less dense a 40mph limit is often posted, while in town centres 20mph zones are becoming common. Take special care:

- on busy high streets where people may not have their mind on traffic
- in zones with a 20mph speed limit where there are pedestrians or children playing
- near schools, especially around school opening and closing times. Roads outside schools can become chaotic when parents are dropping off and picking up their children so slow down and give way to manoeuvring vehicles. You must not park or stop to drop off passengers where road markings indicate a school entrance.

traffic calming

Physical obstructions such as humps, chicanes and constrictions are becoming more common in urban streets. Their purpose is to slow down traffic in residential areas, and discourage drivers from using 'rat-runs' – short cuts through backstreets.

Drive smoothly and slowly through these areas. Don't accelerate and then brake harshly between humps, and don't try to overtake a slower-moving vehicle. Not all humps are of uniform size so be prepared to slow to a walking pace to pass over them without causing discomfort to your passengers or damage to your car.

congestion charging

Car drivers must pay a congestion charge (currently £5) to enter London's central zone between 7am and 6.30pm, Monday to Friday (excluding Bank Holidays). You can pay on the day of travel at www.cclondon.com, or by phone on 0845 900 1234. Cameras monitor the zone and if you do not pay by midnight you will be liable for a fine of £80.

confidence

Drivers in busy cities can be assertive to the point of seeming aggressive – which can be intimidating to anyone not used to city driving. You need to be alert and decisive when joining a busy stream of traffic, or you could end up waiting for ages and holding up a queue of frustrated drivers. It helps to get some experience of city driving with your instructor beside you, and to avoid the rush hour the first time you drive into a city.

The fact is that driving on busy, congested city streets is no fun, and with congestion charges being introduced it is set to become costly too. If possible, park on the outskirts of town and use public transport instead.

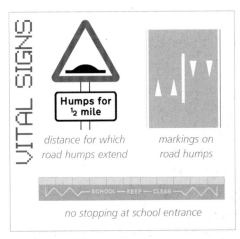

VITAL SIGNS

Humps for ½ mile

distance for which road humps extend

markings on road humps

no stopping at school entrance

Drive slowly where traffic calming measures are in force and be prepared to give way where indicated

07
COUNTRY ROADS

Country roads may look open, traffic free and safe, but appearances can be deceptive. That country bend could hide a horse and rider, a slick of mud left by a tractor, or a sudden sharp turn onto a narrow hump bridge. Although you should make progress where it is safe to do so on country roads, always be ready to encounter slow-moving vehicles, cyclists and pedestrians.

narrow lanes

On country roads wide enough for only one vehicle, be prepared to pull over where there is a passing place to let an oncoming vehicle through, or to let a following vehicle overtake. If the passing place is on your right-hand side then wait opposite it. If you meet a vehicle in between two passing places you may need to reverse back to the nearest passing place to let the other vehicle through. Never park in a passing place.

Use extreme caution when approaching a blind bend on a single-track road. In this situation you should be able to stop in half the distance you can see to be clear, which allows space for an approaching vehicle to stop too.

On narrow country roads be prepared to stop in half the distance you can see to be clear

special hazards

Take care when overtaking slow-moving agricultural vehicles as the driver may have difficulty seeing or hearing you.

Look out for pedestrians who may be approaching on your side of the road.

Animals – both domestic and wild – are another hazard on country roads (see p148).

Look out for slow-moving agricultural vehicles – and for the slippery mud they leave on the road

VITAL SIGNS

agricultural vehicles

falling or fallen rocks

hump bridge

uneven road

opening or swing bridge ahead

quayside or river bank

KNOW THE CODE

HIGHWAY CODE RULE 132

Country roads. Take extra care on country roads and reduce your speed at approaches to bends, which can be sharper than they appear, and at minor junctions and turnings, which may be partially hidden. Be prepared for pedestrians, horse riders and cyclists walking or riding in the road. You should also reduce your speed where country roads enter villages.

DUAL CARRIAGEWAYS

On dual carriageways the lanes in either direction are separated by a central reservation. Driving on a dual carriageway is similar to driving on a motorway, with a speed limit of 70mph unless otherwise signed, but there can be extra hazards such as slow-moving vehicles and right turns across the carriageway which would not be encountered on a motorway.

joining a dual carriageway

At many dual carriageway junctions you join by using a slip road. The purpose of the slip road is to let vehicles build up speed so they can merge smoothly with the traffic on the main carriageway.

As you drive onto the slip road try to assess the speed at which traffic in the inside lane of the dual carriageway is moving and accelerate to match it. Use the mirror-signal-manoeuvre routine, signal right to show that you intend moving across from the slip road and glance over your right shoulder just before you join the main carriageway to make sure there is nothing in your blind spot.

Don't expect traffic to make space for you and be prepared to use the full length of the slip road to merge safely. You should not have to stop and wait at the end of the slip road unless traffic on the main dual carriageway is very slow moving.

Where there is no slip road you join the dual carriageway as you would a normal road at a stop or give way junction. Be sure to take into account the higher speed of vehicles on the dual carriageway before moving out.

leaving a dual carriageway

Where there is a long slip road at the exit to a dual carriageway you can use this to lose speed. But some slip roads are short and end in a sharp bend, so be prepared to start losing speed before you leave the main carriageway. Where no slip road is provided you should start signalling and slowing early to give following traffic plenty of warning that you are turning off.

When joining from a slip road you must be prepared to give way to vehicles already on the dual carriageway. Adjust your speed and position to blend in smoothly with the traffic flow

Exit slip roads may be short and busy so watch your speed when leaving a dual carriageway

TEST TIPS

DO
➜ use the length of the slip road to build up your speed to match that of traffic on the dual carriageway

➜ take into account higher traffic speeds on dual carriageways and check your mirrors frequently

DON'T
➜ get too close to vehicles you intend to overtake. Remember the two-second rule

➜ leave it till the last moment before returning to the left-hand lane when you see that the dual carriageway is about to end.

right turns

Keep in the left lane of the dual carriageway unless you are overtaking slower-moving traffic or turning right. If you want to carry out a right turn, you need to consider the high speed of traffic and start planning your turn at an early stage. Check your mirror carefully, signal well in advance, and consider a gentle pressure on the brake pedal at an early stage to signal to following traffic that you are slowing. Position your car accurately inside the turning bay in the central reservation, and take care to check that the road you are entering is clear before turning across the right-hand carriageway.

Be careful when overtaking large vehicles as your car may be obscured in the driver's blind spot

dual carriageway ends

When you see the dual carriageway ends sign, check your speed because, unless signposted otherwise, the speed limit is about to drop back from 70 mph to 60 mph – the national speed limit for single carriageway roads. If you are overtaking, make sure you get back into the left-hand lane in good time before the dual carriageway ends. Be alert for other vehicles cutting past to pull in front of you at the last moment, and leave plenty of room from the vehicle in front so they have space to pull in safely.

When approaching a roundabout on a dual carriageway, reduce speed in good time, look at the signs and follow the 'get in lane' instruction

Finish overtaking and return to the inside lane in good time when you see the dual carriageway ends sign

overtaking

On dual carriageways you need to plan your overtaking manoeuvres well in advance and give clear signals in good time because other vehicles may be coming up fast behind you.

1 Carry out the mirror-signal-manoeuvre routine and look well down the road to check for hazards in front of the vehicle you will be overtaking. Let the indicator flash at least three times before you start to move out to give other road users time to respond to your signal. Give a signal even if there is no one behind as it indicates your intentions to the driver you are overtaking.

2 When it is safe to move out, pull across into the right-hand lane of the dual carriageway. This should be carried out as a smoothly flowing manoeuvre – don't steer harshly or change lanes abruptly.

(Remember that on a dual carriageway you may overtake only on the right, unless traffic is moving slowly in queues and your queue is quicker than the one in the right-hand lane).

3 Accelerate and overtake briskly, always keeping within the speed limit. Avoid lingering in the blind spot of the vehicle you are overtaking where the driver may not be able to see you, especially when you are overtaking a large vehicle.

4 Don't cut in sharply once you're past the front of the vehicle you've overtaken – you mustn't leave it with less than a two-second separation distance once you've pulled back in. Check your mirrors to make sure you've left enough room before pulling back into the inside lane.

MOTORWAYS

You aren't permitted to drive on motorways until you get your full driving licence, but the theory test includes plenty of questions about motorways, so don't overlook this section. Motorways are great for covering long distances quickly, but driving on them demands discipline and responsibility. Although motorways are statistically the safest of all roads, because of their higher speeds and volume of traffic, when accidents do occur they are often serious ones.

Keep in the left-hand lane of the motorway unless you need to pull out to overtake slower traffic

planning your journey

Motorways are laid out to avoid sharp bends or steep hills, and there are no stop or give way junctions to halt the traffic flow. This means it's possible to make swift progress, and if you're planning a long journey it makes sense to use the motorway.

You must make sure you are prepared before setting out, because long high-speed journeys put extra strain on both car and driver. Check the car's lights, fluid levels and tyre pressures before setting out. If you do break down, recovery from a motorway is expensive so it pays to be a member of a breakdown recovery service. Don't travel long distances if you are ill or haven't slept well. The hard shoulder is only for stopping in a real emergency – not just if you feel tired – so plan frequent rest stops at service areas.

IT'S THE LAW

MOTORWAYS MUST NOT BE USED BY:

- ➔ learner drivers and riders
- ➔ pedestrians
- ➔ cyclists
- ➔ horse riders
- ➔ motorcycles under 50cc
- ➔ slow-moving vehicles, agricultural vehicles and invalid carriages.

lane discipline

Keep in the left-hand lane unless you need to overtake slower-moving vehicles. Where there is a stream of slower-moving traffic, don't weave in and out of the left-hand lane. It's better to stay in the middle lane until the left-hand lane clears (but do keep an eye on your mirror and be prepared to move over to let faster-moving vehicles pass).

Use the outer lane to overtake when the inner and middle lanes are occupied with slower traffic, but again be ready to move back as soon as it is clear to do so.

If a vehicle which is clearly exceeding the speed limit comes up behind you, never try to make it slow down or hold it up: pull over at the first safe opportunity and let it overtake. If you are held up by a slower vehicle, never try to intimidate your way past: wait patiently until it pulls over.

Large goods vehicles, buses, coaches and vehicles towing a trailer or caravan are not allowed to use the outer lane of a motorway, so take care not to block their progress by neglecting to pull back into the left-hand lane as soon as it is clear for you to do so.

junctions

As you approach a junction be prepared for vehicles exiting the motorway to cut across in front of you at the last moment.

There is usually a slip road entering the motorway immediately after you pass an exit. Anticipate that vehicles may be joining here. If there is space to do so then pull into the middle lane to give vehicles joining the motorway room to move across from the slip road into the inside lane.

stopping

Stopping is not permitted on a motorway except in an emergency, or if you are directed to by a sign with flashing red lights, or by the police. If you feel in need of a break then go on to the next exit or service station. You must not pick up or put down hitch hikers, even on a slip road.

joining and leaving

When joining a motorway, use the slip road as you would when joining a dual carriageway. Once you have joined, keep in the left-hand lane until you have adjusted to the traffic conditions on the motorway.

Motorway exits are clearly marked, with signs at one mile and half a mile, and then countdown markers at 300, 200 and 100 yards (270, 180 and 90 metres) before the slip road. Don't pull across to the exit at the last second. You should aim to be in the left-hand lane by around the half-mile warning sign. Where other traffic might benefit from a signal, start indicating left at the 300 yard marker.

If you go past your junction by mistake you must continue to the next junction and leave the motorway to rejoin in the opposite direction. You must never reverse on a motorway or slip road.

Keep a careful eye on your speedometer after leaving a motorway, as you may feel as though you are driving more slowly than you really are.

It is illegal (except in an emergency) to drive into the triangular area of chevrons within a solid white line which separates a motorway slip road from the main carriageway

anticipation

Anticipating what is happening far ahead of your vehicle is vital when driving at high speed on the motorway. Too many drivers follow too closely behind the vehicle in front. When one brakes, it sends a chain reaction of panic braking back down the motorway. Leave at least a two-second gap between your car and the vehicle in front – more in wet weather or poor visibility. Keep looking well ahead and ease off the accelerator if you see brake lights in the distance. Be ready to slow down or stop if you see hazard warning lights flashing ahead, and if you encounter slow or stationary traffic consider switching on your hazard warning lights briefly to warn drivers behind you.

Take special care when entering service stations as slip roads can be shorter than at normal junctions, and you will need to slow to a walking pace when you enter the service station car park

Avoid getting boxed in behind slow traffic; look well ahead so you can anticipate in advance when you will need to move out to overtake

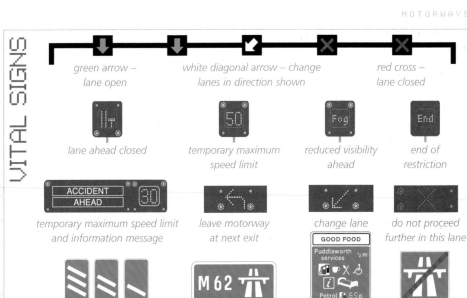

green arrow –
lane open

white diagonal arrow – change
lanes in direction shown

red cross –
lane closed

lane ahead closed

temporary maximum
speed limit

reduced visibility
ahead

end of
restriction

temporary maximum speed limit
and information message

leave motorway
at next exit

change lane

do not proceed
further in this lane

countdown markers at
exit from motorway

start of motorway (motorway
regulations now apply)

service area in
half a mile

end of
motorway

bad weather

Because of the high traffic speeds it is essential to make yourself visible on the motorway. Always use your headlights at night and in rain or poor light, even when the motorway is well lit.

In wet conditions, beware of spray thrown up from the road, particularly as you overtake large goods vehicles and coaches. Look out also for the effect of crosswinds on exposed stretches of motorway. Be prepared for the wind to drop as you come alongside a high-sided vehicle, then increase violently as you pass it.

Use your fog lights if visibility falls below 100 metres – but remember to turn them off again as soon as it clears. Fog patches are a special danger on motorways as you may encounter them at high speed with little warning. Reduce your speed in conditions where fog patches may be likely to form and take heed of fog warning signs, even if it is quite clear where you are.

ROADWORKS

Roadworks are an occupational hazard for drivers, and the delays they cause can be frustrating. For safety's sake, stay calm and follow all signs to the letter. You may have to merge with other traffic where lanes are closed off, follow a deviation over an uneven temporary road surface, and give way to workmen and machinery crossing in front of you. Take particular care on motorway contraflows.

roadwork precautions

⮕ take care when you see the roadworks ahead sign, and look out for further signs
⮕ temporary speed limits posted at roadworks are mandatory and you must obey them, even if there is no work taking place
⮕ if one or more lanes are closed, carry out the mirror-signal-manoeuvre routine and get into the correct lane in good time. Leave plenty of space and be alert for vehicles cutting across at the last moment
⮕ do not switch lanes to overtake queuing traffic. When queuing in lines of traffic, obey merge in turn signs where posted
⮕ lanes may narrow through roadworks so look for width restriction warnings. Use the hard shoulder if signs direct you to
⮕ be prepared to stop where traffic at roadworks is controlled by a stop-go board, a police officer or temporary traffic lights
⮕ do not enter areas cordoned off by cones
⮕ try not to be distracted by work going on around you, but be prepared to give way to works vehicles or staff
⮕ slow down for ramps, rough road surfaces or loose chippings
⮕ at the end of motorway roadworks there may be a national speed limit sign or an end of roadworks sign: both indicate that the speed limit has returned to the national limit (70mph for cars)
⮕ where the pavement is closed due to street repairs, look out for pedestrians walking in the road.

contraflows

On motorway contraflow systems traffic from both directions share the same carriageway. Lanes are separated by temporary red and white marker posts, and may be narrower than usual. You may need to select a lane some way in advance if you intend leaving at the next junction. Make sure you:

⮕ reduce speed in good time and obey any speed limit signposted
⮕ get into an appropriate lane early
⮕ keep a generous separation distance.

roadworks

loose chippings

manually operated temporary stop and go signs

temporary hazard at roadworks

roadworks one mile ahead

lane restrictions at roadworks ahead

temporary lane closure

one lane crossover at contraflow roadworks

Mandatory reduced speed limit ahead

end of roadworks and any temporary restrictions

When minor roadworks are carried out on motorways and dual carriageways these signs may be shown on the back of a slow-moving or stationary works vehicle blocking a traffic lane. The four amber lamps flash in alternate horizontal pairs. Pass the vehicle in the direction shown by the arrow. Where a lane is closed there will be no cones to separate it

08
ROAD SENSE

Unfortunately there's no equivalent to an aircraft's auto-pilot when you're driving a car. Every moment you are behind the wheel, you need to concentrate one hundred per cent on your driving. Not only do you need to observe what is happening on the road all around you, you need to think hard about what you're seeing too, identifying hazards and assessing what sort of risk they represent. That way you can anticipate risks in advance, not react to them at the last moment. You must also watch your speed on the road: speeding is both illegal and responsible for many serious road accidents.

One reason why inexperienced drivers have a higher accident rate is that they take more time – up to two seconds longer – to detect a hazard as it is developing on the road ahead. Hazard perception is tested in a special video-clip based exam that forms part of the theory test. Get into the habit of trying to identify potential hazards every time you are on the road, even as a passenger, and ask yourself what action you would need to take to deal with them safely.

what is a hazard?

simply any potential danger you encounter on the road which may cause you to change your speed or direction.

Types of hazard include:

static hazards

These are stationary features such as bends, junctions, traffic lights and crossings. They are the easiest type of hazard to recognise, as they do not change as you approach them, but you often have to deal with them while concentrating on what other road users – such as pedestrians using a zebra crossing – are doing as well

moving hazards

These may be pedestrians, cyclists, animals, horse riders, motorcyclists and large vehicles as well as other cars. Each type of road user is likely to react differently to situations on the road, and you need to understand why this is in order to anticipate how they are likely to react and so share the road safely with them

road and weather hazards

Rain, ice or snow, mud or loose gravel on the road all make it more likely that harsh steering, braking or acceleration will cause a skid. Bright sunshine can dazzle, and darkness makes it harder to spot hazards. Fog dangerously reduces visibility and high winds make it more hazardous to drive near cyclists, motorcyclists and high sided vehicles.

prioritising hazards

Hazards on the road don't come neatly one at a time. It's important to assess how serious each hazard is so you can decide which one takes priority. For instance, a parked car on a wide road with no oncoming traffic is a minor hazard. But if you spot that there is a driver sitting in the car and exhaust fumes show that the engine is running, then it becomes a more serious hazard, and you must anticipate that the driver might pull out in front of you.

The sooner you recognise a hazard, the sooner you are able to take the action needed to negotiate it safely. If ever you have to take emergency action to avoid a collision on the road, ask yourself whether you could have recognised and anticipated the hazard earlier, and what steps could you take to avoid the same thing happening again in the future.

OBSERVATION

Effective observation is a vital driving skill to develop. You can only react to what you see happening on the road around you, and the sooner you see a hazard, the more time you will be able to give yourself to deal with it safely.

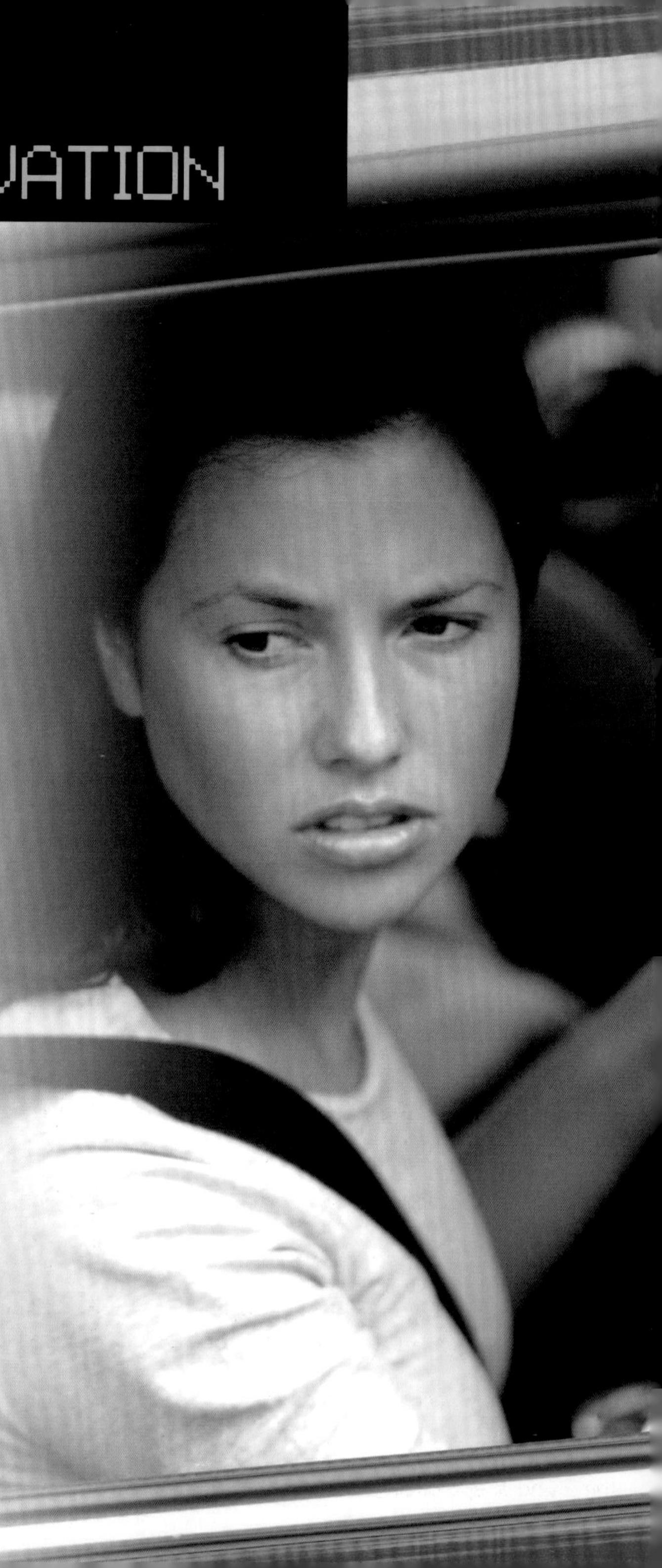

looking or seeing?

If you let your attention wander you may find you are looking at hazards without really seeing them. And you may be surprised how easy it is to drive past a road sign without actually taking in what it means. It's important to train your sense of observation so you really are seeing and thinking about everything on the road around you.

scanning

Keep your eyes moving, so you are seeing what is happening in all directions. Scan to the left and right of the road, then shift the focus of your eyes into the far distance. By looking well ahead of the vehicle in front you can see any hazards that it may have to react to, and anticipate in advance when you will need to slow down. Don't wait till you see the brake lights of the car in front come on before starting to take action.

Remember to use your mirrors to keep an eye on what is happening behind your vehicle too, and be sure to carry out the mirror-signal-manoeuvre routine every time you encounter a hazard.

improve your view

- following too closely behind the vehicle in front can drastically reduce your view. Keep well back, especially when you are behind a large vehicle, so you can see around it
- scan to your left and right as you approach a crossroads or roundabout to see if you can spot other vehicles which will arrive there at the same time you do
- look at rows of trees or lamp posts along the road ahead to see if they curve to indicate a bend in the road
- look underneath parked cars to spot the feet of pedestrians who may be about to cross the road
- don't rely just on your eyes. In fog or where high hedges obscure a junction, wind down your window and listen for the sound of approaching vehicles.

Keep your eyes constantly moving and shifting focus from the foreground into the far distance

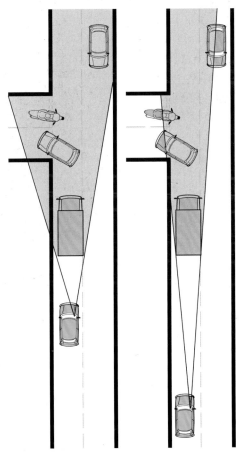

Keeping well back from the vehicle in front can dramatically improve your view and give you earlier warning of any hazards ahead

131

Some people think that a good driver is one who has the quick reactions to get out of trouble. This isn't true. The good driver is the one who anticipates trouble and avoids getting into it in the first place. Ask yourself 'what if?' as you drive along the road. What if that pedestrian walks onto the zebra crossing? What if that taxi does a U-turn? What if that driver waiting to pull out hasn't seen me? If you always anticipate the worst that may happen, you won't be taken unawares when it does.

Anticipating hazards

Hazards on the road come in all sorts, shapes and sizes. The situations pictured opposite illustrate the sort of questions you need to ask yourself in order to anticipate what hazards might develop on the road ahead.

No footway for 530 yds

This is a HomeWatch Area

Approaching pedestrian crossing
Scan the pavements on either side and ask yourself whether any of the pedestrians may be about to use the crossing ahead

Cyclist approaching junction
Ask yourself if this young cyclist might swerve across the road to turn right at the junction. Hold back until you are certain what he intends to do

Approaching a school entrance
Extra care is needed at school opening and closing hours in term time. Ask yourself if there are likely to be children about whenever you approach a school

Car following slow truck on motorway
Ask yourself if the driver is likely to pull out in front of you in order to overtake the slow truck, with or without giving a signal beforehand

Stationary vehicle on hard shoulder
Ask yourself whether this vehicle may start to move out without warning, or if the driver may open the door and jump out without looking. This situation needs particular care as most of your attention is focused on joining the motorway

VITAL SIGNS

stationary traffic is likely ahead (always make sure that you can stop in the distance you can see to be clear)

danger ahead

reduce speed warning shown beneath some signs

CONCENTRATION

Driving is a serious business. If you walk along a footpath chatting to a friend and not concentrating on where you're going, you may trip over a fallen branch and stub your toe. It's irritating but no disaster. But if you're driving along lost in conversation, or fiddling with the radio, or daydreaming about your next holiday, and you fail to see a cyclist pull out in front of you, then the outcome could be devastating.

staying alert

To maintain your concentration:

- don't drive when you are feeling distracted or emotional. Delay setting out until you have calmed down or, take a cab instead
- keep your eyes on the road. At 70mph you are travelling over 30 metres (100 feet) every second – so if you glance away for just three seconds to fiddle with the car stereo, you have covered nearly 100 metres (330 feet) without looking where you are going
- avoid eating or drinking behind the wheel. It's not only bad for concentration, it's bad for the digestion too. On a long journey you need regular breaks, so plan a lunch stop and don't try to refuel on the move
- don't listen to excessively loud music
- avoid arguing with passengers
- if you need to consult a map, find a safe place to pull over. Never try to read a map and drive at the same time
- never use a mobile phone while driving. Even hands-free phones are a serious mental distraction – you can't concentrate properly on a telephone discussion and your driving at the same time
- don't drive when you are tired, or when under the influence of drugs or alcohol.

fatigue

Driving when tired is a major cause of death on the road. Crashes involving drivers who doze off at the wheel are usually serious, because a sleeping driver isn't able to slow down or take avoiding action. But no one falls asleep without warning. As soon as you start to feel drowsy and lose concentration you should:

- make sure there is plenty of fresh air coming into the car – but remember that if you are really tired then opening a window will not stop you falling asleep
- pull over as soon as you can into a lay-by or service area (but not the hard shoulder of a motorway) and take a break
- have a drink high in caffeine, such as two cups of strong coffee
- recline your seat and take a short nap.

You can reduce the risk of becoming seriously sleepy while you are driving by:

- avoiding long drives during your body's natural sleep periods (the early hours of the morning and just after lunch)
- taking regular breaks during a long drive. Stop for at least 15 minutes for every two hours you are on the road
- not driving a long distance after a poor or interrupted night's sleep.

Using a hand-held mobile while driving is illegal, so park up safely before making or receiving calls

Take regular breaks when driving long distances to avoid losing concentration behind the wheel

135

Most cars are capable of exceeding 100mph. Many could easily double the maximum speed permitted on the motorway. With so much power on tap it takes discipline to keep your speed under control. But using speed safely is one of the most vital driving skills. The stark truth is that if you have to stop in an emergency and you are driving too quickly then you will crash. The higher your speed, the more serious that crash will be.

speed limits

You must always keep your speed below the maximum speed limit for the road and vehicle you are driving. These general rules govern the speed limit for cars on most roads:

- the national speed limit on single carriageway roads is 60mph
- the national speed limit on dual carriageways and motorways is 70mph
- the speed limit on roads with street lighting is 30mph.

These speed limits apply at all times if there are no speed limit signs indicating otherwise. There will not necessarily be signs to remind you that one of these speed limits is in force.

These limits are overridden if there are signs which indicate a specific speed limit, such as 40mph on a road with street lighting or 50mph on a dual carriageway. Where other speed limits apply there will be regular speed limit repeater signs placed along the road.

safe speeds

Speed limits represent the maximum speed permitted. They are not targets to be achieved at all costs. There are many occasions where it is not safe to drive as fast as the speed limit. For instance, when driving near children running along the pavement, or where parked cars obscure your vision on either side, 30mph could be recklessly fast.

Too many drivers routinely ignore the speed limit in town. It's true that 30mph feels slow from inside a car, but you must always put the safety of pedestrians and cyclists first. The fact is that if a car hits a pedestrian while travelling at 20mph, nine times out of ten the pedestrian will survive the impact; at 40mph, the pedestrian has only a one-in-ten chance of living.

national speed limits

Type of vehicle	Built-up area	Single carriageway	Dual carriageway	Motorway
Cars & motorcycles	30	60	70	70
Cars towing caravans or trailers	30	50	60	60
Buses & coaches	30	50	60	70
Goods vehicles * 60 if articulated or towing a trailer	30	50	60	70*
Goods vehicles (exceeding 7.5 tonnes maximum laden weight)	30	40	50	60

In busy town centres (above) or on narrow country lanes (below) you may need to keep your speed well below the speed limit to stay safe

20 mph	6 metres 6 metres	3 car lengths or **12** metres
30 mph	9 metres 14 metres	6 car lengths or **23** metres
40 mph	12 metres 24 metres	9 car lengths or **36** metres
50 mph	15 metres 38 metres	13 car lengths or **53** metres
60 mph	18 metres 55 metres	18 car lengths or **73** metres
70 mph	21 metres 75 metres	24 car lengths or **96** metres

Thinking distance   Braking distance   Average car length = 4 metres

stopping distances

The diagram above gives typical stopping distances from varying speeds. There are a number of important points to bear in mind when you are considering these stopping distances:

- it takes a long way to bring a car to a complete halt even from a low speed: six car lengths are needed from 30mph, which is a lot more space than most drivers allow when driving in town
- it takes time to react and press the brake pedal before you even start to slow down. At 40mph you will travel three car lengths during the time it takes you to react. This assumes that it takes about 0.7 seconds to react before braking, a time that could easily treble if you aren't concentrating
- stopping distance doesn't increase uniformly with speed: double your speed from 30mph to 60mph, and you need not twice but three times the distance in which to stop
- these are stopping distances on a dry road in good weather: in the wet, allow twice the distance to stop; on icy roads, ten times further may be needed
- a car with worn brakes or tyres may take much further to stop, particularly on a wet road, even if the tyre tread depth is still above the legal minimum
- always remember the driving rule which cannot be repeated too often: you must be able to stop in the distance you can see to be clear.

how fast?

Sometimes your senses can trick you into thinking you are driving more slowly than you really are. A speed of 40mph feels much slower on an open road than it does through an avenue of trees, because the objects flashing past on the edge of your vision give you a sensation of speed. This means it is particularly difficult to judge your speed when the reference points around you are obscured, for instance at night or in foggy weather.

Take particular care to monitor your speed at times when you may feel you are going more slowly than you really are, such as:
- at night or in poor visibility
- on long, open stretches of road, especially motorways
- when you enter a speed limit after a spell of fast driving on the open road
- when driving an unusual car, particularly if it is quieter and more powerful than the one you are used to.

other vehicles

Remember that drivers of other vehicles are not necessarily permitted to travel as quickly as you are in your car. Make allowance for this and don't get frustrated when you are following, for instance, a caravan doing 50mph on the open road – it's going as fast as it is allowed.

minimum speed

Minimum speed limits are not common, but are sometimes posted on roads where it is important for traffic to keep flowing smoothly.

Don't race up to hazards and brake at the last moment: anticipate them and lose speed smoothly

It's good driving to make progress when it is safe to do so, but you must stay within the speed limit

acceleration sense

Never accelerate towards a hazard. If you spot brake lights coming on ahead, or see advance warning for a give way sign, lift your foot off the accelerator pedal. The sooner you start to lose speed as you approach a hazard the more time you give yourself to deal with it. Accelerating up to a hazard and braking at the last minute is bad practice for other reasons too: it wastes fuel and causes unnecessary brake wear, as well as being unnerving for passengers (including your driving examiner) who may think you haven't noticed there's a hazard ahead.

making progress

If safety is the most important consideration when driving, and the higher your speed the greater the potential danger, wouldn't the best plan be to drive everywhere at 10mph? Unfortunately this would be a sure route to failing your driving test. Although you must at all times drive safely, you should also make progress when it is safe to do so. Drivers who crawl along the road when it would be safe to drive at the speed limit obstruct other road users, making them feel frustrated and more likely to take risks to overtake. Where it is safe to drive at the indicated speed limit, then it is good driving practice to do just that.

national speed
limit applies

end of 20
mph zone

maximum
speed limit

maximum speed
limit within traffic
calming scheme

minimum
speed limit

end of minimum
speed limit

area with traffic
enforcement cameras

09
OTHER ROAD
USERS

From the smooth, warm, quiet comfort of your car, it can be hard to put yourself in the position of other road users who are exposed to harsher conditions. Such as the pedestrian hurrying to get home through blinding rain, the cyclist swerving to avoid a broken drain cover, or the rider trying to calm a horse spooked by a tin can rattling across the road. But you should never forget that you are at the wheel of a potentially lethal weapon and it is your responsibility to look out for the safety of these more vulnerable road users.

PEDESTRIANS

Cars and pedestrians make an uneasy mix and where the two come into conflict it's the pedestrian who comes off worst. You simply cannot take risks where pedestrians are around. That means slowing down when there are people on the pavement and always being prepared to give way for pedestrians crossing the road.

vulnerable people

Take special care around those pedestrians who may fail to be aware of your presence, such as:

- ➡ elderly pedestrians, who can find it harder to judge the speed of approaching vehicles
- ➡ children, who may run into the road unexpectedly
- ➡ blind and deaf pedestrians, who may be unaware of your approach. If a person is holding a white stick, or leading a guide dog on a harness, it means they are blind. If the white stick has a red band around it, they are deaf as well. There are guide dogs for the deaf too, and these usually wear a burgundy-coloured coat
- ➡ wheelchair users. Be patient when a wheelchair user needs to cross the road, and don't obstruct them by parking where the kerb is lowered to allow wheelchair access.

Look out for powered vehicles used by disabled people. These small vehicles travel at a maximum speed of 8mph. When used on a dual carriageway they must by law have a flashing amber light, but on other roads you may not be given any such warning of their presence

pedestrian crossings

Pedestrian crossings are points designed to allow pedestrians to cross the road in safety. Always be prepared to stop when approaching a crossing, and take special care if your view as you approach the crossing is obscured by queuing traffic or badly parked vehicles.

Treat pedestrians using a crossing courteously. Consider giving a slowing down arm signal as you approach to let waiting pedestrians know you are stopping, but do not beckon them to cross – this may be dangerous if other vehicles are approaching. Wait patiently while they are crossing, especially for elderly or disabled pedestrians who may not be able to get across before the lights change.

Never park on a crossing or in the area marked by zig-zag lines. When approaching a crossing in a slow-moving queue, hold back so you do not stop where you would obstruct the crossing. It is illegal to overtake the moving vehicle nearest to a pedestrian crossing or a vehicle which has stopped to give way to pedestrians at the crossing.

Pedestrians don't always use crossings, so drive carefully wherever there are people on foot

Approach zebra crossings with caution and be prepared to stop and give way to pedestrians

zebra crossings

Be ready to slow down or stop as you approach a zebra crossing. You must by law give way when someone has stepped on to a crossing, but you should also be prepared to stop and let waiting pedestrians cross. Scan the pavements as you approach for anyone who looks like they might want to cross and slow down well before you get to the crossing. If a pedestrian does not cross immediately, be patient and remain stationary until they do. Be prepared for pedestrians to change their mind halfway across and walk back in front of you.

Where the zebra crossing is divided by a central island you should treat each half as a separate crossing.

pelican crossings

Pelican crossings are controlled by lights. Unlike normal traffic lights, these have a flashing amber phase in between red and green. When the amber light is flashing, you must give way to pedestrians who are on the crossing. If there are no pedestrians on the crossing when the amber light is flashing, you may proceed across it with caution. If pedestrians are still crossing after the lights have changed to green you should continue to give way to them.

Pelican crossings which go straight across the road are one crossing, even when there is a central island. This means you must wait for pedestrians who are crossing from the other side of the island. However, if the crossings are staggered on either side of the central island they should be treated as separate crossings.

144

Pelican crossings (above), toucan crossings and puffin crossings are all controlled by traffic lights

Hold back in a queue of traffic so you do not stop where you would obstruct a pedestrian crossing

toucan crossings

These are also used by cyclists, who are permitted to ride across a toucan crossing. They are operated by push buttons and follow the normal traffic light sequence, with no flashing amber phase. Take care when preparing to move off when the lights turn green, in case a pedestrian has left it late to cross or is an elderly person crossing slowly.

school crossings

You must stop when a school crossing patrol shows a stop for children sign. Always be courteous to school crossing patrols.

There may be a flashing amber signal below the school warning sign to alert you that children may be crossing the road ahead. Drive very slowly until you are clear of the area. Be cautious also when passing a stationary bus showing a school bus sign. You may have to give way to children running across the road to and from the bus.

puffin crossings

These have automatic sensors which detect when pedestrians are on the crossing and delay the green light until they have safely reached the other side. Like the toucan crossing, puffins have a normal traffic light sequence with no flashing amber.

VITAL SIGNS

pedestrian crossing

elderly people (or blind or disabled as shown) crossing road

stop at school crossing patrol

school crossing patrol ahead

Patrol

No footway for 400 yds

no footway (there may be pedestrians walking in the road)

145

HORSE RIDERS

Horses are easily alarmed and unpredictable. When you encounter a horse rider on the road, slow right down and be prepared to stop. Don't become irritated with horse riders for slowing your journey – they aren't riding on the road for the fun of it, but have no other option to get to and from local bridleways.

passing horses

Treat all horses as a potential hazard. Slow to a walking pace as you approach a horse rider and give them plenty of space. Be prepared to stop and wait if other vehicles are approaching, as you will need to move well onto the other side of the road to pass a horse rider. Never try to squeeze by when a vehicle is coming the other way. Remember that horses are easily startled and may shy into the middle of the road if surprised by something – which may be just a rustling crisp packet – in the hedge.

Slow right down when passing horse riders and always leave them plenty of space

avoid noise

Never sound your horn or rev your engine while approaching a horse. If the horse looks skittish, pull over and turn off your engine until it has gone by.

Take extra care if you are driving a larger and more noisy vehicle such as a van or car and trailer which may be more likely to alarm the horse. More caution is also needed in wet weather when your tyres make more noise, and you need to avoid startling the horse by splashing it with spray.

Take special care when you encounter horse riders who may be young or inexperienced

inexperienced riders

Be particularly careful when horses are being ridden by children, or where there is a line of inexperienced riders. Riders may be in double file when escorting a young or inexperienced horse rider. Look out for signals from horse riders, and always heed a request to slow down or stop.

right turns

Take care when following a horse and rider at the approach to a right-hand turn or roundabout. The rider may signal right but stay on the left of the road at the approach to the turn, so slow down and be prepared to stop and wait to let the rider cross the road in front of you and make the right turn.

KNOW THE CODE | HIGHWAY CODE RULE 191

Horse riders. Be particularly careful of horses and riders, especially when overtaking. Always pass wide and slow. Horse riders are often children, so take extra care and remember riders may ride in double file when escorting a young or inexperienced horse rider. Look out for horse riders' signals and heed a request to slow down or stop. Treat all horses as a potential hazard and take great care.

ANIMALS

Animals – both wild and domestic – are unpredictable and represent a serious hazard when they stray onto the road. Observe signs warning of animals, and keep your speed down, especially where there are no fences to keep cattle, sheep or ponies off the road.

domestic animals

In country areas, especially moorland, there may be no fences keeping cattle, sheep and horses from straying onto the road. Exercise great caution in these areas and keep your speed down, especially at night or in misty conditions. Where there are animals on or near the road, drive past them at walking pace. Do not sound your horn, flash your lights, or rev your engine loudly as this may cause them to panic. Bear in mind that if an animal such as a sheep crosses the road in front of you then several others may follow it, and that young animals will run to their mother if they feel threatened, even if that means darting in front of your car.

Sometimes sheep or cattle have to be led across the road. If your way is blocked by a herd of animals, stop, switch off your engine and wait until they have left the road.

wild animals

Colliding with a large wild animal like a deer is distressing, and can cause serious damage to your car and possibly you too. Keep your speed down wherever there is likely to be wildlife near the road, and slow down when you see warning signs. Take special care at dawn and dusk when deer are most active.

Cattle grids are often placed at the entrance to areas of open country: cars can cross them but cattle cannot. Slow down when driving across a grid as they can be loose and slippery

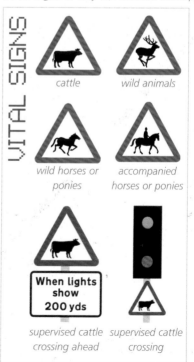

VITAL SIGNS

cattle

wild animals

wild horses or ponies

accompanied horses or ponies

When lights show 200 yds

supervised cattle crossing ahead

supervised cattle crossing

If you have ever cycled on a busy road you'll know how intimidating it is when cars speed by leaving only a couple of feet to spare. Cyclists have every much right to use the road as car drivers – maybe more right, as they are doing so at less cost to the environment – so treat them with courtesy, and be conscious of their extra vulnerability compared with a motor vehicle.

overtaking cyclists

Leave as much room when overtaking a cyclist as you would when overtaking a car. Remember that a cyclist may swerve to avoid something you can't see, such as a pothole or rubbish in the road. Never try to squeeze past a cyclist when another vehicle is coming towards you, and slow right down when passing a cyclist on a narrow road.

Be prepared for cyclists to do the unexpected. Although most cyclists are responsible road users, remember that no training is needed to ride a bicycle and riders of any age are allowed to use the road. Situations where you should be particularly alert for cyclists include:

Take special care to look out for cyclists who may be riding past on the inside when you make a left turn at a junction or into a driveway

➡ **slow-moving traffic**
Cyclists may overtake on your inside, so check your nearside mirror before pulling into the kerb or turning left

➡ **junctions and roundabouts**
Cyclists can find it daunting to pull across the road to turn right in busy traffic, and may feel safer keeping to the left when turning right at a roundabout. Be cautious whenever you see a cyclist looking over their shoulder as they could be about to turn right. Give them time and space to do so safely

➡ **left turns**
Never overtake a cyclist just before a left turn so you have to cut in front to make the turn. Slow down and hold back until the cyclist has passed the turning

➡ **country lanes**
You may encounter slow-moving cyclists around any bend

➡ **at night or dusk**
Cyclists may not be showing lights, or their lights may be hard to spot among other vehicle lights

➡ **windy weather**
In strong winds cyclists may find it hard to keep a straight course and you should leave more space when overtaking them.

VITAL SIGNS

cycle route ahead

no cycling

route for cycles only

route for pedestrians and cyclists

recommended route for cycles

with-flow cycle lane

KNOW THE CODE

HIGHWAY CODE RULE 119

Cycle lanes. These are shown by road markings and signs. You MUST NOT drive or park in a cycle lane marked by a solid white line during its times of operation. Do not drive or park in a cycle lane marked by a broken white line unless it is unavoidable. You MUST NOT park in any cycle lane whilst waiting restrictions apply.

MOTORBIKES

Motorcyclists are seriously vulnerable road users. They are up to 20 times more likely than car drivers to be killed or seriously injured in a road accident. Many collisions involving bikers are caused by car drivers who aren't thinking about motorbikes approaching. Always look out for motorbikes, give them plenty of room and do what you can to let them get past easily and safely.

check your mirrors

Motorcyclists use the small size, acceleration and manoeuvrability of their machine to make progress by overtaking streams of slower vehicles. This means you need to be alert at all times to the possibility of a motorbike overtaking, especially when you are making a right turn.

junctions

Motorbikes aren't always easy to see. Many riders wear bright clothing and use a dipped headlamp during the day to make themselves more visible, but even so it can be easy to overlook a motorbike on the road. Be vigilant at junctions. Before pulling out in front of a large vehicle or bus, always consider the possibility that an overtaking motorbike may be hidden from your view by the larger vehicle.

overtaking

When you overtake a motorbike allow as much room as you would when overtaking a car. Bear in mind that the rider may swerve to avoid debris or potholes. Take special care in the wet when a rider may swerve to avoid skidding on a metal drain cover or tram lines, and in windy weather when a strong gust could blow the bike across the road in front of you.

Make sure before overtaking a slow-moving motorbike that it is not about to make a turn, or quickly pick up speed again. Motorcyclists often look over their right shoulder to check their blind spot just before turning right, so if you see a rider doing this, hang back and give them room.

traffic queues

It is perfectly legal for a motorcyclist to filter between lanes of queueing traffic. Keep an eye on your mirrors when queueing, consider edging to one side to give motorcyclists space to get past safely, and leave enough room for them to cut in front of you. Be extra vigilant for filtering motorbikes before you change lanes in slow-moving traffic.

Use your mirrors to look out for motorcyclists who may be filtering past queues of slower traffic

LARGE VEHICLES

If you have any difficulty with manoeuvring your car, you can't fail to be impressed by the skills demonstrated by drivers of large articulated vehicles as they thread their vehicles through narrow streets and reverse into tight spaces. But LGV drivers can't work miracles, and there are times when they need extra space and consideration from other road users.

take care

Driving situations where you need to take extra care around large vehicles include:

- **left turns**: a long vehicle may need to pull on to the right side of the road to be able to make a sharp left turn without cutting the corner. Don't overtake until it has completed the manoeuvre

- **roundabouts**: a long vehicle may not be able to keep entirely inside its own lane markings on a tight roundabout. Don't pull alongside it or you may get squashed

- **low bridges**: a high lorry or bus may have to pull into the middle of the road to squeeze under a low bridge. Slow down and be prepared to stop at a bridge with a height restriction

- **overtaking**: it can be difficult to see past large vehicles to overtake. Keep well back to improve your view, and look past the nearside of the vehicle as well as the offside. Remember you will need extra space to overtake a long vehicle. Be cautious about overtaking a heavily laden truck after it crests a hill – it may pick up speed quickly when heading downhill

- **blind spots**: you may be hidden in the driver's blind spot while driving past a truck or coach, particularly if it's a left-hand drive vehicle. Remember, if you cannot see the driver's eyes in their offside mirror, they cannot see you. Don't linger in this blind spot: get past trucks on multi-lane roads briskly. You will also be hidden from the driver's view if you get too close behind a large vehicle, so always maintain a generous separation distance

- **bad weather**: in the wet take care to avoid being blinded by spray thrown up by large vehicles. Be careful when passing high vehicles in windy weather as wind gusting around them may cause your car to veer off course.

VITAL SIGNS

no goods vehicles over maximum weight shown in tonnes

risk of grounding

markers displayed on a vehicle with an overhanging load

low bridge – beware of oncoming high vehicles in middle of road

vehicles more than 13 metres long must display these warnings to the rear. The vertical markings are also required to be fitted to builders' skips left in the road

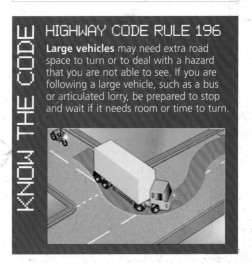

KNOW THE CODE

HIGHWAY CODE RULE 196

Large vehicles may need extra road space to turn or to deal with a hazard that you are not able to see. If you are following a large vehicle, such as a bus or articulated lorry, be prepared to stop and wait if it needs room or time to turn.

One thing you know for sure when following a bus is that it's soon going to stop to let down or pick up passengers. Keep well back so when the bus does pull in you are not held up behind it but are in a position to see beyond and pass it if it is safe to do so.

bus stops

Exercise great care when passing a stationary bus as passengers getting on or off may walk into the road without checking for traffic. Take care when a bus has stopped on the other side of the road too: passengers may run across to get on it, and oncoming vehicles may pull onto your side of the road to overtake it.

As you approach a bus at a bus stop try and assess whether it is about to move off. (If there is a long queue waiting, it will probably be stopped for a while; if no-one is queuing, it may have loaded its passengers and be ready to leave.) Be ready to slow down and give way to a bus which indicates that it wants to pull out.

Do not park at or near a bus stop.

bus lanes

These are special lanes at the side of the road which only buses (and taxis or cycles if indicated) are permitted to use. Check if there is a sign showing times of operation because the lane may be restricted at rush hours only; outside the times indicated, you are allowed to drive in the lane. Where there are no signs it means the lane is reserved for buses 24 hours a day.

If you have to turn across a bus or cycle lane to enter a side road or driveway, always give way to vehicles using it.

Slow down and give way when you see a bus at a bus stop with its right-hand indicator flashing

VITAL SIGNS

school bus: take extreme care passing a stationary school bus as children may run from or towards it without looking

other vehicles may use this bus lane outside the times shown

bus lane on road at junction ahead

with-flow bus lane ahead

no buses (over eight passenger seats)

bus lane road markings

bus stop road markings

buses and cycles only

contra-flow bus lane

In recent years trams or Light Rapid Transit (LRT) systems have made a comeback and are now established in several British cities. They are an environmentally efficient public transport system which runs on electricity and helps to reduce noise and traffic congestion in town. Trams move quickly and quietly, and cannot steer to avoid you, so they need to be treated with special caution. Be particularly careful the first time you drive where there are trams, and anticipate the unexpected from other road users who are coming across trams for the first time.

tram lanes

Do not enter a lane reserved for trams and indicated by white lines, yellow dots or a different colour or texture of road surface.

Always give way to trams and do not try to overtake a moving tram – wait until it is stationary at a tram stop. Take extra care where a tram track crosses from one side of the road to the other and where the road narrows and the tracks come close to the kerb.

Where a tram line crosses the road, treat it in the same way as a railway level crossing.

Take care when driving across tram rails. They can be slippery when wet so avoid braking or steering while crossing them. Look out for cyclists and motorcyclists who may swerve suddenly to avoid tram rails.

traffic signals

Tram drivers usually have their own traffic signals. These may give a different instruction to the signal for other road users, and a tram may be permitted to move when cars are not. Diamond-shaped road signs give instructions to tram drivers only.

tram stops

Follow the route indicated by signs and road markings where the tram stops at a platform, either in the middle or at the side of the road. Do not drive between a tram and the left-hand kerb when it has stopped to pick up passengers at a stop with no platform. Look out for pedestrians, especially children, running to catch a tram which is at or approaching a stop.

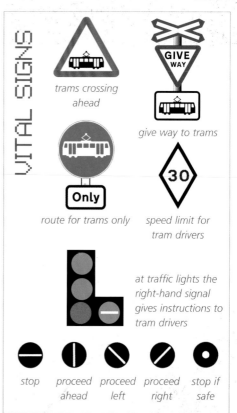

VITAL SIGNS

trams crossing ahead

give way to trams

route for trams only

speed limit for tram drivers

at traffic lights the right-hand signal gives instructions to tram drivers

| stop | proceed ahead | proceed left | proceed right | stop if safe |

IT'S THE LAW

TRAM RULES

It is illegal to:
- park your vehicle where it would get in the way of trams or where it would force other drivers to do so
- drive in a lane reserved for trams
- drive between the left-hand kerb and a tram which has stopped to pick up passengers.

Extra care is needed near a tramway, especially where trams are stopping or crossing the road

Level crossings are situated where a railway line crosses the road. Trains approach them at high speed, which means accidents involving vehicles on a crossing are serious ones. Never take risks when approaching a level crossing, and make sure you do not get stranded on a level crossing when a train is approaching. Only drive onto a crossing if you can see the exit is clear on the other side, and never stop or park on or near the crossing.

controlled crossings

Most crossings have traffic light signals with a steady amber light, twin flashing red stop lights and an audible alarm for pedestrians. They may have full, half or no barriers. Never try to zig-zag around half-barriers or drive over a crossing without barriers when the lights show.

When a train approaches, the amber light will show, followed by the red lights. If the amber light comes on after you have passed the stop line you should keep going. Otherwise, stop and wait at the line. Turn off your engine as you may be waiting for a few minutes. If a train goes by and the red lights continue to flash, or the alarm changes tone, you must carry on waiting as this means another train is approaching. Only cross when the lights go out and the barriers open.

Some crossings do not have warning lights. In this case you should stop and wait at the barrier or gate when it begins to close, and wait until it opens again before crossing.

user-operated crossings

These crossings have stop signs and small red and green lights. Only cross if the green light is on, and wait when the red light shows. To cross, open the gates or barriers on both sides of the crossing, check that the green light is still on and drive quickly across. Then pull up well clear of the crossing, walk back and close the gates or barriers.

If there are no lights, stop, look both ways and listen before you cross. If there is a railway telephone, use it to contact the signal operator to make sure it is safe to cross. Inform the signal operator again when you are clear of the crossing.

open crossings

These require special care as they have no gates, barriers, attendant or traffic lights (but do have a give way sign). Look both ways, listen and make sure there is no train coming before crossing.

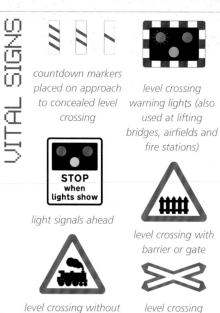

VITAL SIGNS

countdown markers placed on approach to concealed level crossing

level crossing warning lights (also used at lifting bridges, airfields and fire stations)

STOP when lights show

light signals ahead

level crossing with barrier or gate

level crossing without barrier or gate

level crossing without barrier

accidents and breakdowns

If your vehicle breaks down or you have an accident on a level crossing you should get everyone out of the vehicle and clear of the crossing immediately.

If there is a railway telephone then use it to tell the operator what has happened. Follow any instructions you are given. If there is time before a train arrives then try to move your car clear of the crossing. If you are on your own and cannot push the car clear, you may be able to move it by putting it in first gear with the handbrake off and engaging the starter motor repeatedly. Take care as the engine may start unexpectedly. If the alarm sounds, or the amber light comes on, leave the vehicle and get clear of the crossing immediately.

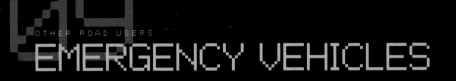

EMERGENCY VEHICLES

It's easy to panic when you see an emergency vehicle bearing down on you with lights flashing and siren blaring. In this situation it's important to stay calm and do your best to help the driver of the emergency vehicle get past quickly and safely.

You must pull over and stop if signalled to do so by a police officer, and produce your driving documents for inspection on request

warning lights

In an emergency, drivers of police, fire and ambulance vehicles are permitted to use flashing blue lights and sirens. They are also exempt from certain road regulations and may lawfully exceed the speed limit and drive through red traffic lights.

Certain other organisations, including mountain rescue, coastguard, mines rescue, bomb disposal, blood transfusion, lifeboat and medical transplant services are also permitted to drive under blue lights. A doctor answering an emergency call may display a flashing green beacon.

(A flashing amber beacon indicates a slow-moving vehicle.)

giving way

When you see an emergency vehicle in your rear-view mirror it's important to keep your cool and not slam on the brakes. This will only make it more difficult for the driver to get by quickly. Look ahead and find a safe place where you can pull over, and signal clearly to let the driver of the emergency vehicle know what you are doing.

If you see an emergency vehicle coming from the other direction, pull over to make room for it to drive on your side of the road if it needs to. If you are approaching a junction and can hear the emergency vehicle but are uncertain where it is coming from, hold back till you can see it.

Remember that several vehicles may attend the same emergency. Don't pull straight out after letting an emergency vehicle pass without checking there isn't another one following it. It makes sense anyway to pause for a few moments after having an emergency vehicle rush by to calm your nerves before continuing your journey.

stop – police

You must by law stop your car if signalled to do so by a police officer. The officer will usually signal you to stop by flashing their headlights and indicating and pointing to the left. Stop in the first safe place, then switch off your engine. Carrying a gun is thankfully not commonplace in the UK, but even so keeping your hands in clear view and avoiding making sudden gestures will help to reassure the officers that you are unarmed. Stay calm and courteous, listen carefully to what the officers have to say, and be prepared to produce your driving documents for inspection (see p198).

10

MANOEUVRING

During your driving test you will be asked to perform two of the following manoeuvres:
➡ turning in the road
➡ reversing into a side street
➡ reverse parking at the side of the road or into a parking bay.

For many candidates, performing these manoeuvres under the watchful eye of the examiner is the most nerve-racking part of the driving test. The only way to build up your confidence is practice. Try these manoeuvres in as many different locations as possible. Remember that this is a test not just of technical skill but of safety. It's essential to keep looking out for other vehicles and pedestrians at all times when manoeuvring.

REVERSING

Reversing isn't a difficult skill to master, although it takes a bit of practice to get used to the different way a car responds to the steering when going backwards. The key to carrying out reversing manoeuvres is to do them slowly, giving yourself plenty of time to make any steering adjustments needed to keep on course.

steering

Find a comfortable position to adopt while reversing. You may need to shift your body around in your seat so you can see clearly over your left shoulder. Adjust your grip on the steering wheel so you are holding it with your right hand at the top of the wheel and your left hand low down on the wheel. If it feels more natural, you may prefer to keep just your right hand on the wheel and rest your left arm on the back of the seat while reversing in a straight line. However, when you are changing direction while reversing, you will probably find that keeping both hands on the wheel gives you more accurate control over your steering.

seatbelt

You are permitted by law to undo your seatbelt while you are carrying out a manoeuvre that involves reversing, and you may wish to do this if you find your belt restricts your movements. However, it is easy to forget to put the seatbelt back on when you have finished reversing – particularly during your driving test when you have so much else to think about – and for this reason it is advisable to keep your seatbelt on wherever possible.

Be prepared to stop and give way to other vehicles or pedestrians when you are reversing

Check all round when reversing

Continual all-round observation is essential when carrying out any sort of reversing manoeuvre

observation

Reversing is a potentially dangerous manoeuvre which needs to be carried out with care. This is partly because your view when going backwards is restricted, but also because when you steer the front of the car swings outwards, posing a hazard for oncoming traffic. Take these precautions when reversing:

- look all round your car before starting to reverse to check for approaching vehicles, cyclists or pedestrians
- stop and give way to pedestrians crossing the road while you are reversing
- be alert for children, who may be harder to see when you are reversing
- don't reverse using your mirrors alone – you need to perform continual all round observation when reversing
- never reverse anywhere if you cannot clearly see what's behind you. If necessary get out of your car and have a look, or ask someone else to guide you.

VITAL SIGNS

 no U-turns permitted

 *no through road
(If you drive down a road with this sign on it, you will have to turn round and come out again, which may be difficult if you are towing a trailer)*

A car is easier to manoeuvre when reversing so it is almost always better to reverse into a parking space than to try and drive straight in

Remember when reversing that the front of your car will swing out as you start to turn. Look forwards up and down the road as well as behind you to check that this will not cause an obstruction or endanger other road users

reversing manoeuvres

Always choose a safe, legal and convenient place to carry out any reversing manoeuvre. Consider whether you really need to reverse or if there might be a simpler alternative. For instance, if you need to turn around, and there is a roundabout ahead, drive all the way around that to turn round.

A car is easier to manoeuvre when reversing, which is why it usually makes sense to reverse into parking spaces and parking bays.

Never reverse from a side road into a main road. This includes your driveway at home – always reverse in at night so you can drive out forwards in the morning.

U-turns

Where the road is very wide and there is no traffic, it may be easier to carry out a U-turn instead of turning by reversing in the road or reversing into a side street. You should only carry out a U-turn where it is safe and legal to do so, with no signs or road markings prohibiting it. Take special care to make sure the road is clear in both directions, and don't forget to look over your shoulder for a final check before starting the U-turn.

TEST TIPS

Do

→ be prepared to stop and give way if other road users want to go by. If drivers have clearly stopped to let you finish your manoeuvre then continue with it – but don't rush what you are doing because they are waiting or you may end up making mistakes

→ if you have taken off your seatbelt to carry out a reversing manoeuvre, remember to put it back on once you have finished

Don't

→ stop where you would inconvenience or endanger another road user when asked by your examiner to pull over to carry out any manoeuvre

→ 'dry steer' by turning the steering wheel while the car isn't moving.

Turning in the road using forward and reverse gears is one of the reversing manoeuvres that you may be required to perform during your driving test. This is sometimes called the three-point turn. In fact, on a narrow road you may need to make five or even seven turns, though you should always aim to make as few turns as possible.

turning in the road

1 Stop by the kerb in a safe, legal and convenient place and apply the handbrake. Avoid stopping where trees or lamp posts by the kerb make the manoeuvre more difficult.

2 Engage first gear. Check it is clear all round. Release the handbrake and slowly move forward using clutch control. Once the car is moving apply full right steering lock.

3 As you drive over the centre of the road be careful not to let the car run away if there is a downhill camber. Apply the footbrake gently if necessary. Keep looking all round.

4 Just before you reach the other kerb, apply as much left steering lock as possible. Stop before your front wheels touch the kerb and apply the handbrake.

5 Select reverse gear and check the road is clear in all directions. Remember you may be making an uphill start against the slope of the road camber. Use clutch control to keep the car moving slowly and steer quickly to your left. Keep looking all round.

6 Look over your right shoulder as you near the other kerb and apply right steering lock. Stop before the rear wheels touch the kerb and apply the handbrake. Engage first gear. Check it is clear all round. Drive forward into a normal position on the left side of the road.

REVERSING INTO SIDE ROADS

Reversing into a side road is often the safest and most convenient way to turn round. It's a manoeuvre which needs great caution: not only are you reversing against traffic emerging from the junction, but as you reverse the front of your car will swing out into the road. This means you must continually check not only what's behind your car but also what is happening to the front and side as you carry out the manoeuvre.

reversing to the left

1 As you drive past the road you want to reverse into take a good look down it for potential hazards. Pull up about half a metre from the kerb in a safe, legal and convenient place at least two car lengths past the corner and apply the handbrake.

2 Engage reverse gear. Check the road is clear in all directions and take note of any pedestrians or cyclists approaching on the pavement. Release the handbrake and use clutch control to move slowly backwards.

reversing to the right

Reversing to the right is useful when your rear view is restricted, for instance if you're driving a van. It gives you a clearer view down the side road through the driver's door window. All round observation is especially important because you are on the wrong side of the road facing oncoming traffic. Look out for vehicles wanting to turn into the junction while you are reversing. Once you straighten up after turning, reverse back about twice as far as you would when reversing to the left. This gives you space to cross to the left of the road before emerging at the junction.

Make sure you also practise reversing to the right, which can be easier if your rear view is restricted

3 As your rear wheels come level with where the road starts to curve, begin to steer to the left. Look in all directions, not just behind, as the front of the car will swing out as you turn.

4 Keep looking all around. If a vehicle wants to emerge from the junction as you are reversing, be prepared to stop, drive back to your original position, and wait for the road to clear before continuing.

5 As the road straightens begin to wind off the steering lock, ensuring that the car stays parallel to the kerb.

6 Continue reversing back about three car lengths, then and stop and apply the handbrake, taking care not to block any driveways or other entrances.

173

10 REVERSE PARKING

Parking in the gap between two vehicles is an essential driving skill. Although it might look easier to drive straight into the space, it's almost impossible to park neatly this way. What you need to do is take advantage of your car's increased manoeuvrability when going backwards by driving past the space and then reversing into it. If you are required to carry out this manoeuvre on your driving test, you will not necessarily be required to park between two vehicles, but may be asked to park behind a single vehicle as though you are reversing into a space of about two car lengths.

reverse parking

1 Stop slightly ahead of the front vehicle and no more than a metre away from it. Don't get too close or it will make reversing into the space more difficult. Apply the handbrake if necessary and engage reverse gear (your reversing lights will help to signal to other road users what you intend to do).

Don't park so close to other vehicles that they have difficulty getting out of the space you have left

2 Check in all directions before you start to turn because the front of your car will swing out, posing a hazard for other road users. Pause and wait if you need to give way to other vehicles or pedestrians.

3 Looking over your left shoulder, use clutch control to move backwards slowly. Quickly apply left steering lock as your rear wheels pass the back of the car. Aim for an angle of around 45 degrees to the kerb.

4 Check that the front nearside of your car is going to clear the back of the vehicle in front, then apply full right steering lock. Just before you come parallel to the kerb, straighten the wheels by steering left. If you find that you have misjudged the angle, pull forward and correct the steering – don't wait until your rear wheels hit the kerb.

5 Adjust the position of your car so you are close to and parallel to the kerb, and not too near to the vehicles in front or behind.

10

REVERSING INTO A PARKING BAY

Most car parks have rows of parking bays neatly marked out with white lines. Reversing into a bay is normally the best option as it's easier to manoeuvre in reverse, and it's also safer to drive out forwards than backwards. But there are occasions when it makes more sense to drive straight in – for instance, when you're visiting the DIY store and need access to the boot to load bulky items.

reversing into a parking bay

1 After checking all round to make sure it is clear, stop in front of the parking bay. This manoeuvre is easier to perform if you turn away from the parking bay before pulling up as you will then be steering into the bay at an easier angle.

2 Release the handbrake and use clutch control to reverse slowly back while steering to the left. Aim to make the sides of the car line up parallel to the white lines that mark out the parking bay.

Pull up in the middle of the parking space and parallel to the white lanes that mark out the bay (right)

3 You can use your mirrors or glance out of the driver's window to check your position as you are reversing, but don't forget to keep observing all around as well. Remember that the front of your car will swing out as you turn, causing a possible hazard for other vehicles and pedestrians.

4 Park squarely in the middle of the parking bay and apply the handbrake. If you find that you are not entering the space straight, pull forwards to straighten the steering before trying again. Don't leave your car with its front or rear end sticking out of the parking space.

When you need to park your car you must make sure you find a safe and legal place. Parking regulations can be complicated, so if you plan to leave your car for any length of time check road markings and signs to make quite sure that it is permitted. If you park where you shouldn't the penalties can be severe – including points on your licence for an offence such as parking on the zig-zag lines at a pedestrian crossing.

where to park

When looking for somewhere to leave your car, try to use a secure off-street car park. If you have to park in the street use a marked parking bay wherever possible. Do not park on the pavement unless there are signs which specifically permit this.

If you do have to park on the road, stop so that passengers, especially children, can get out of the vehicle on the side next to the kerb. Always check your door mirror for approaching vehicles before opening your door.

You must by law apply the handbrake and switch off the engine, headlights and foglights when leaving your car on the roadside, even if you're just popping into a shop for a couple of minutes.

parking at night

When leaving your car at night, remember the following rules:

- you are not allowed to leave your car facing against the direction of traffic flow on a road at night
- vehicles must display parking lights when parked on a road (or a lay-by on a road) with a speed limit over 30mph
- cars, small vans and motorcycles may be parked without lights on a road (or a lay-by on a road) with a speed limit of 30mph or less as long as they are at least ten metres away from any junction, close to the kerb and facing in the direction of the traffic flow, or in a recognised parking place or lay-by
- trailers must not be left on a road at night without lights.

Always lock your car securely and remove the key, even if you're leaving it for just a few moments

Parking on the road against the direction of traffic flow is permitted only during daytime

179

signs and markings

Whenever you park your car, check signs and road markings to ensure you are legally entitled to do so.

On a clearway you are not permitted to stop at any time. On an urban clearway, you may stop only to set down and pick up passengers.

Double yellow lines along the edge of the road mean no waiting at any time (although in places such as seaside towns this restriction may be eased out of season). A single yellow line indicates no waiting during the times shown on the nearby yellow plate. If no days are shown on the plate, then the restrictions are in force every day including sundays and bank holidays.

You may stop on yellow lines for a short time to load and unload, or to let passengers on and off, unless yellow lines on the kerb and accompanying black and white plates indicate that no loading is allowed.

Red routes have been introduced in some cities to improve the traffic flow. These have red lines in place of yellow lines along the side of the road. You must not stop even to unload or drop off passengers on a red route except in marked bays or at the times indicated by accompanying signs.

disabled parking

You must display a blue or orange disabled badge to park in a space reserved for disabled people. If you do not have a badge, do not park there even if all other spaces are occupied. Leave extra space if you park next to a car displaying a disabled badge. The driver may need more room to get a wheelchair alongside the car.

car parks

Car parks are full of hazards such as manoeuvring vehicles, pedestrians walking to and from their cars and excited children running around. The golden rule in car parks is to drive dead slow. Observe what is going on all around and look out for children running out from between parked cars. Show courtesy when parking – don't leave your car so close to another vehicle that it will be difficult for its driver or passengers to get in.

Leave enough space when parking: even if you can squeeze out of your car, the occupants of the other car may not be able to get back into theirs

VITAL SIGNS

no stopping
(clearway)

no waiting

no stopping at times shown
(except to set down or pick up
passengers)

controlled
parking zone
(pay at meter at
times shown)

end of
controlled
parking zone

distance to
parking place
ahead

vehicles may
park fully on
the verge or
footway

parking place
for solo
motorbikes

parking
restricted to
permit holders

direction to
car park

direction to
park and ride
car park

No loading at
any time

no loading at
times shown

no waiting
at any time

no waiting at times
shown

loading allowed only
at times shown

parking limited as
indicated by sign

no stopping
at any time

no stopping
at times shown

waiting limited as
indicated by sign

loading bay

parking space reserved
for vehicles named

11

ADVERSE CONDITIONS

Driving is easiest in clear, bright weather on dry roads. Once night falls, it starts to rain, or the thermometer drops below zero, the hazards start to multiply alarmingly. You need to slow down, concentrate harder and sharpen your anticipation skills to stay safe. Inside a warm car you can become insulated from what's happening outside. It's easy to keep driving at the same pace while conditions deteriorate, and only discover when an emergency develops that you have no safety margin left. Recognise that in atrocious weather conditions it is best to avoid driving altogether. If you wake up to find the roads covered in snow, ask yourself whether your journey is really worth risking an accident to accomplish, and stay at home instead until conditions improve.

11 DRIVING AT NIGHT

Night driving can feel strange and unnerving at first. It's a good idea to get your first taste of night driving with your instructor alongside you. If you're learning to drive in winter time then you may get plenty of opportunity to drive at night. But if you start in the summer when daylight hours are longer, it's worth trying to arrange a special late evening lesson.

night vision

On unlit roads at night, what we can see is limited to the range of our car headlights. Reduce speed to compensate, and never drive so fast that you are unable to stop within the distance your lights show to be clear. If you find driving at night particularly difficult this can be a sign that your eyesight needs checking, so arrange a visit to an optician.

using lights

Car lights serve two purposes: they help you to see at night, and they help other road users to see you. Put your headlights on anytime light levels are low, even if street lamps are not yet lit and most other drivers are not yet using lights. Put them on earlier still if you are driving a dull coloured car which doesn't stand out against the background.

Check and clean your lights regularly, and remember it is a requirement for your side lights and numberplate light as well as your headlights to function properly.

Use the main beam setting on unlit roads at night. But remember that main beam headlights will dazzle oncoming drivers, so dip your headlights when you see another vehicle approaching. Road users such as cyclists or pedestrians will also be dazzled by main beam lights so dip your headlights for them too.

Just before you dip your lights look along the left-hand verge to check that there is nothing on the road ahead. Immediately the oncoming vehicle has passed, switch back to main beam. If there is a stream of traffic approaching you will need to leave your headlights dipped until the road clears.

Main beam headlights can also cause discomfort for drivers you are following, so switch to dipped beam when you approach a vehicle ahead. When following at night, you should adjust your following distance so that your lights are not shining on the vehicle in front.

overtaking at night

If you need to overtake at night, exercise great caution. Switch your lights to main beam as soon as you have pulled past the car you are overtaking so you get the maximum view of the road ahead. Beware of bends and dips in the road ahead which may hide an oncoming vehicle.

If a driver wants to overtake you, help them see the road ahead by keeping your lights on main beam while the driver is preparing to overtake, and dip them only as the overtaking vehicle comes level with you.

avoiding dazzle

- don't stare at oncoming headlights, or you may be dazzled. Look slightly towards the left-hand side of the road. Slow down and if necessary stop if you cannot see. Keeping your windscreen clean will help reduce dazzle
- anticipate when your vision may be reduced by oncoming lights. When a car approaches round a bend, slow down in advance if you think that you may be dazzled by its lights
- following headlights reflected in your rear-view mirror can be dazzling. Flick the lever beneath the mirror to adjust its angle and reduce dazzle. Some cars have photochromatic mirrors which react automatically to reduce dazzle
- turning down the instrument panel illumination and switching off any interior lights can also help reduce distraction
- never wear tinted glasses to try to reduce dazzle at night.

noise at night

Remember that people are trying to sleep at night. Avoid revving your engine and slamming car doors.

It is illegal to use your horn in a built-up area between 11.30pm and 7.00am, except in an emergency. Flash your headlights instead if you need to give a warning signal.

185

Bad weather makes driving more hazardous in many ways. Winter is a time to be especially cautious on the road, as it brings a number of hazards including icy roads, snow, fog, heavy rain and high winds. When bad weather threatens check the forecast before leaving and if possible postpone your journey until conditions improve.

driving in winter

Make sure you and your car are prepared for wintry conditions before setting out:

- get your antifreeze and battery checked. Flat batteries are the main cause of breakdowns in winter
- check your screenwash. The cleaning solution you put in your washer reservoir acts as anti-freeze as well as helping to clean the windscreen. Fill it with screenwash to the concentration recommended on the bottle
- inspect your tyres to ensure they have plenty of tread: to be sure of staying safe on winter roads you need more than the legal 1.6mm minimum
- carry windscreen de-icer, a scraper and a brush for sweeping snow off the car. In very wintry conditions make sure you have plenty of warm clothes, a spade, some emergency food and a mobile phone in case you get stranded
- if you do a lot of driving on snow-covered roads, consider buying a set of winter tyres, designed to give more grip on frozen surfaces. Alternatively, you can fit snow chains which help to improve grip
- never start driving before your car is completely defrosted. When the windows are covered in ice, start the engine and switch the heater to maximum defrost. Scrape the ice off the windows all round the car – not just the windscreen – and make sure the lights, door mirrors and numberplates are clear too. If your windscreen wipers can't keep the screen clear of falling snow when you are driving then stop and clear it by hand.

Driving in snow is extremely hazardous: try to postpone your journey until conditions improve

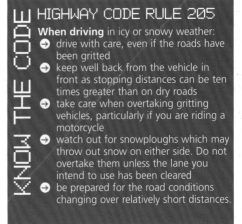

KNOW THE CODE — HIGHWAY CODE RULE 205

When driving in icy or snowy weather:
- drive with care, even if the roads have been gritted
- keep well back from the vehicle in front as stopping distances can be ten times greater than on dry roads
- take care when overtaking gritting vehicles, particularly if you are riding a motorcycle
- watch out for snowploughs which may throw out snow on either side. Do not overtake them unless the lane you intend to use has been cleared
- be prepared for the road conditions changing over relatively short distances.

wet weather

Driving is more dangerous when it's raining for several reasons:

➲ reduced vision

Rain makes it more difficult to see, and other road users may find it harder to see you too. Windows become obscured by raindrops, and they mist up more readily. As a general rule you should switch on your dipped headlights whenever it is raining. Keeping your windows clean makes it easier to see clearly in wet weather. Make sure you keep your windscreen washer bottle topped up and use the washers whenever your screen becomes dirty. Don't forget that most cars have a washer jet and wiper to keep the rear screen clear too. If the windows

Put on your headlights as soon as it starts to rain

mist up, switch your heater fan to maximum, and if you have air conditionin turn it on. If necessary open a window to get the air moving and reduce misting

➲ slippery roads

Water on the road acts as a lubricant whic reduces tyre grip, making it easier to skid and lose control. If you have to brake in a emergency you will take further to stop th in the dry, even if your car has anti-lock brakes. Reduce your speed in wet weathe and increase your separation distance fror the car in front, leaving at least a four-second gap. Be careful when cornering, especially where the road surface is worn greasy, such as on roundabouts

➲ spray

In wet weather vehicles send up spray fro their tyres which can drastically reduce yo vision. Keep well back from other vehicles particularly large vehicles which can throw up huge quantities of spray. Flick your wipers to full speed before you start to overtake so they can cope with the spray thrown on your windscreen as you go pas the other vehicle.

➲ standing water

Aquaplaning can occur on standing wate the tyres surf on the water and lose thei grip. You may feel a tug at the steering wheel as you start to aquaplane, then th wheel will feel strangely light. Don't attempt to steer or brake which could cause loss of control. Ease off the accelerator, and as the car loses speed th wheels will regain contact with the road surface. The higher your speed on a wet road, the more likely you are to aquapla so slow down in conditions where aquaplaning is likely. Be careful too whe driving through puddles at the side of th road – the drag of the water can tug at steering and cause you to swerve

Drive through a ford only if you are certain the water level is low enough to allow safe passage

⟿ flooding

You may have to drive through water either where the road has flooded, or at a ford where a river runs across the road). Driving through deep water can cause your engine to stall if water blocks the exhaust, and if water enters the engine air intake it can cause serious damage.

Fords may deepen after heavy rain or in winter and become unsafe to cross. Never attempt to drive through water unless you are certain how deep it is. Watch another vehicle make the attempt first, or check the depth on the gauge located beside many fords. If the water is too deep, turn round and find another route.

When you are driving through standing water, try to choose the shallowest route. This is usually the middle of the road, because the camber makes the edges slope away. Don't rush at the water – you want to avoid creating a wave that could flood your engine. Proceed slowly and steadily in first gear but keep the engine revs high by slipping the clutch (this helps prevent water entering the exhaust).

Once out the other side, drive slowly while applying the brakes gently to make sure they are dry and working properly.

KNOW THE CODE

HIGHWAY CODE RULE 202

Wet weather In wet weather, stopping distances will be at least double those required for stopping on dry roads. This is because your tyres have less grip on the road.

In wet weather

- ➡ you should keep well back from the vehicle in front. This will increase your ability to see and plan ahead

- ➡ if the steering becomes unresponsive, it probably means that water is preventing the tyres from gripping the road. Ease off the accelerator and slow down gradually

- ➡ the rain and spray from vehicles may make it difficult to see and be seen.

Driving in fog is dangerous, so slow down and leave plenty of extra time to complete your journey

Foglights should be used only when visibility falls below 100 metres, and switched off once it clears

fog

Fog is a major road hazard. Serious motorway pile-ups occur most winters because motorists carry on driving too fast and too close in foggy conditions. If you can avoid making your journey, stay off the road when it is foggy.

If you do have to drive in fog:

- leave more time for your journey as you will have to reduce your speed to stay safe
- make sure your windows are clean and your lights – including your foglights – are working properly
- use your windscreen wipers and keep the windows demisted
- switch on your dipped headlights, plus your foglights when visibility falls below 100 metres (328 feet). Avoid using main beam headlights as they reflect off the fog and can make it harder to see. Remember that your rear foglights are designed to alert following drivers to your presence. Keeping them switched on when you are in dense traffic will just dazzle the driver behind you. Don't leave your foglights on once visibility improves – it's illegal, it makes your brake lights less clear and it dazzles and annoys other drivers

- always make sure you can stop in the distance you can see to be clear. With all usual reference points outside the car obscured it can be harder to gauge how quickly you're travelling, so keep an eye on your speedometer
- don't overtake unless you can be absolutely sure nothing is coming
- when waiting to emerge at a junction it can help to wind down the window and listen for the sound of approaching vehicles which may not be visible till the last moment
- remember that in dense fog the reflective studs separating lanes on a motorway can help you tell which lane you are in:
  red studs to left, white studs to right mean you are in the left-hand lane
  white studs to both left and right mean you are in a middle lane
  white studs to left, amber studs to right mean you are in the right-hand lane
  green studs to left mean you are passing a slip road
- avoid parking your car on the road on a foggy day. If you have to do this, then leave the side lights on

HIGHWAY CODE RULES 207-8

Windy weather High sided vehicles are most affected by windy weather, but strong gusts can also blow a car, cyclist or motorcyclist off course. This can happen at open stretches of road exposed to strong cross winds, or when passing bridges or gaps in hedges.

In very windy weather your vehicle may be affected by turbulence created by large vehicles. Motorcyclists are particularly affected, so keep well back from them when they are overtaking a high-sided vehicle.

Be careful when driving with the sun low in the sky, as it can dazzle you and obscure other vehicles

be alert to the possibility of encountering unexpected fog patches. Slow down in conditions where fog might occur, and anticipate that fog may form on higher ground, or in valleys on cold winter mornings. Always slow down on the motorway when you see a fog warning sign, even if it is clear where you are.

high winds

Windy conditions can make driving hazardous. Take care on exposed open sections of road where crosswinds may gust across the road. On country lanes expect to encounter fallen branches or even trees in the road.

Take care when overtaking cyclists and motorcyclists who could be blown in front of you by a fierce gust. Choose a sheltered place to pass high-sided vehicles, and as you pass anticipate that you may need to correct your steering to compensate for eddying wind currents.

If you are towing a trailer or caravan your vehicle may be unstable in high winds and you should stay off the road till conditions improve.

sunshine

Wear tinted glasses to reduce dazzle in bright sunshine, particularly when the sun is low in the sky in the morning and evening, and in winter time. If you need corrective lenses to drive, make sure your sunglasses are made up to match your prescription.

Remember that you can pull the windscreen visor down to reduce dazzle from the sun. The visor can also be twisted around to shield the side window if the sun is causing you discomfort from that direction

When driving with the sun setting behind you, be aware that oncoming drivers may find it harder to see you, although from your perspective you can still see clearly. Put your headlights on to make yourself more visible.

hot weather

Keep your car well ventilated in hot weather to avoid getting drowsy. When it's very hot you may find that the road surface becomes soft, reducing the grip of the tyres and affecting the steering and braking.

Take particular care when it rains after a period of dry weather: the water can combine with the film of grease, rubber and oil deposited on the road to make driving treacherous.

191

Skidding is more likely in bad weather, but it's important to understand that the fundamental cause of a skid is the driver. A car only skids if it's being driven too fast for the conditions, or if a skid is provoked through harsh steering, braking or acceleration.

avoiding skids

Skids can be avoided by never asking your car to do more than it can with the grip available from its tyres in the prevailing road conditions. This means that in poor weather you must:

- slow down
- increase your stopping distance, so if the vehicle in front of you stops unexpectedly you have enough space to brake to a halt without skidding
- take extra care when approaching a bend which may be slippery
- be gentle and progressive in your use of the steering, accelerator and brakes.

slippery roads

Just as you're more likely to slip when walking on frosty pavements, when the roads are icy or it is snowing your car is more likely to skid. You need to slow right down, steer and brake very gently and leave a much greater stopping distance – up to ten times further than normal.

Be alert for ice forming on roads whenever you drive on a winter evening with clear skies. Look for signs of frost forming on verges or parked cars. Take special care where the road is exposed, such as on motorway bridges, because ice often forms here first. If your car has an outside temperature gauge, take extra care as this nears zero.

Beware of rain falling in freezing conditions and forming black ice, which is particularly treacherous because it is invisible.

On icy roads you may notice a reduction in tyre noise, and the steering will feel unusually light. Do not attempt to brake or steer. Lift gently off the accelerator and let your car slow down gradually. Drive slowly and cautiously, stay in a high gear and avoid harsh acceleration which could cause the wheels to spin.

The best way to avoid a skid is to read the road and slow down wherever grip might be reduced

You may need to leave up to ten times more distance to stop when braking on an icy road

VITAL SIGNS

risk of ice *slippery road*

193

HIGHWAY CODE RULE 99

Skids Skidding is caused by the driver braking, accelerating or steering too harshly or driving too fast for the road conditions. If skidding occurs, ease off the brake or accelerator and try to steer smoothly in the direction of the skid. For example, if the rear of the vehicle skids to the right, steer quickly and smoothly to the right to recover.

Rear of car skids to the right

Driver steers to the right

Too much power can cause the wheels to spin if you try to pull away from a junction in a hurry

skidding when accelerating

If you accelerate too hard when moving off on a slippery road, the driven wheels will spin frantically with little or no forward motion. This can be dangerous when you are trying to move out into a stream of traffic, or on a bend or slope when it can cause the car to slide across the road.

On an icy surface you may find it difficult to avoid wheel spin however gentle you are with the accelerator. It may help to engage a higher gear before moving off. Spinning the wheels in snow can cause the car to dig itself in. Try using reverse then forward gears in quick succession to free it. Fitting skid chains will improve traction on snow-covered roads.

If you have to stop on an uphill slope in icy conditions you may find it difficult to get moving again. Leave a long separation distance from the car in front so if it slows you have a better chance to keep moving.

skidding when braking

If you brake hard on a slippery surface the wheels may lock up and you will slide onwards with little or no braking effect. With the wheels locked you are also unable to steer the car. If the wheels lock up, release the brake pedal so they start to rotate again, then reapply the brake less harshly.

If your car has ABS fitted it will prevent the wheels locking up (see p47). But even ABS can't work miracles on snow or ice. You still need to allow a much longer stopping distance than you would if you were driving on dry tarmac.

Be extra cautious when heading downhill on a slippery road. Engage a low gear and approach the incline very slowly, as you may find it difficult to slow down again if your car starts to pick up speed.

A practice session on a skid pan can help to boost your confidence in dealing with skids

skidding when steering

If you approach a corner too fast on a slippery road there is a danger that the car will skid. This is even more likely if you brake or use the accelerator harshly while cornering.

In a front-wheel drive car (most small cars), the most common skid is caused when the front wheels lose grip. You turn the steering wheel on the approach to a bend but there is no response and the car carries straight on no matter how much steering lock you apply. If this starts to happen, come off the power. This throws the weight balance of the car forwards and helps the front wheels find more grip. Don't touch the brake pedal. As the car slows you should feel the tyres start to regain grip, and you can carefully steer the car back on course.

A rear-wheel skid can be more dramatic and if uncontrolled may develop into a spin. This type of skid is normally caused when the car is unbalanced mid-corner by lifting off the power or harsh braking, or by excessive acceleration in a rear-wheel drive car. If you feel the rear of the car starting to slide round, take your foot off the accelerator and brake, and steer in the direction that the rear of the car is sliding. This should bring the rear of the car back into line, but take care not to overcorrect so that it starts to slide the other way.

four-wheel drive

Some high-performance cars are fitted with four-wheel drive which improves traction in slippery conditions, although these cars are not designed to be used off road. True off-roaders or 4x4s have special features such as raised ground clearance and a low-ratio gearbox which allow them to tackle rough or muddy conditions. However, the higher centre of gravity of these models makes them less stable than a conventional car when driven on the road. Specialised tuition is recommended to get the most out of driving a 4x4 off-road. Remember that 4x4s can cause extensive damage to the countryside and should be used responsibly off-road and only where it is legal to do so.

traction control

Electronic traction and skid control systems are becoming a common feature of modern cars. Traction control senses when a wheel starts to lose grip, and automatically cuts the power or applies the brake to stop the wheel spinning. Skid control is a more sophisticated version which uses sensors to anticipate the onset of a skid and cuts the power or brakes individual wheels to counter it. If your car has traction or skid control, always leave it switched on.

Remember that even the best skid control system cannot overcome the laws of physics and will not prevent a crash if a car is driven too fast for the conditions. Aim to drive within the limits of your car's grip so that even if traction or skid control is fitted you never give it cause to activate.

195

12

YOU AND
YOUR CAR

As a driver you have legal responsibilities. You must ensure that you have a valid signed driving licence, that you are insured for the car you are driving, and that the car is properly registered and taxed. It is your responsibility to keep the car in a roadworthy condition, and ensure it is not overloaded. You should keep your vehicle secure from theft, and take steps to minimise its impact on the environment. And if you take your car abroad you are responsible for making sure you remain safe and legal whatever the local driving conditions.

There are a number of documents required to keep you and your car legal on the road. You must by law produce your driving licence and counterpart, a valid insurance certificate and (if appropriate) a valid MOT certificate if requested to do so by the police. If you can't produce these documents on the spot, you will be asked to take them to a police station of your choice within seven days.

driving licence

You must have a valid signed driving licence for the category of vehicle you are driving.

The photocard driving licence consists of a photo ID card and a counterpart. You must be able to show both parts if you are asked to produce your licence by a police officer. You must by law inform the Driver and Vehicle Licensing Agency (DVLA) if you change your name or address – there is a section on the licence to fill in and return to the DVLA to do this.

All drivers have regular contact with the Driver and Vehicle Licensing Authority, which administers driving licences and car registrations. You can contact them at DVLA, Swansea SA6 7JL. (For drivers in Northern Ireland, the equivalent organisation is Driver and Vehicle Licensing Northern Ireland, County Hall, Castlerock Rd, Coleraine BT51 3TB)

registration document

Every car has a registration document (sometimes called a logbook or V5) which lists identification details including the name and address of its registered keeper, the make, model, colour and engine size, and identifying marks such as registration, chassis and engine numbers.

You must by law notify the DVLA if you change any of the details listed on the V5, including your name or your permanent address, or the car's colour or engine size. When a car is sold, both buyer and seller must complete the top part of the V5 and the seller must forward this immediately to the DVLA (for a V5 issued before March 27, 1997, the buyer must fill in the change of keeper section and send it to the DVLA).

The V5 is not proof of ownership of a car – which is something worth bearing in mind when you are buying a second-hand car.

You must notify the DVLA of any changes to your car's details on the registration document (V5)

insurance certificate

You are legally required to be insured for the car you drive. There are three types of motor insurance:

- **third party insurance** is the minimum legal requirement. It means that if you injure or cause damage to the property of a third party (that is, another person), your insurance will cover the cost of their repairs and medical treatment – but you will receive nothing for your own injuries or damage to your own car
- **third party fire and theft insurance** means that in addition to having third party cover you will be compensated if your car is stolen or damaged by fire
- **Fully comprehensive insurance** means that your costs, as well as those of any third party, will be covered if you have an accident, even if it is your own fault. Fully comprehensive is the most expensive sort of insurance cover but it is well worth the extra cost.

Modified or high-performance cars can cost a lot to insure. All cars have insurance ratings from 1 to 20: choose a group 1 or 2 car to get the best insurance deal in your early years on the road

When you take out motor insurance you will be given a detailed policy document, plus an insurance certificate which acts as legal confirmation of your insurance cover (you may initially receive a cover note, which is legally recognised as a substitute for your certificate until this reaches you).

Check your insurance cover if you wish to drive someone else's car. Your insurance may not cover you and even if it does, a fully comprehensive policy often limits you to third party cover when you are driving another person's car.

You must always inform your insurer of any changes to your circumstances, or modifications to your car, otherwise you may invalidate your insurance policy.

Many factors influence the cost of motor insurance. You will pay more:

- to insure a high-performance car
- if you live in a high-risk area such as an inner city
- if you are a young driver – premiums fall significantly for drivers over 25
- if you get penalty points on your licence – insurance is particularly expensive and difficult to get after a drink-driving conviction.

You may reduce your insurance premium by:

- completing the Pass Plus scheme after passing your driving test (see p253)
- not having accidents – every year that you don't claim on your insurance earns you a no-claims bonus, which knocks a set percentage off your insurance premium (usually up to a five-year maximum). If you have to make a claim you lose a year's no-claims bonus, and your next premium may also rise
- opting for a higher excess (this is an amount you have to pay when you make a claim. If you have an excess of £100, it means you have to pay the first £100 of any claim you make).

MOT certificate

Your car must take an MOT test three years after the date it was first registered. The MOT test checks that the car is safe to use on the road, and that exhaust noise and emissions are within specified limits. Items examined include bodywork, suspension, steering, brakes, lighting, tyres, indicators, windscreen wipers and washers, horn and seatbelts. If your car passes you will be given an MOT certificate which is valid for one year. You can get your car tested up to one month before its current MOT expires, and the new certificate will still run from the original expiry date. Remember that an MOT certificate shows simply that the items examined were found to be satisfactory on the day the test was carried out, and it is no guarantee of roadworthiness.

You are breaking the law if you drive a car without a current MOT certificate when it requires one (the only exception is if you are driving it to an MOT test which you have already booked). If you drive a car without a current MOT it could invalidate your insurance cover.

Vehicle Excise Duty

This is better known as road tax. You must by law display a tax disc on the left-hand side of the windscreen of any car which is used or parked on the public road. You can apply for a tax disc at the post office. You will need to take along your motor insurance certificate, MOT certificate (if applicable) and either the DVLA road tax reminder form V11, or the registration document (V5).

Tax discs are available for six months or one year. The cost varies on a graduated scale depending on the car's exhaust emissions (or engine size, for cars registered before March 2001).

If you intend to keep your car off the road you must use the road tax reminder form (V11) to make a Statutory Off Road Notification (SORN) declaration at the post office. This must be renewed annually if the car is kept off the road for more than a year.

Cars first registered before 1973 are exempt from road tax but must still display a current nil tax disc.

MOT test examines components which could affect safety, such as suspension and steering

If you drive without road tax you could have your car clamped, or even confiscated and scrapped

The consequences of breaking the law on the road can be severe. Serious offences, such as drink-driving, result in automatic disqualification or even a jail sentence – up to ten years for causing death by dangerous driving. Being convicted for even a minor motoring offence is an unpleasant and expensive experience. It's worth remembering that it is easy to avoid ever coming into conflict with the law, simply by driving in a safe, sensible and responsible manner.

IT'S THE LAW

PENALTY TABLE

MAXIMUM PENALTIES

OFFENCE	Imprisonment	Fine	Disqualification	Penalty points
Causing death by dangerous driving	10 years	Unlimited	Obligatory 2 years minimum	3–11 (if exceptionally not disqualified)
Dangerous driving	2 years	Unlimited	Obligatory	3–11 (if exceptionally not disqualified)
Causing death by careless driving under the influence of drink or drugs	10 years	Unlimited	Obligatory 2 years minimum	3–11 (if exceptionally not disqualified)
Careless or inconsiderate driving	–	£2500	Discretionary	3–9
Driving while unfit through drink or drugs or with excess alcohol; or failing to provide a specimen for analysis	6 months	£5000	Obligatory	3–11 (if exceptionally not disqualified)
Failing to stop after an accident or failing to report an accident	6 months	£5000	Discretionary	5–10
Driving when disqualified	6 months (12 months in Scotland)	£5000	Discretionary	6
Driving after refusal or revocation of licence on medical grounds	6 months	£5000	Discretionary	3–6
Driving without insurance	–	£5000	Discretionary	6–8
Speeding	–	£1000 (£2500 for motorway offences)	Discretionary	3–6 or 3 (fixed penalty)
Traffic light offences	–	£1000	Discretionary	3
No MOT certificate	–	£1000	–	–

driving offences

ome examples of driving offences and their maximum penalties are shown in the table above. For serious offences, the courts can impose a range of penalties including imprisonment, a fine, disqualification from driving and endorsing the offender's driving licence with penalty points. Minor offences, such as speeding slightly in excess of the limit, may be dealt with by a fixed penalty fine and licence endorsement which can be settled without a court hearing.

penalty points

Under the penalty point system, drivers who break the law have their licence endorsed with points, the number depending on the severity of the offence. A driver who accumulates 12 or more penalty points within a three-year period will be disqualified from driving for a minimum of six months. For every offence which carries penalty points the court has a discretionary power to order the licence holder to be disqualified. This may be for any period the court thinks fit, but is usually between one week and a few months. For serious offences there is a mandatory period of disqualification – 12 months in the case of drink-driving. Serious or repeat offenders may face longer periods of disqualification, and in some cases the offender has to pass an extended driving test before being allowed back on the road.

New Driver Act

Special rules apply to drivers within two years of passing their driving test. If the number of penalty points on their licence reaches six or more as a result of offences they commit before the two years are over (including any they committed before passing their test) their licence is revoked. They revert to learner status and must reapply for a provisional licence and retake both theory and practical driving tests to get their full licence back again.

12

MAINTENANCE

You can't expect your car to function safely with no attention outside its stated service intervals. This is more important than ever now that recommended service intervals are being stretched to 20,000 miles or more. Running a car with worn or wrongly inflated tyres, or which is low on oil or coolant, is dangerous and illegal, as well as being likely to incur serious expense rectifying problems caused by neglect.

regular checks

Every time you drive your car you should ensure that its windows, lights and numberplates are clean. Make sure that everything that is needed to make the car roadworthy is in good working order, including the lights, horn, speedometer, windscreen, wipers/washers and seatbelts.

As part of the practical test from September 2003, driving test candidates are required to show that they can perform basic vehicle safety checks (see p209 for the specific questions you may be asked). Your answers should be relevant for the car you are driving. So as well as reading the advice outlined in this section, you should consult the handbook of the car in which you will be taking your practical test for specific information on the maintenance checks applicable to that model.

Make sure your windows are always kept clean

fault finding

Keep an eye open for any faults your car may develop. Look out for problems such as those listed below, and get the car checked by a garage as soon as possible:

- ⇒ car pulls to one side under braking. This may indicate a puncture or fault in the braking system
- ⇒ smell of petrol or burning rubber. Stop and investigate immediately
- ⇒ loud or unusual knocking or rubbing noises. Any noise indicates that wear is taking place and it needs to be checked.
- ⇒ poor roadholding or body control on bumpy roads may point to worn shock absorbers. Check by pressing down on a wing and releasing. If the car keeps bouncing then the shock absorbers may need replacing.
- ⇒ if the windscreen picks up a chip or crack get it repaired or replaced
- ⇒ vibration through the steering wheel may mean that the wheels are out of balance.

Washers and wipers must be kept in working order

KNOW THE CODE — HIGHWAY CODE ANNEX 6

Vehicle maintenance. Take special care that lights, brakes, steering, exhaust system, seat belts, demisters, wipers and washers are all working. Also:

- ➔ lights, indicators, reflectors, and number plates MUST be kept clean and clear
- ➔ windscreens and windows MUST be kept clean and free from obstructions to vision
- ➔ lights MUST be properly adjusted to prevent dazzling other road users. Extra attention needs to be paid to this if the vehicle is heavily loaded
- ➔ exhaust emissions MUST NOT exceed prescribed levels
- ➔ ensure your seat, seat belt, head restraint and mirrors are adjusted correctly before you drive
- ➔ items of luggage are securely stowed.

lights

To check that lights such as indicators or headlamps are working, switch them on and walk round the car so you can check them visually (you may need to turn the ignition on first). You'll need to get someone to help you to check the brake lights; alternatively, reversing up to a reflective surface (such as a window) and applying the brakes will also show you if the lights are operating correctly. Some cars have a warning light which illuminates in the event of a bulb failure.

horn

Test the horn at regular intervals, but remember to do this somewhere off the highway as it is illegal to sound the horn while the car is stationary on the road.

brakes

As soon as you can after moving off press the brake pedal gently to ensure that the braking system is working properly.

You can also get an indication that the brake servo-assistance is functioning properly if you press your foot on the brake while starting the engine: as the servo activates you should feel a pulse through the pedal.

Make sure that the parking brake is working effectively. The car should not roll on a gradient with the handbrake firmly applied. Check that the travel needed to apply the handbrake does not exceed the amount specified in the car handbook.

steering

Try the steering once you have moved off to check that the power-assistance is working correctly (if it has failed then the steering wheel will feel heavy and hard to turn). As with checking the brakes, you can confim that the power-assistance is working by putting a little pressure on the steering wheel as you start the engine: you should feel the wheel move slightly when the assistance activates.

under the bonnet

opening the bonnet:
- pull the bonnet release handle (usually located under the dashboard)
- release the bonnet latch under the front edge of the bonnet
- raise the bonnet and secure it on its support.

closing the bonnet:
- remove the support and secure it
- lower the bonnet and press down firmly on the leading edge
- check that it is securely shut.

fluid levels

Open the bonnet regularly and inspect the fluid levels. The levels you need to check are:

brake fluid

Never let this drop below the minimum mark on the brake fluid reservoir or braking could be dangerously impaired. Get a garage to investigate if there is any loss of fluid. Brake fluid becomes contaminated with age and must be replaced at the intervals stated in your car's service schedule

battery level

Most batteries are sealed and need no maintenance apart from keeping the terminals secure, clean and greased. If there is a filler cap, remove it and check the fluid level – it should cover the plates in each cell. Use distilled water to top it up if necessary. At the end of its life dispose of a battery by taking it to a local authority site or a garage

windscreen washer bottle

Never let the windscreen washer reservoir run dry. Add a mixture of water and washer solution made up to the concentration indicated on the bottle – this helps clean the screen and prevents the washers freezing in winter. Always use proper washer solution, not washing up liquid which won't do the job and could damage paintwork

⊜ engine coolant

The engine cooling system is pressurised when hot, so never try to take off the filler cap straight after the engine has been running or you could be scalded. Do not let the coolant level fall below the minimum indicated on the coolant reservoir or the engine may overheat and be damaged. Ask a garage to investigate if you have to keep topping up the coolant level, and get the concentration of anti-freeze checked so the system won't freeze solid in winter and cause expensive damage

⊜ engine oil

It is especially important to check the oil before a long journey. If the engine runs short of oil expensive wear may result. With the car on a level surface, take out the dip stick, wipe it clean with a rag, reinsert it and then remove it again. Check that the oil is above the minimum marked on the stick. If necessary, undo the oil filler cap and add more oil (a little at a time so you do not overfill, which could overpressurise the system and cause oil leaks). Some cars have a gauge on the instrument panel which shows the oil level without having to open the bonnet, though it's also a good idea to occasionally double-check the level using the dip stick. Never pour old engine oil down the drain – take it to a local authority waste disposal site.

tyre care

Your tyres are your only contact with the road, so don't skimp on their maintenance or you could regret it. Get in the habit of glancing at your tyres every time you use your car to check for obvious defects such as cuts or bulges.

At least once a week check that the tyres are correctly inflated to the pressures laid down in the car handbook. Do this before a journey, when the tyres are cold, or you may get an inaccurate reading. Having underinflated tyres affects the braking and handling of the car, makes the steering feel heavy, and causes increased fuel consumption and tread wear. Overinflated tyres also affect handling, give a harsh ride and cause increased tread wear.

Tyres fitted to cars, vans and trailers must have a tread depth of at least 1.6mm across the central three-quarters of the breadth of the tread and around the entire circumference. But you should regard this as the absolute legal minimum. Worn tyres greatly reduce roadholding on damp, flooded or icy roads. For safety's sake you should start thinking about replacing a tyre when its tread gets below 3mm, especially if winter is approaching. A deep cut in the sidewall also makes a tyre unsafe and illegal.

If your tyres are wearing excessively or unevenly it may indicate that the wheels are out of alignment or that there is a fault with the braking or suspension systems. Get them checked as soon as possible.

Most everyday road tyres are the radial type. It illegal to mix cross-ply and radial tyres on the same axle.

Some cars have a space saver spare tyre which is narrower then the normal tyre. If you have a space saver fitted after a puncture, remember that it will affect your car's handling and braking performance, and restrict you to a lower maximum speed. Check the car handbook for further information and get the space saver replaced by a proper tyre as soon as you can.

reducing tyre wear

To get the best use from your tyres:

- keep them correctly inflated
- avoid fierce braking, hard cornering and harsh acceleration
- steer around pot holes and slow down on poorly surfaced roads
- don't drive over kerbs or scrape your tyres along them while parking. This could weaken the wall of the tyre. Hitting the kerb can also put the wheels out of alignment, leading to uneven tread wear.

It's essential to check tyre pressures regularly to keep your car safe on the road and to prevent unnecessary extra tyre wear and fuel consumption

practical test vehicle safety check questions

As part of the practical driving test from September 2003, candidates are required to answer two questions about vehicle maintenance checks based on the following set of questions.

One of these two questions will ask you to tell the examiner how you would carry out a procedure, such as checking the engine oil. The second question will require you to show the examiner how you would carry out a safety check, such as inspecting the indicator lights to make sure they are working. You will not be asked to touch any hot engine parts, but you may be required to open the bonnet and identify where you would check the various fluid levels.

Your answers should refer specifically to your vehicle, so practise these maintenance checks on your driving test car and study its handbook before taking your test. If your car has electronic diagnostic systems which display information such as tyre pressures or oil level on the instrument panel, it is acceptable to refer to these in your answer.

In your practical test you will be asked how you would carry out two vehicle safety checks, such as checking that your indicators are working

what you may be asked

- ❷ open the bonnet, identify where you would check the engine oil level and tell me how you would check that the engine has sufficient oil

- ❷ open the bonnet, identify where you would check the engine coolant level and tell me how you would check that the engine has the correct level

- ❷ identify where the windscreen washer reservoir is and tell me how you would check the windscreen washer level

- ❷ open the bonnet, identify where the brake fluid reservoir is and tell me how you would check that you have a safe level of hydraulic brake fluid

- ❷ tell me how you would check that the brake lights are working on this car

- ❷ tell me how you would check that the brakes are working before starting a journey

- ❷ tell me where you would find the information for the recommended tyre pressures for this car and how tyre pressures should be checked

- ❷ tell me how you would check the tyres to ensure that they have sufficient tread depth and that their general condition is safe to use on the road

- ❷ tell me how you would check that the power-assisted steering is working before starting a journey.

- ❷ show me how you would check that the headlights and tail lights are working

- ❷ show me how you would check that the direction indicators are working

- ❷ show me how you would check that the horn is working (off road only)

- ❷ show me how you would check the handbrake for excessive wear.

LOADING AND TOWING

It is your responsibility to ensure that you do not overload your car. For larger loads you should consider using a trailer. Towing is not difficult but there are important rules to be aware of, and if you intend to tow a trailer or caravan you would be well advised to take some expert instruction in towing. Reversing in particular is something that towing novices find difficult, and it pays to practise first somewhere safe off the road.

loading

Always follow these loading rules:

- you, the driver, are responsible for making sure that your vehicle is not overloaded. Overloading can seriously affect a car's steering and handling
- check your car handbook to see if you need to increase tyre pressures when driving with a heavy load
- don't load the rear of the car higher than the top of the rear seats, or heavy items could fly forward dangerously during an emergency stop
- distribute any load as evenly as possible
- take care when loading a roof rack. The load must be securely fastened when driving. A heavy load on the roof rack can reduce stability, so take special care when cornering
- if anything falls from your vehicle on to the road, retrieve it only if it is safe to do so. If you are on a motorway, do not try to remove the obstruction yourself. Go to the next emergency telephone and call the police
- the front of a heavily laden car can be angled upwards so that its headlights are likely to dazzle other road users even on dipped beam. Adjust the headlamp angle to compensate, from its normal setting (0) to 1, 2 or 3 depending on the load
- if carrying domestic pets such as dogs, make sure they are properly restrained in a cage or behind bars in the rear.

Use a special rack for bicycles. If a rear-mounted carrier is used it must not obscure the numberplate

Make sure pets are safely constrained while being carried in the car, for both their safety and yours

If a heavy load distorts your headlamp beam angle, use the adjustment switch to compensate

KNOW THE CODE

HIGHWAY CODE RULE 74

Vehicle towing and loading. As a driver

- you MUST NOT tow more than your licence permits you to
- you MUST NOT overload your vehicle or trailer. You should not tow a weight greater than that recommended by the manufacturer of your vehicle
- you MUST secure your load and it MUST NOT stick out dangerously
- you should properly distribute the weight in your caravan or trailer with heavy items mainly over the axle(s) and ensure a downward load on the tow ball. Manufacturer's recommended weight and tow ball load should not be exceeded. This should avoid the possibility of swerving or snaking and going out of control. If this does happen, ease off the accelerator and reduce speed gently to regain control.

Towing is a specialised skill and taking some training before setting out is highly recommended

caravans and trailers

Before starting your journey, check that:

- your car is capable of towing the trailer. The maximum weight of the laden caravan/trailer should be no more than 85% of the towcar's kerbside weight

- the caravan/trailer is loaded evenly. Stow heavy items low down over the axle. With the caravan/trailer hitched up, run your eye along the outfit from the side: if properly loaded, it should be level or make a slight V-shape towards the coupling

- the caravan/trailer is correctly hitched up and the breakaway cable (which applies the trailer brakes if the towbar fails) is connected

- the noseweight is correct. This is the weight at the front towbar coupling and it plays an important role in maintaining stability. The noseweight is generally around 7% of the caravan or trailer's laden weight, and you need to check that this doesn't exceed the noseweight limit set by your car manufacturer

- all lights on the car and caravan/trailer are working correctly

- the caravan/trailer brakes are working

- the handbrake of the caravan/trailer is off, corner steadies are up, jockey wheel fully retracted, gas cylinders turned off and all windows and skylights closed

- any trailer load is securely fastened and not protruding dangerously

- your door mirrors give a good view down the side of the caravan/trailer. If not, fix a set of extension mirrors (but remember these must be removed when you are not towing)

- all tyres are in good condition and inflated to the correct pressure.

towing licence

A car driving licence allows you to use your car to tow a small caravan or trailer. However, for combinations exceeding 3.5 tonnes (or where the weight of the laden trailer exceeds the unladen weight of the car) you need to obtain a category B+E licence by taking a separate towing test (this does not apply to drivers who passed their driving test before January 1997).

towing guidelines

- passengers are not permitted to travel in a moving caravan
- speed limits are lower when towing: 50mph on single carriageways, 60mph on dual carriageways and motorways
- you are not allowed to use the right-hand lane of a motorway with more than two lanes when towing, unless other lanes are closed
- remember the extra size of your vehicle when towing and look out for warning signs, especially when entering a car park or lay-by with height/width restrictions
- consider the extra length of your vehicle when emerging from junctions and overtaking
- allow extra space for braking and watch your speed on corners
- avoid obstructing other traffic. If a queue of vehicles forms behind you, pull over somewhere safe and let them pass
- beware of crosswinds on bridges and exposed motorway sections which can cause the outfit to sway or 'snake'. If this happens don't try to brake or correct the steering. Instead, ease off the accelerator gently to reduce speed. Fitting a stabiliser to the towbar can help improve handling and stability, but don't use one to compensate for poor weight distribution
- when reversing, begin by steering in the opposite direction to where you want the caravan/trailer to go.

VITAL SIGNS

no towed caravans

no vehicle or combination of vehicles over length shown

overhead electric cable: no vehicles over height shown

no vehicles over width shown

no vehicles over maximum gross weight shown (in tonnes)

no vehicles over height shown

Caravans can become unstable in high winds so stay off the road during bad weather conditions

Remember that size restrictions which wouldn't apply to a car may affect you when you tow

In the last hundred years the motor car has transformed the way we live. It allows us to go where we want when we want, and to travel long distances for work and leisure. The downside is that this mobility has been achieved at a considerable cost to the environment we live in.

environmental issues

The growth in motor traffic has had wide-ranging effects on the environment. These include:

- depletion of natural resources such as oil reserves
- air pollution which causes health problems, damages historic buildings, and on a wider scale contributes to global warming
- road building which degrades the natural landscape
- traffic congestion
- noise pollution.

CO₂ emissions

Every time you drive a car it emits carbon dioxide (CO_2), a gas which is contributing to the atmospheric greenhouse effect and global warming. More efficient cars such as smaller-engined superminis produce less CO_2 than large executive cars and off-roaders. Automatic cars generally use 10% or so more fuel than a manual, although modern automatic designs are becoming more efficient. The government has taken several steps to encourage motorists to produce less CO_2, including:

- car manufacturers must publish CO_2 emission figures for all their models
- road tax (Vehicle Excise Duty) rates are linked to CO_2 emissions, so that cars with lower emissions are taxed less
- company car drivers pay less tax on cars with lower CO_2 emissions
- the MOT test includes a strict emissions test to check that older cars are not producing unnecessary pollution.

Increasing car ownership has raised environmental issues such as traffic congestion and pollution

Exhaust emissions are checked as part of the annual MOT test for cars older than three years

fuel types

➲ petrol

Petrol is the most common car fuel in the UK. Modern cars use unleaded petrol and have exhaust systems with a catalytic converter which helps to remove certain toxic gases including carbon monoxide, nitrogen oxide and hydrocarbons (though it does not reduce CO_2 emissions)

➲ diesel

Quiet and powerful modern diesels are becoming more popular. Diesels consume around 20% less fuel than petrol models and emit 20% less CO_2. But diesels also produce more particulates, which can aggravate breathing disorders (although the latest diesel technology is addressing this)

➲ gas

Cars powered by Liquefied Petroleum Gas (LPG) and Compressed Natural Gas (CNG) are available. Both types are more environmentally friendly than petrol or diesel

➲ hybrid

Hybrid cars combine a conventional engine with battery power which reduces emissions, especially in city driving. But weight and cost are increased and hybrid cars are still rare

➲ fuel cell

Fuel cell cars combine hydrogen with oxygen to generate electricity, giving zero-emissions operation. Several manufacturers are currently developing fuel cell models.

refuelling

Keep an eye on your fuel gauge so you never risk running out during a journey. Always check the gauge when you start a journey and anticipate when you may need to fill up. Where few fuel stations are available, such as on the motorway or when driving at night, don't wait for the fuel warning light to come on before stopping to fill up. Expert help may be needed to restart a diesel car if it runs dry.

There should normally be no need to carry spare fuel with you, but if you do, it must be in an approved container.

When you visit a fuel station, remember that petrol is highly flammable. Smoking is strictly forbidden on fuel station forecourts. You must also never use a mobile phone in the vicinity of a fuel station.

If you're driving an unfamiliar car, check whether it takes petrol or diesel before beginning to fill up. If you confuse the two you may need to get the fuel tank flushed out. In a modern petrol-engined car you must only use unleaded petrol (from a pump with a green handle), or you risk damaging the catalytic converter.

If your car uses diesel, take special care not to spill any fuel when refuelling as it will make the ground slippery and hazardous. Check that your filler cap is securely fitted before driving off so there's no danger of diesel splashing out onto the road.

Cars powered by gas are more efficient than petrol models but do not yet sell in large numbers

Make sure you know what type of fuel your car runs on and use the right pump to fill it up

green driving tips

f you follow these tips when driving, not only will you minimise your impact on the environment, but you will also save money by reducing fuel consumption and wear and tear on your vehicle.

drive smoothly
Don't leave your vehicle idling from cold, and use the gears efficiently – 37 mph in third gear uses 25% more fuel than in fifth.

maintain your vehicle
An unserviced engine can waste fuel and produce unnecessary emissions, and catalytic converters need checking regularly to ensure they're working effectively.

strick to the speed limit
The higher your speed, the more fuel your car uses. At 70 mph fuel consumption is up to 30% higher than at 50 mph.

accelerate gently
Racing the engine in the lower gears wastes fuel.

avoid short journeys
Short journeys – less than two miles – don't give the exhaust catalyst a chance to warm up and cause a disproportionate amount of pollution. Walking or cycling these short journeys cuts pollution – and is better for your health.

check tyre pressures
Wrongly inflated tyres can cause fuel consumption and tread wear to increase.

cut wind resistance
A fully loaded roof rack increases fuel consumption by up to 30%. Even an unladen rack causes extra drag, so remove it when it's not in use. Keep windows closed too, but remember that air conditioning also consumes power so use it sensibly.

travel light
Remove unnecessary items from the boot to reduce weight and improve fuel consumption. Avoid adding heavy accessories or wider tyres that increase rolling resistance.

plan your journey
Work out your best route in advance, make sure you know the way so you don't waste time and fuel by getting lost, and try to travel off-peak to avoid congestion.

share your car
Sharing a car for commuting or the school run halves your fuel costs and reduces urban pollution and congestion.

use public transport
If more people took the train or bus, traffic congestion would be reduced.

don't idle
Switch off your engine if you have to wait in a traffic queue.

anticipate
Planning ahead avoids the need for unnecessary braking and acceleration.

If you have a roof rack or box, leaving it attached to the car when it's not being used wastes fuel

Avoid revving your engine unnecessarily, as it increases fuel consumption and mechanical wear

CAR THEFT

A car is many people's most valuable possession.
Treat yours accordingly. Always be alert to the
possibility of it being stolen or broken into. Even if
you have fully comprehensive insurance, car theft
is still a costly, inconvenient and unpleasant
experience. And don't think that if you car is
older and not of great value it won't interest
thieves – they often target older cars because
these are easier to steal.

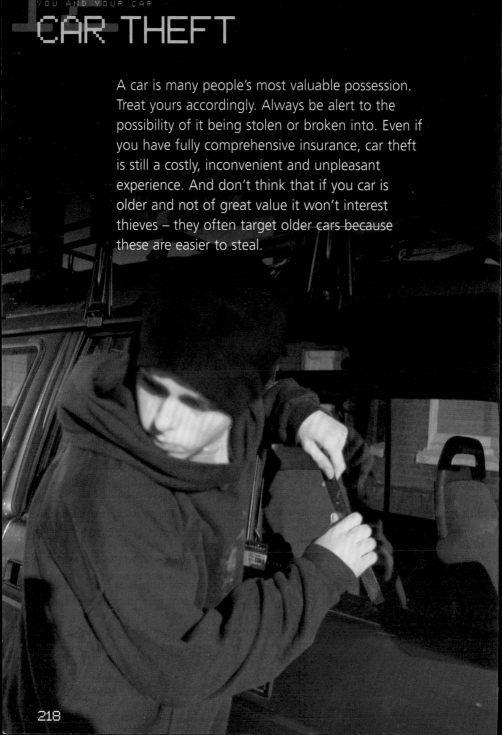

beat the car thief

- if you have a garage always keep your car locked inside it overnight
- if you don't have a garage, park your car where a thief would draw attention to himself. Leave it under a lamp post on the main road and not in a dark side street where the thief could work uninterrupted
- lock your car and remove the key, even if you are leaving it for just a few seconds outside your home or at a petrol station
- most cars have an engine immobiliser and often an alarm too. Check what is fitted to your car and consider extra deterrents – such as fitting a manual steering lock, or getting the registration number etched on the windows
- make sure you always activate any anti-theft devices you have, and ensure the steering column lock is engaged by twisting the wheel until it clicks
- Fit a security coded radio. If your radio has a removable front section, always take this with you or lock it securely in the boot when you park your car

- check that you know how your central locking works – you may have to press the remote control button twice to activate deadlocks if fitted
- never leave valuables on display in the car, or even items such as jackets or briefcases which look as though they might contain something of value. If you can't remove these items when parking, conceal them in the boot
- don't leave your vehicle paperwork (such as the registration document or MOT certificate) in the car when it is left unattended
- consider joining a vehicle watch scheme. This means you place a sticker in your car which informs the police they should flag it down if they see it being driven by someone who looks under 25 years old, or (depending on the scheme) if it is being driven between midnight and 5am
- look after your car keys. Don't leave them near the front door at night where they are vulnerable to break-ins.

Always make sure you lock your car even if you're leaving it unattended for just a few seconds

Don't leave valuables on display in the car. Lock up everything securely in the boot out of sight

219

DRIVING ABROAD

Although questions about driving in other countries aren't included in the driving test, it's important to be aware of the issues involved. Many of us now routinely hire a car when on holiday, or take our own car across the channel, and you should prepare yourself before you set out for the different laws and driving conditions you will encounter overseas.

driving on the right

In Europe, America and much of the rest of the world, traffic travels on the right-hand side of the road and local vehicles are left-hand drive. Adapting to driving on the right isn't difficult, but you must be alert for situations – such as emerging from a lay-by or petrol station – where you may drive onto the wrong side of the road without thinking.

accessories

In many countries it is a legal requirement to carry in the car a:

- warning triangle (two in Spain)
- set of spare light bulbs
- first aid kit
- fire extinguisher.

Carrying spare fuel in a can is illegal in some countries, and is not permitted when using the channel tunnel or car ferries.

You will also need to obtain headlamp converters, or get your headlamps adjusted so they will not dazzle oncoming traffic when driving on the right.

documents

You must take your full valid UK driving licence and keep it with you at all times in case the police ask to see it. For some countries outside the EU you also need an International Driving Permit. When taking your car abroad make sure you also have the registration document, written authorisation that you are permitted to drive the car if it is a lease, hire or company car, and an MOT certificate if the car is over three years old.

Unless your car has 'Europlate' style numberplates (which show the letters GB below the Euro symbol) you must display a GB sticker on your car, as near as possible to the rear number plate.

Well in advance of leaving check with your insurance company that you will be covered to drive your car abroad. A green card may be required if you are visiting a country outside the EU.

local laws

Speed limits and drink-drive laws vary from country to country. For instance, in France the maximum motorway speed limit is 130km/h (81mph), while in Norway it is 90km/h (56mph). The maximum blood-alcohol limit varies from 0.08% in Switzerland through 0.05% in France to 0.02% in Sweden. To stay safe, always keep to the speed limit, and do not drink at all when you are driving.

In many countries the police are empowered to hand out a fine which must be paid on the spot. Local laws include:

- where two roads meet and there is no priority sign, in many countries you must automatically give way to the right
- in Austria and Switzerland you must purchase and display a vignette (tax disc) before driving on the motorway
- if you need to wear spectacles when driving, in Spain and Switzerland you must keep a spare pair in the car
- in Scandinavian countries you must keep your headlamps switched on at all times
- in the US, vehicles may use any lane to overtake on multi-lane highways, and they are permitted to turn right through a red traffic light if it is safe to do so.

For fuller advice on driving techniques and regulations overseas see the Haynes book, Driving Abroad *(ISBN 1 84425 048 2)*

Check which accessories you will need to carry with you when driving your car overseas

221

Driving is the most dangerous thing most people do. Each of us has about a 1 in 200 chance of being killed in a road accident. You probably know of someone who has been killed or badly hurt on the road. And as a driver you don't just put yourself at risk. A car is a lethal weapon and every time you take to the road you have the capability to kill or maim. But it is reassuring to know that crashes don't happen for no reason. The overwhelming majority of road accidents are caused by bad driving. If you follow the advice in this book and become a good driver who always puts safety first, there is no reason why you should not enjoy an accident-free driving career.

Society has a blind spot about road casualties. When a train or plane crashes, it makes headline news, yet the toll of death on the roads goes largely unreported. Ten people die on British roads every day. In total each year over 300,000 people – equivalent to the population of a large town – are killed or injured on the road. And the sad truth is that the vast majority of the crashes that cause these deaths and injuries are caused by bad driving and are completely avoidable.

causes of accidents

Something like 95% of road accidents are caused by driver error. These are all crashes which could have been avoided.

You might think that the way to avoid accidents is to have highly developed car control skills. This is actually not the case. The sort of abilities which make a good racing driver – quick reactions, the ability to corner a car at its limits of grip, skid control and so on – are of little value when it comes to staying safe on the road. What really counts is having the right mental attitude. On the road good drivers are those who put safety first. They always drive within their limits and do not let their emotions influence their behaviour behind the wheel.

Driving a car quickly can be exciting. But the public road is not the place to do it. If you'd like to find out what it's like to push your car to its limits, then take it along to a track day at a racing circuit where you can drive quickly without endangering anyone.

risk taking

One in five drivers involved in an accident in which someone is injured is aged under 25. Young drivers, particularly men, are more likely to be involved in car crashes because they take more risks on the road.

Sometimes young drivers take risks to try to impress their friends. Research has shown that young male drivers are much more likely to crash when they have other young men in the car with them.

Drivers of all ages are more likely to take risks when they're in a bad mood. If they've just fallen out with a friend, or are anxious because they're running behind schedule, they may allow this to cloud their judgement, become aggressive towards other road users and overtake when it isn't safe. It's important to realise how your mood can affect your driving and try to stay cool behind the wheel even when you're feeling under pressure.

bad habits

When drivers do something wrong and get away with it they start to develop bad habits. They may get too close to the car in front on the motorway, or not bother to signal when turning right at a roundabout. They keep doing this and getting away with it so it becomes part of their everyday driving. Until the day that the car in front on the motorway slams on its brakes unexpectedly, or a lorry pulls onto the roundabout thinking they are heading straight ahead.

Research shows that even when these drivers have a crash it may not be enough to break their bad habits. Drivers who crash tend to have the same sort of crash again and again.

To prevent yourself developing bad habits, you need to:

- realise that driving is a life-long skill which you should never stop trying to improve. Don't fall into the trap of getting two or three years' experience after passing your test and thinking you have no room for improvement. The best drivers – such as police class 1 drivers – recognise that however well trained they are, they are not perfect and are always working to improve their driving
- be critical towards your own driving. If you have to slam on the brakes to avoid another vehicle, or have a close shave when overtaking, ask yourself what you could do to avoid such a situation happening again in the future
- put your imagination to work when you are driving. Continually ask yourself 'what if?' What if a car pulls out of that driveway? What if there's a queue of stationary traffic round this bend? What if a child runs out between those two cars? If the answer is that there would be a nasty accident, then you're going too fast for the conditions and you need to slow down.

13

SHARING THE ROAD

There are some 27 million vehicles on our increasingly congested roads, and the only place you're likely to see an empty road nowadays is in a car advert. In the real world, whenever you get behind the wheel you need to interact with other road users. As in any other sphere of life, you can't expect these people to think or act exactly like you do – but you should make it your aim to get along with them courteously and harmoniously.

road rage

It's strange how some of the most mild-mannered people undergo a Jekyll-and-Hyde personality change when they get behind the wheel. They swear at other drivers, curse their stupidity, and generally get hot and bothered. This seriously compromises their ability to drive safely, as well as being unpleasant for their passengers.

Why does this happen? Visualise this scenario. An elderly lady walking along the pavement stops suddenly because she's just forgotten she meant to go to the greengrocers. A young man following behind has to stop and walk around her. She apologises for getting in his way; he smiles back and says 'no problem'.

Now imagine the same scene on the road. The lady realises she has missed her turning so slows down and looks for somewhere to turn. The young man in the car behind starts swearing under his breath, pulls right up behind her and flashes his lights. The lady complains to her passenger about the irresponsible young hooligan following and slows down even more to teach him a lesson. Finally he blasts past at the approach to a blind corner, honking his horn and waving his fist furiously.

The explanation for such different responses to an essentially similar situation is that driving a car has an unfortunate effect on the way we interact with other people. We have a strong sense of our car being an extension of our personal space, and become threatened and angry if we think others are encroaching on this space. We can't hear other drivers or see their facial expressions, so we stop seeing them as human beings and start treating them like mere objects which have the annoying habit of getting in our way.

Losing your cool on the road can lead to potentially lethal situations. However irritating other drivers seem, you must always put safety first and keep your emotions under control

Tailgating is aggressive, dangerous and illegal. If a following vehicle gets too close behind you, increase the safety gap in front of your car to compensate and let it overtake as soon as you can

keeping calm

If you find yourself getting angry with other road users:

- try and recognise how the isolated environment of your car is preventing you from reacting to other people as you would normally. In your daily life you probably meet all sorts of people, and even when they seem difficult you will make an effort to get along with them and create a pleasant atmosphere. Aim to do the same on the road
- remember that if someone seems to be getting in your way, it's almost certain they're not doing it on purpose. Other people get distracted, or lose their way, or make a mistake – just as we do ourselves on occasion
- don't get into stressful situations where you're more likely to lose control over your emotions. Plan your journey in advance and leave plenty of time so you don't find yourself running late and getting tense
- recognise that getting upset over someone else's bad driving serves no useful purpose. You can't control how other people drive, so let them get on

with it and concentrate on what you *can* control – your own driving. If you think someone is driving dangerously, let them get on their way and have their accident somewhere else, not near you
- remind yourself that however important your appointment may be, it's not worth having a crash because you're rushing to get there on time.

communication

Communicating with other road users can help to defuse a tense situation. If you have done something to inconvenience another driver, consider holding up your hand, palm out and fingers together, to acknowledge you have made a mistake. When another driver gives way to you, always give a wave and a smile of acknowledgement. This sort of simple communication with other road users can make life on the road a lot more pleasant and unstressed.

Conversely, never use hand signals or your horn or lights to rebuke another road user. It will have no positive effect whatsoever, but it could annoy them and provoke them to retaliate, putting you and other road users at risk.

Don't get annoyed or frustrated if you are held up by a slow-driven vehicle. Wait until you reach a safe place before attempting to overtake

Politeness makes driving more pleasant for everyone. If someone does you a favour on the road, acknowledge it with a friendly wave

elderly drivers

e patient with elderly drivers. They may no
onger possess the sharp reactions of youth,
ut statistically they are still a lot safer on
he road than young drivers. Accident rates
or drivers aged 74 and over are lower than
hose of drivers aged 21 to 24, and less
han half of those aged 17 to 21.

Don't blame an elderly driver who seems
low and hesitant behind the wheel. They
nay hate driving and share your wish that
hey weren't on the road, but for many
lder people without access to public
ansport driving is their only way of staying
n touch with friends and family and getting
o the shops.

earner drivers

's hard to believe anyone could forget what
 feels like to learn to drive, but as you'll
iscover there are other drivers who become
adly impatient with learners. Make a vow
ot to do this once you have passed your
est. Give learners plenty of space to do
omething unpredictable, and don't hassle a
arner who is holding you up – they may
ist get more nervous and take even longer
o move out of your way.

*nce you've passed your driving test, don't
rget to make allowances for people who are
ll learning and who may be hesitant or slow*

vulnerable road users

Never forget the fact that other road users
such as pedestrians, horse riders, cyclists and
motorcyclists are not cocooned in a shell of
protective steel and need extra care and
courtesy to ensure their safety. Pay particular
attention to children who may act
unpredictably and not follow the rules of the
road. Remember that you, as an individual
driving a car, have no more right to use the
road than another individual riding a bicycle
or a horse. Show them courtesy and be
prepared to follow behind them, even if it
means driving at a walking pace, rather than
squeezing past where there is not enough
room to overtake safely.

KNOW THE CODE · HIGHWAY CODE RULE 125

Be considerate. Be careful of and
considerate towards other road users.
You should:

- ➔ try to be understanding if other
  drivers cause problems; they may
  be inexperienced or not know the
  area well

- ➔ be patient; remember that anyone
  can make a mistake

- ➔ not allow yourself to become
  agitated or involved if someone is
  behaving badly on the road. This
  will only make the situation worse.
  Pull over, calm down and, when you
  feel relaxed, continue your journey

- ➔ slow down and hold back if a
  vehicle pulls out into your path at a
  junction. Allow it to get clear. Do
  not over-react by driving too close
  behind it

PERSONAL SAFETY

If you adopt a responsible attitude towards your driving, minimise risk-taking, put safety first at all times and do not venture onto the road when tiredness or ill health reduce your alertness, or bad weather makes conditions treacherous, then you can dramatically reduce your chances of being involved in a road accident. But there are further measures you can take to ensure that if the worst does happen, you are protected as fully as possible.

car safety

Great progress has been made by car manufacturers in recent years to ensure that you do have a crash your car will help to protect you from injury. When you buy a car, look for the following safety features:

- anti-lock brakes (ABS) which prevent the wheels locking up in an emergency stop, and allow you to steer and brake at the same time to avoid an obstacle
- air bags which inflate to cushion the body in a crash. Most new cars have driver and passenger airbags, but look also for side impact bags and curtain bags which protect the head
- active head restraints which are more effective than normal head restraints at preventing whiplash injuries if you are hit from behind
- traction control which prevents the wheels spinning in slippery conditions
- skid control which automatically cuts the power and activates the brakes on individual wheels if it senses a skid developing
- crash resistance. Check the model's Euro NCAP rating, a measure of how well it has performed under independent crash testing. Aim for a car which has been awarded four or five stars. Look at the car's rating in tests which simulate a collision with a pedestrian too – few manufacturers do as much as they could to minimise the risk to vulnerable road users in a collision.

belt up

The most important safety item in the car is the seatbelt. Always wear your seatbelt when driving, even if you're going just a few hundred yards down the road.

Check your posture so you're not sitting too close to the steering wheel, which could be dangerous if the airbag activates. Never put a rear-facing child seat on a passenger seat which has an active airbag. Make sure that your head restraint is properly adjusted (see p34).

lock up

Your car may be a tempting target for thieves even while you are driving it. They may try to open a door and reach in to grab a handbag or jacket while you are waiting at traffic lights. Make it a habit to keep the doors locked while you are driving. Some people don't like the feeling of being locked in a car; if you feel this way you should at least keep the doors locked while you are in town, and unlock them when you get out on the open road.

carjacking

Carjacking – when a thief hijacks your car while you are in it – is thankfully rare in this country. Be cautious if a driver gestures or flashes at you to stop on a deserted road, maybe pointing to a pretend fault on your car. Drive on till you get to a well-lit, busy garage, shopping area or a police station before stopping to check. The same applies if another vehicle runs into you for no apparent reason – if you have any doubts then drive on to the nearest safe place before pulling over. If you do get in a carjacking situation, on no account put up resistance. Let the assailant get into your car and move quietly away from it.

Airbags are an important safety feature fitted as standard equipment to many new cars

lone women drivers

There are times when all women driving on their own feel intimidated or uncomfortable about their safety, particularly if their car breaks down or when using dark, deserted car parks. Take the following steps to ensure your safety:

- always carry a mobile phone. Nothing beats the reassurance of knowing that you can immediately call for help wherever you may be

- join a breakdown recovery service so if you do break down somewhere you'd rather not linger, you can get help as soon as possible. Always tell the operator when you ring for assistance that you are a woman travelling alone – you will be given priority

- if you break down on a motorway, remember that the hard shoulder is a very dangerous place and staying in your car is far more risky than getting clear of the carriageway. Wait on the embankment and only return to your car and lock the doors if you feel you are in personal danger. As soon as you feel safe to do so then get out of the car and continue waiting well away from the carriageway

- when parking your car think about whether the car park will be dark or deserted by the time you return. If so, park near the exit, or find somewhere else which will be better lit or busier. Reverse into your parking space so you are able to drive straight out again without manoeuvring.

Carrying a mobile phone with you is a useful precaution in case of breakdown or accident

carrying children

As the driver you are not legally responsible for adult passengers who choose to break the law by not wearing a seat belt (though you should insist they do: in a high-speed crash an unrestrained rear seat passenger can be catapulted forwards with such force that they crush anyone in the front seat).

But where children under 14 are concerned you as the driver are responsible for seeing that they are properly restrained (see *It's the Law*).

Other safety factors to remember when carrying children are:

- a child under three years old should be restrained in a child seat, a harness or a baby carrier
- choose the correct size of restraint for the child and get advice from the supplier on how to fit it properly
- never place a rear-facing child seat on the front passenger seat if an airbag is fitted – if the bag inflates it could be fatal. Some cars allow the airbag to be deactivated when a child seat is fitted, but the safest option is to put it on the rear seat
- if child safety locks are fitted to the rear doors (preventing the door from being opened from the inside) they should be used whenever children are carried.

When carrying children under the age of 14 as passengers, it is the driver's responsibility to ensure they are properly restrained

IT'S THE LAW

SEATBELTS, CHILDREN AND THE LAW

OCCUPANT	FRONT SEAT	REAR SEAT	WHO IS RESPONSIBLE?
Driver	must wear seat belt if fitted		driver
Child aged under 3	child restraint must be worn	child restraint must be worn if available	driver
Child aged 3 to 11 and under 1.5m tall	child restraint must be worn if available; if not seat belt must be worn	child restraint must be worn if available; if not seat belt must be worn if available	driver
Child aged 12 or 13 or over 1.5m tall	seat belt must be worn if available	seat belt must be worn if available	driver
Passenger aged over 14	seat belt must be worn if available	seat belt must be worn if available	passenger

Cars rarely break down unless they have been poorly maintained or abused. Never ignore any faults which your car develops. Be alert for unusual noises or smells, and stop immediately to investigate. Keep a warning triangle and a fire extinguisher in the car for use in emergencies. Think about joining a breakdown service. Even if you are a competent home mechanic you will not want to try fixing your car on a busy road in bad weather, and the membership fee is worth paying for peace of mind alone.

safety first

your car breaks down, your first
esponsibility is to ensure that it is not
ausing a hazard for other road users. Try to
et it off the road if possible. If it is on the
oad, turn on the hazard warning lights,
nd keep the side lights on at night or in
oor visibility.

Place a warning triangle on the road at
east 45 metres (147 feet) behind your car on
he same side of the road. If you have broken
own on a bend or after the crest of a hill,
lace the triangle so it can be clearly seen by
ther drivers before they reach the bend or
ill crest. On a very narrow road put the
iangle on the verge or nearside footway.

Make sure your passengers get off the
oad to a place of safety. Never stand
etween your broken-down car and
ncoming traffic, or stand where you might
revent other road users seeing your lights.

Be prepared for the possibility of your car
uffering a breakdown, including:

engine failure

the engine cuts out while you are driving
ou will lose power assistance to the brakes
nd steering. This means you will need to
se more force to steer the car, and will have
o press the brake pedal harder to stop

tyre blow-out

a tyre deflates while you are driving, grip
he steering wheel firmly and allow the car
o roll to a stop at the side of the road. Try
o avoid using the brakes or steering harshly,
hich may cause you to lose control

puncture

nly change a flat tyre if you can do so
ithout putting yourself or others at risk – if
ot, call for professional assistance. Make
ure the parking brake is on and chock the
heels. Also take care that the car is secure
n its jack before removing the wheel, and
ouble check that all nuts are properly
ghtened before driving off

overheating

If your engine overheats, stop and let it
cool down before investigating further.
Only when it is cool should you remove
the filler cap and top up the coolant level
if required

fire

Reduce the risk of fire by carrying a fire
extinguisher and always stopping and
checking for the cause if you smell petrol
fumes while driving. If your vehicle catches
fire, immediately get the occupants out of
the vehicle and to a safe place. Call the fire
brigade. Do not try to extinguish a fire in the
engine compartment, as opening the
bonnet may make the fire flare. If it is safe
then you may be able to direct a fire
extinguisher through the small gap which
opens up at the front of the bonnet when
the bonnet catch is released.

*Joining a breakdown service makes a lot of
sense: it's easier and much safer to leave
roadside repair and recovery to the professionals*

motorway breakdowns

The motorway is a hazardous place to break down, so if your car develops a fault, move to the inside lane and try to carry on to the next exit or service station. If you do have to stop on the motorway:

- pull on to the hard shoulder and stop as far to the left as possible. Turn your front wheels to the left so if your car is hit by another vehicle it will not be pushed back onto the carriageway. Switch on your hazard warning lights and at night or in poor visibility keep your side lights on. (If you aren't able to get your car to the hard shoulder, switch on your hazard warning lights and make certain it is safe before getting out of the car and making your way clear of the carriageway.)
- on the hard shoulder exit the vehicle by the left-hand door and ensure your passengers do the same. Tell them to stay on the verge well away from the hard shoulder, and make sure that children are kept under control

- leave any animals in the vehicle or, in an emergency, keep them under proper control on the verge
- do not try to make even simple repairs such as changing a tyre
- do not place any warning device such as a warning triangle on the hard shoulder
- phone the emergency services. Use an emergency phone rather than your own mobile, as this allows the police control operator to pinpoint your location exactly. The direction of the nearest emergency telephone is given on marker posts situated every 100 metres along the hard shoulder. Face the oncoming traffic while you are using the phone so you can see danger approaching. The operator will ask you for the number of the telephone you are using, details of yourself and your vehicle, and whether you belong to a motoring organisation. Tell the operator if you are a vulnerable motorist such as a woman travelling alone

The motorway hard shoulder is a dangerous place to be. If you break down on the hard shoulder, get out of your car and move well clear of the carriageway while you wait for assistance to arrive

- if you do decide to use your mobile phone to call for help, take note of the number on the nearest marker post as this can also help to identify your location
- wait near your vehicle on the embankment away from the carriageway and hard shoulder
- if you feel at risk from another person, return to your vehicle by a left-hand door and lock all doors. Leave your vehicle again as soon as you feel safe to do so
- if you have a disability which prevents you from following the above advice, you should stay in your vehicle, switch on your hazard warning lights and either use a mobile phone to contact the emergency services or display a 'help' pennant
- when you rejoin the carriageway after a breakdown, build up speed on the hard shoulder before pulling out into a safe gap in the traffic
- if your car needs to be towed off the motorway, leave this job to a professional garage or breakdown service.

tunnels

A tunnel is a particularly hazardous place in which to break down or have an accident. Take extra care by observing all road signs and signals on the approach to a tunnel, and consider tuning in to a local radio station to listen for traffic warnings. Always switch on your dipped headlights in a tunnel, and if you are wearing sunglasses stop and remove them before you enter it.

Leave a generous separation distance from the vehicle in front, especially if you have to stop in a tunnel in congested traffic. Follow any instructions given on variable message signs.

If you break down in a tunnel, put on your hazard warning lights and telephone for help. If fire breaks out try to extinguish it with your own extinguisher or an emergency fire extinguisher situated in the tunnel, but if you cannot put it out or in the case of a serious fire developing, make your way to the nearest emergency exit and safety.

*ake special care if you break down where there
*re motorway roadworks being carried out

VITAL SIGNS

emergency telephone box on motorway (use the number to tell the operator the location of the box)

direction to nearest emergency telephone shown on marker post on motorway hard shoulder

tunnel ahead

direction to emergency pedestrian exit in tunnel

13

ACCIDENTS

If you are involved in a road accident you have certain legal responsibilities. You should also try to gather as much information as possible for insurance purposes. Where you come across the scene of an accident involving other vehicles, you should stop to give assistance. It is useful to carry a first aid kit and take some training in how to use it in case you ever have to give emergency first aid to road casualties.

getting information

Even a minor accident may involve an insurance claim. You should gather as much information on the spot as you can. Draw a sketch map of the scene, and if you are carrying a camera take some photographs. Make a note of:

- the other driver's name, address and telephone number
- whether the driver owns the other vehicle
- the make, model and registration number of the other vehicle
- details of the other driver's motor insurance
- names and addresses of witnesses
- road and weather conditions
- what vehicles were doing at the time of the accident (such as whether their lights were on and if they were signalling)
- what other people say to you
- identification numbers of police officers attending the accident.

accident scenes

If other people have already stopped to give assistance, try not to let yourself be distracted by an accident scene. Where an incident has occurred on the other side of a motorway or dual carriageway, keep your attention on the road ahead as further accidents are often caused by drivers 'rubbernecking' at accidents instead of concentrating on their own driving.

If you need to stop to give assistance:

- first stop and warn other traffic
- switch on your hazard warning lights
- make sure someone telephones for an ambulance if people are badly injured
- get people who are not injured clear of the scene
- place a warning triangle on the road at least 45 metres behind the crash scene
- switch off all engines
- make sure no one is smoking
- do not put yourself at unnecessary risk.

If you are involved in a accident which causes damage or injury then you have a legal obligation to provide certain personal details (see below)

IT'S THE LAW

IN AN ACCIDENT

If you are involved in an accident which causes damage or injury to any other person, vehicle, animal or property, you must by law:

- stop
- give your own and (if different) your vehicle owner's name and address, and the registration number of your vehicle, to anyone having reasonable grounds for requiring them
- if you do not give your name and address at the time of the accident, report the accident to the police as soon as reasonably practicable, and in any case within 24 hours
- if another person is injured and you do not produce your insurance certificate at the time of the accident to a police officer or to anyone having reasonable grounds to request it, you must report the accident to the police as soon as possible (and in any case within 24 hours), and produce your insurance certificate for the police within seven days.

first aid

Do not move injured people out of their vehicles unless you have to do so to protect them from further danger (moving them could aggravate a back injury). Do not remove a motorcyclist's helmet unless it is essential to clear their airway as it could make their injury worse. Casualties may be suffering from shock, so keep them warm and comfortable, give them constant reassurance and make sure they are not left alone. Do not give them anything to eat, drink or smoke. Stay at the scene until emergency services arrive. If a casualty is unconscious:

- first check their breathing. Clear any obstruction to the airway and loosen tight clothing. If breathing does not restart when the airway has been cleared, give mouth to mouth resuscitation. Lift the chin and tilt the head backwards. Pinch the casualty's nostrils and blow into the mouth until the chest rises. Repeat every four seconds until the casualty can breathe without assistance.

- stop heavy bleeding by applying firm hand pressure over the wound, preferably using some clean material. Don't press on any foreign body in the wound. Secure a pad with a bandage or length of cloth. Raise the limb to lessen the bleeding, provided it is not broken.

- douse any burns with cool liquid but do not remove anything sticking to the burns.

If any vehicle catches fire, stay well clear and call for the fire brigade to deal with it

VITAL SIGNS

POLICE ACCIDENT	POLICE SLOW

temporary police warning signs at scene of accident or other danger

H A & E not 24 hrs	H No A & E

hospital with accident and emergency facilities / *hospital without accident and emergency facilities*

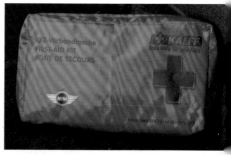

Carry a first aid kit in your car and learn how to use it – it could save someone's life

hazard warning plates

hazard information panel displayed by tanker carrying dangerous goods (in this case flammable liquid)

diamond symbols indicating other hazardous substances include:

toxic substance

oxidising substance

non-flammable compressed gas

radioactive substance

spontaneously combustible substance

corrosive substance

panel displayed by vehicle carrying dangerous goods in packages

dangerous goods

Learn to recognise the markings displayed on vehicles carrying hazardous goods. If an accident involves a vehicle containing dangerous goods, it is essential that all engines are switched off and no one smokes. Do not use a mobile phone nearby. Keep well clear of the vehicle and stay away from any liquids, dust or vapours. Call the emergency services and give as much information as possible about the labels and markings on the vehicle.

Keep at a safe distance if a tanker carrying a dangerous substance is involved in an accident

14
TAKING YOUR TEST

DRIVING STANDARDS AGENCY
DRIVING TEST CENTRE

There are two parts to the driving test. The first part is a theory test and the second a practical test. You cannot take your practical test until you have passed the theory test, and you must take your practical test within two years of passing the theory test. The theory test includes a multiple-choice examination, plus a separate hazard perception test based on video clips. The practical test involves driving for around 40 minutes in the presence of a driving examiner who will assess your driving. It includes an eyesight test and several set manoeuvres, and from September 2003 candidates also have to answer two questions about vehicle safety checks. The driving test is administered by the Driving Standards Agency (DSA) and you'll find useful information on applying for and taking your tests on their website: www.dsa.gov.uk.

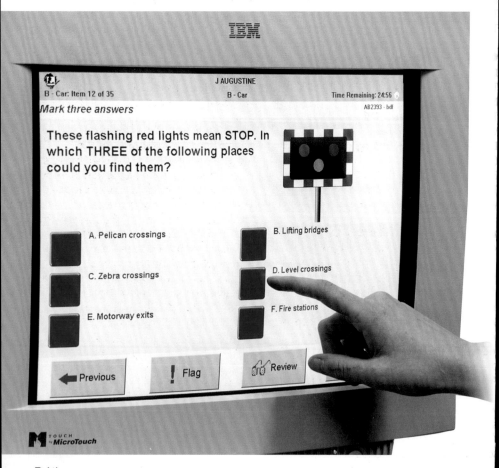

The theory test consists of two elements. Firstly, a multiple-choice examination in which you have to answer correctly 30 out of 35 questions (all of which are listed at the back of this book) on a touch-screen computer. Secondly, you have to identify the road hazards shown on 14 video clips by clicking a mouse button.

IBM

J AUGUSTINE

B - Car: Item 12 of 35   B - Car   Time Remaining: 24:55

Mark three answers   AB2393 - bdf

These flashing red lights mean STOP. In which THREE of the following places could you find them?

A. Pelican crossings

B. Lifting bridges

C. Zebra crossings

D. Level crossings

E. Motorway exits

F. Fire stations

Previous   ! Flag   Review

TOUCH
MicroTouch

booking your test

You can book a theory test by postal application, telephone, or on the internet. The cost of the theory test is currently £20.50.

Weekday, evening and saturday test sessions are available in addition to daytime appointments. If you need to cancel your theory test appointment, you must give at least three whole working days notice, or you forfeit your theory test fee. If you have hearing difficulties, dyslexia or light-sensitive epilepsy then let the DSA know at the time of making your booking and special arrangements will be made for you.

In Northern Ireland, driving tests are administered by the Driver and Vehicle Testing Agency (see contact details below). The tests follow the same format.

Contact details

Driving Standards Agency (DSA)
Test and booking enquiries: PO Box 280, Newcastle-upon-Tyne NE99 1FP
Telephone: 0870 0101 372
Website: www.dsa.gov.uk
Driver and Vehicle Testing Agency (Northern Ireland)
Balmoral Rd, Belfast BT12 6QL
Telephone: 0845 600 6700
Website: www.doeni.gov.uk/dvta

what to take with you

At the test centre you will need to show:
- both parts of your photocard driving licence
- your appointment card or booking number.

If you have one of the older style driving licences which doesn't include a photograph, you will need to bring additional photographic identity, such as a passport or workplace identity card, or a photograph signed and dated by an authorised person such as an Approved Driving Instructor, teacher or doctor.

If you forget to bring the correct documents with you on the day, you won't be able to take your test and you will lose your fee.

Arrive in plenty of time for your theory test so that you don't feel rushed or stressed.

multiple-choice test

The theory test begins with a multiple-choice exam. To pass this you must answer at least 30 out of 35 multiple-choice questions correctly within the 40 minutes allowed (people with special needs can apply for additional time when they are booking their test).

You select your answers by touching the button on the screen beside the answer you want to select. You will be given the opportunity to practise this before starting the test.

If you think you have selected the wrong answer you can change it by touching the screen again. If you are unsure which answer is correct you can mark questions with a flag to help you go back to them. The system also prompts you to go back to questions you have not answered fully.

After the multiple-choice exam, you have a break of up to three minutes before taking the hazard perception test.

preparing for the multiple-choice test

The 35 questions in the multiple-choice test are selected from a bank of around 900. All these questions are listed, along with their answers, in the back of this book. You should not have to learn these questions by heart in order to pass the test. All the information you need to pass the multiple-choice test is included in this book. If you read and make sure you understand all the preceding chapters, then you will know everything you need to answer any of the questions you may be asked.

hazard perception test

Before you sit the hazard perception test you will be shown a short tutorial video demonstrating how it works.

The test consists of 14 video clips, each about one minute long, showing driving situations involving other road users. You should press your mouse button as soon as you see a hazard which may require you to change speed or direction. The earlier you spot the potential danger and respond, the higher the score you receive. The video will not stop or slow down when you respond but a red flag appears at the bottom of the screen each time you press the mouse button to show your response has been recorded. You can click the right or left button on the mouse to show you have identified the hazard.

There are a total of 15 scoreable hazards: 13 clips contain one scoreable hazard and one clip contains two of them. You can score up to five marks for each hazard depending on how quickly you identify it. Unlike the multiple-choice test, in this section you are not able to go back or change your response. You will not lose points for identifying non-scoring hazards.

You must score at least 44 out of 75 points to pass the hazard perception test.

preparing for the hazard perception test

The video clips you will see show real-life hazards of the sort you come across on the road every day. Whenever you are in a car, even as a passenger, test yourself by scanning the road ahead and identifying potential hazards. Read through this book carefully, paying special attention to chapter 8 which deals with hazard perception, observation and anticipation. You may also find it useful to talk through some practice video sessions with your driving instructor.

pass or fail?

After completing both sections of the theory test you should receive your results, and feedback, within 30 minutes.

You must pass both the multiple-choice and hazard perception elements to pass your theory test. If you fail one element but pass the other, you still have to take the whole test over again.

When you pass the theory test you will receive a pass certificate which is valid for two years. This means that if you don't pass your practical test within two years you will have to retake the theory test.

TEST TIPS

DO

→ prepare properly beforehand by studying and making sure you understand the answers to all the theory questions listed in the back of this book

→ listen carefully to all the instructions you are given before and during the theory test

DON'T

➔ arrive at the test centre late and feeling flustered

➔ forget to take along your driving licence and appointment card.

video clip example 1

The hazard is the school crossing patrol with children ready to cross the road. You should click on the mouse button as soon as you realise that the patrol might walk into the road to stop traffic in front of you and let the children cross

video clip example 2

The hazard is the small child on a bicycle who cycles across the road. You should click on the mouse button as soon as you realise that the child might ride across the road, causing the motorcyclist in front of your car to brake

PRACTICAL TEST

Taking the practical test isn't as daunting as you may think. You won't be asked to do anything you haven't already practised many times before with your instructor. But it's a fact that fewer than half of those who take the test pass it. Make sure you get as much practice as you can before booking your test, because taking the test before you're properly prepared will certainly result in a costly and confidence-denting failure.

booking your test

You can book your practical driving test by telephone, on 0870 0101 372, or via the internet at www.dsa.gov.uk.

The cost of the practical test is currently £39 when taken during a weekday. If you would prefer a saturday or weekend evening booking, then the cost is £48. There's usually a waiting time of six to eight weeks for practical tests.

If you have hearing difficulties, dyslexia or any disability or restricted mobility which may affect your driving then you should let the DSA know at the time of booking.

If the date or time you are given for your driving test isn't suitable, or for any reason you need to postpone your test, you must give the DSA at least ten working days notice (not counting the day of the test and day of notification) or you will lose your fee.

what to take with you

When you arrive at the test centre you will need to show:

- both parts of your photocard driving licence
- your theory test pass certificate.

If you have one of the older style driving licences without a photograph, you will need to bring additional photographic identity, such as a passport or workplace identity card, or a photograph signed and dated by an authorised person such as an Approved Driving Instructor, teacher or doctor.

If you forget to bring the right documents with you on the day, your test will be cancelled and you will lose your fee.

your test car

The car you intend to drive must be legally roadworthy and have a current MOT certificate, if applicable. It must be insured for you to drive and you will be asked to sign a declaration that your insurance is in order (you should contact your insurance company in advance to tell them you will be taking a driving test in the car).

If you are planning to take your test in a hire car, you should check with the hire company that you are authorised to do so – some do not permit it.

The car must have:

- a valid tax disc
- L plates (or D plates, if taking your test in Wales) displayed front and rear
- a clear view to the rear other than by the exterior mirrors
- a fully functional front passenger seatbelt
- a head restraint fitted to the front passenger seat
- an additional interior rear-view mirror suitable for use by the examiner.

If a dual accelerator is fitted it must be removed before the test. A car fitted with a temporary 'space-saver' spare wheel cannot be used for the test.

If you overlook any of these you won't be able to take your test and will lose your fee.

coping with nerves

Of course you'll be nervous on your driving test – everyone is. But you will feel a lot happier if you have put in plenty of practice and have reached the stage where you are fluent and confident behind the wheel. Make sure on the day that you arrive for your test in good time to avoid any last minute panics. Look out all the documents you'll need the day before, and get an early night.

A reasonable degree of nervousness on your driving test isn't necessarily a bad thing as it sharpens up your senses and concentration. If it helps to ease the tension, you can have your instructor or a friend accompany you, but they are not allowed to interfere in the test in any way and they must wear a seatbelt during the test.

test procedure

The driving test lasts around 40 minutes. It begins with an eyesight examination. You must be able to read a new-style numberplate from a distance of 20 metres. You can wear spectacles or contact lenses to do so, but if so you must keep them on when you are driving. The examiner will select a parked vehicle probably a little further away than 20 metres and ask you to read the numberplate. If you cannot read it, the examiner will measure the distance exactly and ask you to repeat the test. If you still cannot read it, you have failed and your driving test will go no further.

As part of the practical test, candidates have to answer two questions about the vehicle checks they would carry out before driving, such as of tyres, brakes, fluids, lights, reflectors and direction indicators. See p209 for the questions you may be asked. If you answer one or both of these questions incorrectly this counts as a single driving fault (see *fault assessment* opposite).

The examiner will then ask you to proceed when you are ready. Remember to carry out all the necessary checks before driving off. You will be expected to keep driving ahead, unless the examiner asks you to turn or traffic signs direct you otherwise. So if you receive no other instruction at a roundabout or crossroads, take the road straight ahead. If a road sign instructs you to turn left or right ahead, the examiner will expect you to obey this without being told to do so.

The test takes in a wide range of the driving situations covered in this book, although it excludes motorway driving. Your test may include an emergency stop. The examiner will demonstrate to you in advance the signal for you to stop. When the examiner makes this signal, pull up as you would in a real emergency (see p47). The examiner will check that the road behind is clear before giving the signal, so you should not check your mirrors before performing the emergency stop.

Your test will include two of the reversing manoeuvres described in chapter 10. Remember, whenever you are asked to stop at the side of the road to perform a manoeuvre the examiner will expect you to select somewhere safe and legal to stop. If you are asked to reverse into a parking bay, this manoeuvre may well be carried out at the driving centre car park at the beginning or end of your test.

Although you wouldn't be penalised for talking during your driving test, your examiner won't make small talk while you're driving because this could be distracting. It might feel strange to have someone sitting next to you saying nothing but by sitting quietly the examiner is giving you the best opportunity to concentrate on your driving and pass the test. You might notice that the examiner marks the test form occasionally – this doesn't necessarily mean that you are making mistakes, so just keep driving normally.

Eyesight test: if what you see when asked to read a numberplate from a distance of 20 metres looks more like the picture on the right than the one on the left, you will fail your driving test on the spot

fault assessment

The examiner assesses faults according to three categories:

dangerous faults

This is when a fault committed during the test has resulted in actual danger. Committing one dangerous fault results in test failure. A driving examiner who considers that a candidate is driving dangerously may stop the test on the spot

serious faults

This is when a potentially dangerous incident occurs, or the candidate reveals a habitual driving fault. Committing one serious fault results in failure

driving faults

These are less serious faults. Accumulating more than 15 driving faults results in failure. Don't panic if you think you have made one or two minor faults, as very few candidates fail through making too many driving faults.

if you pass

Congratulations! But don't be in too much of a rush to get behind the wheel on your own. You've just had a stressful hour and it is best to let your driving instructor drive you back from the test centre and wait till the euphoria has worn off before you drive on your own.

if you fail

Don't be too disheartened. If you failed your driving test first time that's no reason why you shouldn't go on to pass next time and become a good, safe driver. The most common reason why applicants fail is lack of preparation. Have you really clocked up enough hours on the road to feel completely at home in the car and at ease with basic techniques like moving off and changing gear? Have you driven in a wide enough variety of traffic situations and become familiar with the whole range of hazards you are likely to encounter during the test?

The examiner will give you a statement of failure showing all the faults you have made, plus a short debrief, running through the reasons why you failed. Go over these faults with your driving instructor and discuss what you need to do to address them.

It's best to keep the momentum going by booking another test date straight away, arranging more lessons and putting in as much practice as possible. Pay attention to the weak points revealed by your test, but don't concentrate only on the items where you failed, or you may find yourself getting out of practice in other areas.

TEST TIPS

DO

- wear smart, comfortable clothes and sensible shoes for your driving test
- make sure the car you take your test in is one you're really familiar with driving
- get your eyesight checked well before taking the test

DON'T

- arrive late and flustered at the driving test centre
- neglect to ensure that your car is acceptable to use for the test
- forget your driving licence and theory test pass certificate.

11 AFTER THE TEST

Those few seconds as you wait for the examiner's verdict at the end of your test will be as nerve-racking as any in your life. Being told you've passed comes as a massive relief and opens a gateway to a fantastic range of new experiences and opportunities. But passing doesn't mean you should stop thinking about your driving. Your career as a driver is only just beginning, and for a good driver the learning never stops.

passing your test

Once you have passed your driving test you should exchange your test pass certificate for a full licence as soon as possible. Make sure you claim your test pass within two years of the date of your test or it will expire and you will have to take both theory and practical tests again. Complete the declaration on your test pass certificate and send it together with your provisional driving licence (both photocard and counterpart sections) and the appropriate fee to the DVLA.

Pass Plus

Passing your driving test is an achievement to be proud of, but it is still only the first step to becoming a good driver. It means you have reached a basic level of driving competence, yet there are still many driving situations, such as driving on the motorway, that you have not experienced. An excellent way to gain extra experience is to take the official Pass Plus course. You can do this within the first year of passing the practical driving test. Consisting of six special training sessions, including driving in all weathers, at night and on motorways, it not only takes you through a range of more advanced driving techniques, it also qualifies you for cheaper car insurance.

There is no further test to take. When your instructor is satisfied with your performance you receive a certificate from the DSA.

driving on your own

Your first drive alone in the car can be both exhilarating and stressful. Don't be too ambitious in your early journeys – you may tire quickly while driving. If you are still hesitant in some situations you may find it helps to fit P-plates, which indicate to others that you are a newly passed driver. But it is inevitable that when driving, as in other areas of life, you will encounter people who

are rude, aggressive, impatient and bullying. Just concentrate on your own driving, and aim to let them get by without transferring their stress to you.

Beware of overconfidence in your first months and years of driving. It's a fact that this is the most dangerous time of your motoring life. As a new driver, you are more likely to have an accident in the first year after passing your test than at any other time in your motoring career.

Be particularly careful when you have passengers on board. Don't let them distract you or adversely influence your driving.

advanced driving

As you'll be aware from your time on the road, many drivers take little or no pride in their driving. They fail to concentrate and anticipate what is happening, and show little respect for other road users.

Don't become one of these bad drivers. Take your driving seriously and critically assess how you are performing on the road. Take a regular look at the *Highway Code* to check you haven't forgotten anything or missed any revisions to the law. And if you get any chance to improve your driving, take it. Many employers provide defensive driving courses for staff who run a company car. These are a great idea and will help highlight any areas where your driving needs attention. Better still, think about taking an advanced driving test: the largest provider is the Institute of Advanced Motorists (www.iam.org.uk), which has over 110,000 members. Preparing for an advanced test gives you a chance to assess how your driving has progressed since you passed your driving test, and weed out any bad habits that may have crept in.

Taking an interest in your driving has another advantage too – it turns it from a dull but necessary everyday task into a real source of interest, enjoyment and long-term satisfaction.

15
THEORY
QUESTIONS

In your theory test you will have to answer correctly 30 out of 35 questions drawn from the following bank of around 900 questions. Test your knowledge by answering these questions and checking to see if you have answered correctly. If you don't understand one of the answers, go to the page number highlighted beside the question (eg ⓘp69) and read the relevant section again.

01 Before you make a U-turn in the road, you should

mark one answer **ⓘ** p169

- **a** give an arm signal as well as using your indicators
- **b** signal so that other drivers can slow down for you
- **c** look over your shoulder for a final check
- **d** select a higher gear than normal

02 As you approach this bridge you should

mark three answers **ⓘ** p80

- **a** move into the middle of the road to get a better view
- **b** slow down
- **c** get over the bridge as quickly as possible
- **d** consider using your horn
- **e** find another route
- **f** beware of pedestrians

03 When following a large vehicle you should keep well back because this

mark one answer **ⓘ** p155

- **a** allows you to corner more quickly
- **b** helps the large vehicle to stop more easily
- **c** allows the driver to see you in the mirrors
- **d** helps you to keep out of the wind

04 In which of these situations should you avoid overtaking?

mark one answer **ⓘ** p85

- **a** just after a bend
- **b** in a one-way street
- **c** on a 30 mph road
- **d** approaching a dip in the road

05 This road marking warns

mark one answer **ⓘ** p84

- **a** drivers to use the hard shoulder
- **b** overtaking drivers there is a bend to the left
- **c** overtaking drivers to move back to the left
- **d** drivers that it is safe to overtake

06 Your mobile phone rings while you are travelling. You should

mark one answer **ⓘ** p135

- **a** stop immediately
- **b** answer it immediately
- **c** pull up in a suitable place
- **d** pull up at the nearest kerb

07 Why are these yellow lines painted across the road?

mark one answer **ⓘ** p67

- **a** to help you choose the correct lane
- **b** to help you keep the correct separation distance
- **c** to make you aware of your speed
- **d** to tell you the distance to the roundabout

8 You are approaching traffic lights that have been on green for some time. You should

mark one answer p69

- accelerate hard
- maintain your speed
- be ready to stop
- brake hard

9 Which of the following should you do before stopping?

mark one answer *i* p54

- sound the horn
- use the mirrors
- select a higher gear
- flash your headlights

10 What does the term 'Blind Spot' mean for a driver?

mark one answer *i* p53

- an area covered by your right hand mirror
- an area not covered by your headlights
- an area covered by your left-hand mirror
- an area not covered by your mirrors

11 Objects hanging from your interior mirror may

mark two answers *i* p53

- restrict your view
- improve your driving
- distract your attention
- help your concentration

12 Which of the following may cause loss of concentration on a long journey?

mark four answers *i* p135

- loud music
- arguing with a passenger
- using a mobile phone
- putting in a cassette tape
- stopping regularly to rest
- pulling up to tune the radio

13 On a long motorway journey boredom can cause you to feel sleepy. You should

mark two answers p135

- **a** leave the motorway and find a safe place to stop
- **b** keep looking around at the surrounding landscape
- **c** drive faster to complete your journey sooner
- **d** ensure a supply of fresh air into your vehicle
- **e** stop on the hard shoulder for a rest

14 You are driving at dusk. You should switch your lights on

mark two answers p185

- **a** even when street lights are not lit
- **b** so others can see you
- **c** only when others have done so
- **d** only when street lights are lit

15 You are most likely to lose concentration when driving if you

mark two answers p135

- **a** use a mobile phone
- **b** listen to very loud music
- **c** switch on the heated rear window
- **d** look at the door mirrors

16 Which FOUR are most likely to cause you to lose concentration while you are driving?

mark four answers p135

- **a** using a mobile phone
- **b** talking into a microphone
- **c** tuning your car radio
- **d** looking at a map
- **e** checking the mirrors
- **f** using the demisters

ANSWERS			
01 c	06 c	11 a,c	16 a,b,c,d
02 b,d,f	07 c	12 a,b,c,d	
03 c	08 c	13 a,d	
04 d	09 b	14 a,b	
05 c	10 d	15 a,b	

17 You should not use a mobile phone whilst driving

mark one answer   *i* p135

- **a** until you are satisfied that no other traffic is near
- **b** unless you are able to drive one handed
- **c** because it might distract your attention from the road ahead
- **d** because reception is poor when the engine is running

18 Your vehicle is fitted with a hands free phone system. Using this equipment whilst driving

mark one answer   *i* p135

- **a** is quite safe as long as you slow down
- **b** could distract your attention from the road
- **c** is recommended by The Highway Code
- **d** could be very good for road safety

19 Using a hands free phone is likely to

mark one answer   *i* p135

- **a** improve your safety
- **b** increase your concentration
- **c** reduce your view
- **d** divert your attention

20 You should ONLY use a mobile phone when

mark one answer   *i* p135

- **a** receiving a call
- **b** suitably parked
- **c** driving at less than 30 mph
- **d** driving an automatic vehicle

21 Using a mobile phone while you are driving

mark one answer   *i* p135

- **a** is acceptable in a vehicle with power steering
- **b** will reduce your field of vision
- **c** could distract your attention from the road
- **d** will affect your vehicle's electronic systems

22 What is the safest way to use a mobile phone in your vehicle?

mark one answer   *i* p135

- **a** Use hands free equipment
- **b** Find a suitable place to stop
- **c** Drive slowly on a quiet road
- **d** Direct your call through the operator

23 You are driving on a wet road. You have to stop your vehicle in an emergency. You should

mark one answer   *i* p47

- **a** apply the handbrake and footbrake together
- **b** keep both hands on the wheel
- **c** select reverse gear
- **d** give an arm signal

24 When you are moving off from behind a parked car you should

mark three answers   *i* p39

- **a** look round before you move off
- **b** use all the mirrors on the vehicle
- **c** look round after moving off
- **d** use the exterior mirrors only
- **e** give a signal if necessary
- **f** give a signal after moving off

25 You are travelling along this narrow country road. When passing the cyclist you should go

mark one answer   *i* p151

- **a** slowly, sounding the horn as you pass
- **b** quickly, leaving plenty of room
- **c** slowly, leaving plenty of room
- **d** quickly, sounding the horn as you pass

26 Your vehicle is fitted with a hand-held telephone. To use the telephone you should

Mark one answer ⓘ p135

a reduce your speed
b find a safe place to stop
c steer the vehicle with one hand
d be particularly careful at junctions

27 To answer a call on your mobile phone while travelling you should

Mark one answer ⓘ p135

a reduce your speed wherever you are
b stop in a proper and convenient place
c keep the call time to a minimum
d slow down and allow others to overtake

28 Your mobile phone rings while you are on the motorway. Before answering you should

Mark one answer ⓘ p135

a reduce your speed to 30 mph
b pull up on the hard shoulder
c move into the left-hand lane
d stop in a safe place

29 You are turning right onto a dual carriageway. What should you do before emerging?

Mark one answer ⓘ p95

a Stop, apply the handbrake and then select a low gear
b Position your vehicle well to the left of the side road
c Check that the central reservation is wide enough for your vehicle
d Make sure that you leave enough room for a vehicle behind

30 You lose your way on a busy road. What is the best action to take?

Mark one answer ⓘ p65

a Stop at traffic lights and ask pedestrians
b Shout to other drivers to ask them the way
c Turn into a side road, stop and check a map
d Check a map, and keep going with the traffic flow

31 You are waiting to emerge from a junction. The windscreen pillar is restricting your view. What should you be particularly aware of?

Mark one answer ⓘ p94

a Lorries
b Buses
c Motorcyclists
d Coaches

32 When emerging from junctions which is most likely to obstruct your view?

mark one answer ⓘ p94

a Windscreen pillars
b Steering wheel
c Interior mirror
d Windscreen wipers

33 Windscreen pillars can obstruct your view. You should take particular care when

mark one answer ⓘ p94

a driving on a motorway ⓘ p109
b driving on a dual carriageway
c approaching a one-way street
d approaching bends and junctions

34 You cannot see clearly behind when reversing. What should you do?

Mark one answer ⓘ p167

a Open your window to look behind
b Open the door and look behind
c Look in the nearside mirror
d Ask someone to guide you

ATTITUDE

01 At a pelican crossing the flashing amber light means you MUST

mark one answer ⓘ p144
- **a** stop and wait for the green light
- **b** stop and wait for the red light
- **c** give way to pedestrians waiting to cross
- **d** give way to pedestrians already on the crossing

02 You should never wave people across at pedestrian crossings because

mark one answer ⓘ p143
- **a** there may be another vehicle coming
- **b** they may not be looking
- **c** it is safer for you to carry on
- **d** they may not be ready to cross

03 At a puffin crossing what colour follows the green signal?

mark one answer ⓘ p145
- **a** Steady red
- **b** Flashing amber
- **c** Steady amber
- **d** Flashing green

04 The conditions are good and dry. You could use the 'Two-Second Rule'

mark one answer ⓘ p77
- **a** before restarting the engine after it has stalled
- **b** to keep a safe gap from the vehicle in front
- **c** before using the 'Mirror-Signal- Manoeuvre' routine
- **d** when emerging on wet roads

05 'Tailgating' means

mark one answer ⓘ p78
- **a** using the rear door of a hatchback car
- **b** reversing into a parking space
- **c** following another vehicle too closely
- **d** driving with rear fog lights on

06 Following this vehicle too closely is unwise because

mark one answer ⓘ p77
- **a** your brakes will overheat
- **b** your view ahead is increased
- **c** your engine will overheat
- **d** your view ahead is reduced

07 You are following a vehicle on a wet road. You should leave a time gap of at least

mark one answer ⓘ p77
- **a** one second
- **b** two seconds
- **c** three seconds
- **d** four seconds

08 You are in a line of traffic. The driver behind you is following very closely. What action should you take?

mark one answer ⓘ p78
- **a** Ignore the following driver and continue to drive within the speed limit
- **b** Slow down, gradually increasing the gap between you and the vehicle in front
- **c** Signal left and wave the following driver past
- **d** Move over to a position just left of the centre line of the road

09 A long, heavily-laden lorry is taking a long time to overtake you. What should you do?

mark one answer ⓘ p78
- **a** Speed up
- **b** Slow down
- **c** Hold your speed
- **d** Change direction

Which of the following vehicles will use blue flashing beacons?

mark three answers ⓘp163

- Motorway maintenance
- Bomb disposal
- Blood transfusion
- Police patrol
- Breakdown recovery

11 Which THREE of these emergency services might have blue flashing beacons?

mark three answers ⓘp163

- Coastguard
- Bomb disposal
- Gritting lorries
- Animal ambulances
- Mountain rescue
- Doctors' cars

12 When being followed by an ambulance showing a flashing blue beacon you should

mark one answer ⓘp163

- pull over as soon as safely possible to let it pass
- accelerate hard to get away from it
- maintain your speed and course
- brake harshly and immediately stop in the road

13 What type of emergency vehicle is fitted with a green flashing beacon?

mark one answer ⓘp163

- Fire engine
- Road gritter
- Ambulance
- Doctor's car

14 A flashing green beacon on a vehicle means

mark one answer ⓘp163

- police on non-urgent duties
- doctor on an emergency call
- road safety patrol operating
- gritting in progress

15 A vehicle has a flashing green beacon. What does this mean?

mark one answer ⓘp163

- **a** A doctor is answering an emergency call
- **b** The vehicle is slow-moving
- **c** It is a motorway police patrol vehicle
- **d** The vehicle is carrying hazardous chemicals

16 Diamond-shaped signs give instructions to

mark one answer ⓘp159

- **a** tram drivers
- **b** bus drivers
- **c** lorry drivers
- **d** taxi drivers

17 On a road where trams operate, which of these vehicles will be most at risk from the tram rails?

mark one answer ⓘp159

- **a** Cars
- **b** Cycles
- **c** Buses
- **d** Lorries

ANSWERS

01 d	06 d	11 a,b,e	16 a
02 a	07 d	12 a	17 b
03 c	08 b	13 d	
04 b	09 b	14 b	
05 c	10 b,c,d	15 a	

18 What should you use your horn for?

mark one answer **ⓘ** p59
- **a** To alert others to your presence
- **b** To allow you right of way
- **c** To greet other road users
- **d** To signal your annoyance

19 You are in a one-way street and want to turn right. You should position yourself

mark one answer **ⓘ** p75
- **a** in the right-hand lane
- **b** in the left-hand lane
- **c** in either lane, depending on the traffic
- **d** just left of the centre line

20 You wish to turn right ahead. Why should you take up the correct position in good time?

mark one answer **ⓘ** p74
- **a** To allow other drivers to pull out in front of you
- **b** To give a better view into the road that you're joining
- **c** To help other road users know what you intend to do
- **d** To allow drivers to pass you on the right

21 At which type of crossing are cyclists allowed to ride across with pedestrians?

mark one answer **ⓘ** p145
- **a** Toucan
- **b** Puffin
- **c** Pelican
- **d** Zebra

22 A bus has stopped at a bus stop ahead o you. Its right-hand indicator is flashing. You shoud

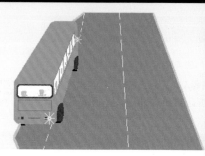

mark one answer **ⓘ** p157
- **a** flash your headlights and slow down
- **b** slow down and give way if it is safe to do so
- **c** sound your horn and keep going
- **d** slow down and then sound your horn

23 You are travelling at the legal speed limi A vehicle comes up quickly behind, flashing its headlights. You should

mark one answer **ⓘ** p78
- **a** accelerate to make a gap behind you
- **b** touch the brakes sharply to show your brake lights
- **c** maintain your speed to prevent the vehicle from overtaking
- **d** allow the vehicle to overtake

24 You should ONLY flash your headlights t other road users

mark one answer **ⓘ** p58
- **a** to show that you are giving way
- **b** to show that you are about to turn
- **c** to tell them that you have right of way
- **d** to let them know that you are there

25 You are approaching unmarked crossroads. How should you deal with this type of junction?

mark one answer **ⓘ** p90
- **a** Accelerate and keep to the middle
- **b** Slow down and keep to the right
- **c** Accelerate looking to the left
- **d** Slow down and look both ways

26 You are approaching a pelican crossing. The amble light is flashing. You must

mark one answer   ❶ p144

- give way to pedestrians who are crossing
- encourage pedestrians to cross
- not move until the green light appears
- stop even if the crossing is clear

27 At puffin crossings which light will not show to a driver?

mark one answer   ❶ p145

- Flashing amber
- Red
- steady amber
- green

28 You should leave at least a two-second gap between your vehicle and the one in front when conditions are

mark one answer   ❶ p77

- wet
- good
- damp
- foggy

29 You are driving on a clear night. There is a steady stream of oncoming traffic. The national speed limit applies. Which lights should you use?

mark one answer   ❶ p185

- Full beam headlights
- Sidelights
- Dipped headlights
- Fog lights

30 You are driving behind a large goods vehicle. It signals left but steers to the right. You should

mark one answer   ❶ p155

- slow down and let the vehicle turn
- drive on, keeping to the left
- overtake on the right of it
- hold your speed and sound your horn

31 You are driving along this road. The red van cuts in close in front of you. What should you do?

mark one answer   ❶ p79

- **a** Accelerate to get closer to the red van
- **b** Give a long blast on the horn
- **c** Drop back to leave the correct separation distance
- **d** Flash your headlights several times

32 You are waiting in a traffic queue at night. To avoid dazzling following drivers you should

mark one answer   ❶ p58

- **a** apply the handbrake only
- **b** apply the footbrake only
- **c** switch off your headlights
- **d** use both the handbrake and footbrake

33 You are driving in traffic at the speed limit for the road. The driver behind is trying to overtake. You should

mark one answer   ❶ p78

- **a** move closer to the car ahead, so the driver behind has no room to overtake
- **b** wave the driver behind to overtake when it is safe
- **c** keep a steady course and allow the driver behind to overtake
- **d** accelerate to get away from the driver behind

34 You are driving at night on an unlit road behind another vehicle. You should

mark one answer **ⓘ**p185
- **a** flash your headlights
- **b** use dipped beam headlights
- **c** switch off your headlights
- **d** use full beam headlights

35 A bus lane on your left shows no times of operation. This means it is

mark one answer **ⓘ**p157
- **a** not in operation at all
- **b** only in operation at peak times
- **c** in operation 24 hours a day
- **d** only in operation in daylight hours

36 You are driving along a country road. A horse and rider are approaching. What should you do?

mark two answers **ⓘ**p147
- **a** Increase your speed
- **b** Sound your horn
- **c** Flash your headlights
- **d** Drive slowly past
- **e** Give plenty of room
- **f** Rev your engine

37 A person herding sheep asks you to stop. You should

mark one answer **ⓘ**p149
- **a** ignore them as they have no authority
- **b** stop and switch off your engine
- **c** continue on but drive slowly
- **d** try and get past quickly

38 When overtaking a horse and rider you should

mark one answer **ⓘ**p147
- **a** sound your horn as a warning
- **b** go past as quickly as possible
- **c** flash your headlights as a warning
- **d** go past slowly and carefully

39 You are approaching a zebra crossing. Pedestrians are waiting to cross. You should

mark one answer **ⓘ**p143
- **a** give way to the elderly and infirm only
- **b** slow down and prepare to stop
- **c** use your headlights to indicate they can cross
- **d** wave at them to cross the road

40 You are driving a slow moving vehicle on a narrow winding road. You should

mark one answer **ⓘ**p78
- **a** keep well out to stop vehicles overtaking dangerously
- **b** wave following vehicles past you if you think they can overtake quickly
- **c** pull in safely when you can, to let following vehicles overtake
- **d** give a left signal when it is safe for vehicles to overtake you

41 You are driving a slow moving vehicle on a narrow road. When traffic wishes to overtake you should

mark one answer **ⓘ**p78
- **a** take no action
- **b** put your hazard warning lights on
- **c** stop immediately and wave it on
- **d** pull in safely as soon as you can do so

42 You are driving a slow-moving vehicle on a narrow winding road. In order to let other vehicles overtake you should

mark one answer **ⓘ**p78
- **a** wave to them to pass
- **b** pull in when you can
- **c** show a left turn signal
- **d** keep left and hold your speed

43 A vehicle pulls out in front of you at a junction. What should you do?

mark one answer *i* p89

a Swerve past it and sound your horn
b Flash your headlights and drive up close behind
c Slow down and be ready to stop
d Accelerate past it immediately

44 You stop for pedestrians waiting to cross at a zebra crossing. They do not start to cross. What should you do?

mark one answer *i* p144

a Be patient and wait
b Sound your horn
c Carry on
d Wave them to cross

45 You are following this lorry. You should keep well back from it to

mark one answer *i* p77

a give you a good view of the road ahead
b stop following traffic from rushing through the junction
c prevent traffic behind you from overtaking
d allow you to hurry through the traffic lights if they change

46 You are approaching a red light at a puffin crossing. Pedestrians are on the crossing. The red light will stay on until

mark one answer *i* p145

a you start to edge forward on to the crossing
b the pedestrians have reached a safe position
c the pedestrians are clear of the front of your vehicle
d a driver from the opposite direction reaches the crossing

47 Which instrument panel warning light would show that headlights are on full beam ?

mark one answer *i* p23

a

b

c

d

ANSWERS

34 b   39 b   44 a
35 c   40 c   45 a
36 d,e 41 d   46 b
37 b   42 b   47 a
38 d   43 c

01 Which of these, if allowed to get low, could cause an accident?

mark one answer   *i* p206

- **a** Antifreeze level
- **b** Brake fluid level
- **c** Battery water level
- **d** Radiator coolant level

02 Which TWO are badly affected if the tyres are under-inflated?

mark two answers   *i* p208

- **a** Braking
- **b** Steering
- **c** Changing gear
- **d** Parking

03 Motor vehicles can harm the environment. This has resulted in

mark three answers   *i* p215

- **a** air pollution
- **b** damage to buildings
- **c** less risk to health
- **d** improved public transport
- **e** less use of electrical vehicles
- **f** using up natural resources

04 Excessive or uneven tyre wear can be caused by faults in which THREE of the following?

mark three answers   *i* p208

- **a** The gearbox
- **b** The braking system
- **c** The accelerator
- **d** The exhaust system
- **e** Wheel alignment
- **f** The suspension

05 You must NOT sound your horn

mark one answer   *i* p185

- **a** between 10 pm and 6 am in a built-up area
- **b** at any time in a built-up area
- **c** between 11.30 pm and 7 am in a built-up area
- **d** between 11.30 pm and 6 am on any road

06 The pictured vehicle is 'environmentally friendly' because it

mark three answers   *i* p158

- **a** reduces noise pollution
- **b** uses diesel fuel
- **c** uses electricity
- **d** uses unleaded fuel
- **e** reduces parking spaces
- **f** reduces town traffic

07 Supertrams or Light Rapid Transit (LRT) systems are environmentally friendly because

mark one answer   *i* p158

- **a** they use diesel power
- **b** they use quieter roads
- **c** they use electric power
- **d** they do not operate during rush hour

08 'Red routes' in major cities have been introduced to

mark one answer   *i* p180

- **a** raise the speed limits
- **b** help the traffic flow
- **c** provide better parking
- **d** allow lorries to load more freely

09 In some narrow residential streets you may find a speed limit of

mark one answer   *i* p113

- **a** 20 mph
- **b** 25 mph
- **c** 35 mph
- **d** 40 mph

0 Road humps, chicanes, and narrowings are

ark one answer ⓘ p113
- always at major road works
- used to increase traffic speed
- at toll-bridge approaches only
- traffic calming measures

1 The purpose of a catalytic converter is to reduce

ark one answer ⓘ p216
- fuel consumption
- the risk of fire
- toxic exhaust gases
- engine wear

2 Catalytic converters are fitted to make the

ark one answer ⓘ p216
- engine produce more power
- exhaust system easier to replace
- engine run quietly
- exhaust fumes cleaner

3 It is essential that tyre pressures are checked regularly. When should this be done?

ark one answer ⓘ p208
- After any lengthy journey
- After travelling at high speed
- When tyres are hot
- When tyres are cold

4 When should you NOT use your horn in a built-up area?

ark one answer ⓘ p185
- Between 8 pm and 8 am
- Between 9 pm and dawn
- Between dusk and 8 am
- Between 11.30 pm and 7 am

5 You will use more fuel if your tyres are

ark one answer ⓘ p208
- under-inflated
- of different makes
- over-inflated
- new and hardly used

16 How should you dispose of a used battery?

mark two answers ⓘ p207
- **a** Take it to a local authority site
- **b** Put it in the dustbin
- **c** Break it up into pieces
- **d** Leave it on waste land
- **e** Take it to a garage
- **f** Burn it on a fire

17 What is most likely to cause high fuel consumption?

mark one answer ⓘ p217
- **a** Poor steering control
- **b** Accelerating around bends
- **c** Staying in high gears
- **d** Harsh braking and accelerating

18 The fluid level in your battery is low. What should you top it up with?

mark one answer ⓘ p207
- **a** Battery acid
- **b** Distilled water
- **c** Engine oil
- **d** Engine coolant

19 You need to top up your battery. What level should you fill to?

mark one answer ⓘ p207
- **a** The top of the battery
- **b** Half-way up the battery
- **c** Just below the cell plates
- **d** Just above the cell plates

20 You have too much oil in your engine. What could this cause?

mark one answer ⓘ p207
- **a** Low oil pressure
- **b** Engine overheating
- **c** Chain wear
- **d** Oil leaks

ANSWERS

01 b	06 a,c,f	11 c	16 a,e
02 a,b	07 c	12 d	17 d
03 a,b,f	08 b	13 d	18 b
04 b,e,f	09 a	14 d	19 d
05 c	10 d	15 a	20 d

21 You are parking on a two way road at night. The speed limit is 40 mph. You should park on the

mark one answer 🛈 p179
- **a** left with parking lights on
- **b** left with no lights on
- **c** right with parking lights on
- **d** right with dipped headlights on

22 You are parked on the road at night. Where must you use parking lights?

mark one answer 🛈 p179
- **a** Where there are continuous white lines in the middle of the road
- **b** Where the speed limit exceeds 30 mph
- **c** Where you are facing oncoming traffic
- **d** Where you are near a bus stop

23 Which FOUR of these must be in good working order for your car to be roadworthy?

mark four answers 🛈 p205
- **a** The temperature gauge
- **b** The speedometer
- **c** The windscreen washers
- **d** The windscreen wipers
- **e** The oil warning light
- **f** The horn

24 New petrol-engined cars must be fitted with catalytic converters. The reason for this is to

mark one answer 🛈 p216
- **a** control exhaust noise levels
- **b** prolong the life of the exhaust system
- **c** allow the exhaust system to be recycled
- **d** reduce harmful exhaust emissions

25 What can cause heavy steering?

mark one answer 🛈 p208
- **a** Driving on ice
- **b** Badly worn brakes
- **c** Over-inflated tyres
- **d** Under-inflated tyres

26 Driving with under-inflated tyres can affect

mark two answers 🛈 p208
- **a** engine temperature
- **b** fuel consumption
- **c** braking
- **d** oil pressure

27 Excessive or uneven tyre wear can be caused by faults in the

mark two answers 🛈 p208
- **a** gearbox
- **b** braking system
- **c** suspension
- **d** exhaust system

28 The main cause of brake fade is

mark one answer 🛈 p47
- **a** the brakes overheating
- **b** air in the brake fluid
- **c** oil on the brakes
- **d** the brakes out of adjustment

29 Your anti-lock brakes warning light stays on. You should

mark one answer 🛈 p23
- **a** check the brake fluid level
- **b** check the footbrake free play
- **c** check that the handbrake is released
- **d** have the brakes checked immediately

30 What does this instrument panel light mean when lit?

mark one answer 🛈 p23
- **a** Gear lever in park
- **b** Gear lever in neutral
- **c** Handbrake on
- **d** Handbrake off

31 While driving, this warning light on your dashboard comes on. It means

mark one answer ⓘ p23
- **a** a fault in the braking system
- **b** the engine oil is low
- **c** a rear light has failed
- **d** your seat belt is not fastened

32 It is important to wear suitable shoes when you are driving. Why is this?

mark one answer ⓘ p31
- **a** To prevent wear on the pedals
- **b** To maintain control of the pedals
- **c** To enable you to adjust your seat
- **d** To enable you to walk for assistance if you break down

33 The most important reason for having a properly adjusted head restraint is to

mark one answer ⓘ p34
- **a** make you more comfortable
- **b** help you to avoid neck injury
- **c** help you to relax
- **d** help you to maintain your driving position

34 What will reduce the risk of neck injury resulting from a collision?

mark one answer ⓘ p34
- **a** An air-sprung seat
- **b** Anti-lock brakes
- **c** A collapsible steering wheel
- **d** A properly adjusted head restraint

35 You are driving the children of a friend home from school. They are both under 14 years old. Who is responsible for making sure they wear a seat belt?

mark one answer ⓘ p233
- **a** An adult passenger
- **b** The children
- **c** You, the driver
- **d** Your friend

36 Car passengers MUST wear a seat belt if one is available, unless they are

mark one answer ⓘ p233
- **a** under 14 years old
- **b** under 1.5 metres (5 feet) in height
- **c** sitting in the rear seat
- **d** exempt for medical reasons

37 You are testing your suspension. You notice that your vehicle keeps bouncing when you press down on the front wing. What does this mean?

mark one answer ⓘ p205
- **a** Worn tyres
- **b** Tyres under-inflated
- **c** Steering wheel not located centrally
- **d** Worn shock absorbers

38 A roof rack fitted to your car will

mark one answer ⓘ p217
- **a** reduce fuel consumption
- **b** improve the road handling
- **c** make your car go faster
- **d** increase fuel consumption

39 It is illegal to drive with tyres that

mark one answer ⓘ p208
- **a** have been bought second-hand
- **b** have a large deep cut in the side wall
- **c** are of different makes
- **d** are of different tread patterns

40 The legal minimum depth of tread for car tyres over three quarters of the breadth is

mark one answer ⓘ p208
- **a** 1 mm
- **b** 1.6 mm
- **c** 2.5 mm
- **d** 4 mm

ANSWERS

21 a	26 b,c	31 a	36 d
22 b	27 b,c	32 b	37 d
23 b,c,d,f	28 a	33 b	38 d
24 d	29 d	34 d	39 b
25 d	30 c	35 c	40 b

41 You are carrying two 13 year old children and their parents in your car. Who is responsible for seeing that the children wear seat belts?

mark one answer ℹ️ p233
- **a** The children's parents
- **b** You, the driver
- **c** The front-seat passenger
- **d** The children

42 When a roof rack is not in use it should be removed. Why is this?

mark one answer ℹ️ p217
- **a** It will affect the suspension
- **b** It is illegal
- **c** It will affect your braking
- **d** It will waste fuel

43 You have a loose filler cap on your diesel fuel tank. This will

mark two answers ℹ️ p216
- **a** waste fuel and money
- **b** make roads slippery for other road users
- **c** improve your vehicles fuel consumption
- **d** increase the level of exhaust emissions

44 How can you, as a driver, help the environment?

mark three answers ℹ️ p217
- **a** By reducing your speed
- **b** By gentle acceleration
- **c** By using leaded fuel
- **d** By driving faster
- **e** By harsh acceleration
- **f** By servicing your vehicle properly

45 To help the environment, you can avoid wasting fuel by

mark three answers ℹ️ p217
- **a** having your vehicle properly serviced
- **b** making sure your tyres are correctly inflated
- **c** not over-revving in the lower gears
- **d** driving at higher speeds where possible
- **e** keeping an empty roof rack properly fitted
- **f** servicing your vehicle less regularly

46 To reduce the volume of traffic on the roads you could

mark three answers ℹ️ p217
- **a** use public transport more often
- **b** share a car when possible
- **c** walk or cycle on short journeys
- **d** travel by car at all times
- **e** use a car with a smaller engine
- **f** drive in a bus lane

47 Which THREE of the following are most likely to waste fuel?

mark three answers ℹ️ p217
- **a** Reducing your speed
- **b** Carrying unnecessary weight
- **c** Using the wrong grade of fuel
- **d** Under-inflated tyres
- **e** Using different brands of fuel
- **f** A fitted, empty roof rack

48 To avoid spillage after refuelling, you should make sure that

mark one answer ℹ️ p216
- **a** your tank is only three quarters full
- **b** you have used a locking filler cap
- **c** you check your fuel gauge is working
- **d** your filler cap is securely fastened

49 Which THREE things can you, as a road user, do to help the environment?

mark three answers ℹ️ p217
- **a** Cycle when possible
- **b** Drive on under-inflated tyres
- **c** Use the choke for as long as possible on a col engine
- **d** Have your vehicle properly tuned and serviced
- **e** Watch the traffic and plan ahead
- **f** Brake as late as possible without skidding

50 As a driver you can cause more damage to the environment by

mark two answers ℹ️ p217
- **a** choosing a fuel-efficient vehicle
- **b** making a lot of short journeys
- **c** driving in as high a gear as possible
- **d** accelerating as quickly as possible
- **e** having your vehicle regularly serviced

51 Extra care should be taken when refuelling, because diesel fuel when spilt is

mark one answer *p216*

a sticky
b odourless
c clear
d slippery

52 To help protect the environment you should NOT

mark one answer *p217*

a remove your roof rack when unloaded
b use your car for very short journeys
c walk, cycle, or use public transport
d empty the boot of unnecessary weight

53 Which THREE does the law require you to keep in good condition?

mark three answers *p205*

a Gears
b Transmission
c Headlights
d Windscreen
e Seat belts

54 Driving at 70 mph uses more fuel than driving at 50 mph by up to

mark one answer *p217*

a 10%
b 30%
c 75%
d 100%

55 Your vehicle pulls to one side when braking. You should

mark one answer *p205*

a change the tyres around
b consult your garage as soon as possible
c pump the pedal when braking
d use your handbrake at the same time

56 As a driver you can help reduce pollution levels in town centres by

mark one answer *p217*

a driving more quickly
b over-revving in a low gear
c walking or cycling
d driving short journeys

57 Unbalanced wheels on a car may cause

mark one answer *p205*

a the steering to pull to one side
b the steering to vibrate
c the brakes to fail
d the tyres to deflate

58 Turning the steering wheel while your car is stationary can cause damage to the

mark two answers *p45*

a gearbox
b engine
c brakes
d steering
e tyres

59 How can you reduce the chances of your car being broken into when leaving it unattended?

mark one answer *p219*

a Take all valuables with you
b Park near a taxi rank
c Place any valuables on the floor
d Park near a fire station

60 You have to leave valuables in your car. It would be safer to

mark one answer *p219*

a put them in a carrier bag
b park near a school entrance
c lock them out of sight
d park near a bus stop

61 How could you deter theft from your car when leaving it unattended?

mark one answer *p219*

a Leave valuables in a carrier bag
b Lock valuables out of sight
c Put valuables on the seats
d Leave valuables on the floor

ANSWERS

41 b	47 b,d,f	53 c,d,e	59 a
42 d	48 d	54 b	60 c
43 a,b	49 a,d,e	55 b	61 b
44 a,b,f	50 b,d	56 c	
45 a,b,c	51 d	57 b	
46 a,b,c	52 b	58 d,e	

62 Which of the following may help to deter a thief from stealing your car?

mark one answer   *i* p219

- **a** Always keeping the headlights on
- **b** Fitting reflective glass windows
- **c** Always keeping the interior light on
- **d** Etching the car number on the windows

63 How can you help to prevent your car radio being stolen?

mark one answer   *i* p219

- **a** Park in an unlit area
- **b** Hide the radio with a blanket
- **c** Park near a busy junction
- **d** Install a security coded radio

64 Which of the following should not be kept in your vehicle?

mark one answer   *i* p219

- **a** A first aid kit
- **b** A road atlas
- **c** The tax disc
- **d** The vehicle documents

65 What should you do when leaving your vehicle?

mark one answer   *i* p219

- **a** Put valuable documents under the seats
- **b** Remove all valuables
- **c** Cover valuables with a blanket
- **d** Leave the interior light on

66 You are parking your car. You have some valuables which you are unable to take with you. What should you do?

mark one answer   *i* p219

- **a** Park near a police station
- **b** Put them under the drivers seat
- **c** Lock them out of sight
- **d** Park in an unlit side road

67 Which of these is most likely to deter the theft of your vehicle?

mark one answer   *i* p219

- **a** An immobiliser
- **b** Tinted windows
- **c** Locking wheel nuts
- **d** A sun screen

68 Wherever possible, which one of the following should you do when parking at night?

mark one answer   *i* p219

- **a** Park in a quiet car park
- **b** Park in a well lit area
- **c** Park facing against the flow of traffic
- **d** Park next to a busy junction

69 When parking and leaving your car you should

mark one answer   *i* p219

- **a** park under a shady tree
- **b** remove the tax disc
- **c** park in a quiet road
- **d** engage the steering lock

70 Rear facing baby seats should NEVER be used on a seat protected with

mark one answer   *i* p233

- **a** an airbag
- **b** seat belts
- **c** head restraints
- **d** seat covers

71 When leaving your vehicle parked and unattended you should

mark one answer   *i* p219

- **a** park near a busy junction
- **b** park in a housing estate
- **c** remove the key and lock it
- **d** leave the left indicator on

72 How can you lessen the risk of your vehicle being broken into at night?

mark one answer   *i* p219

- **a** Leave it in a well lit area
- **b** Park in a quiet side road
- **c** Don't engage the steering lock
- **d** Park in a poorly lit area

73 To help keep your car secure you could join a

mark one answer   *i* p219

- **a** vehicle breakdown organisation
- **b** vehicle watch scheme
- **c** advanced drivers scheme
- **d** car maintenance class

74 Which TWO of the following will improve fuel consumption?

mark two answers **ⓘ** p217

- **a** Reducing your road speed
- **b** Planning well ahead
- **c** Late and harsh braking
- **d** Driving in lower gears
- **e** Short journeys with a cold engine
- **f** Rapid acceleration

75 You service your own vehicle. How should you get rid of the old engine oil?

mark one answer **ⓘ** p207

- **a** Take it to a local authority site
- **b** Pour it down a drain
- **c** Tip it into a hole in the ground
- **d** Put it into your dustbin

76 On a vehicle, where would you find a catalytic converter?

mark one answer **ⓘ** p216

- **a** In the fuel tank
- **b** In the air filter
- **c** On the cooling system
- **d** On the exhaust system

77 Why do MOT tests include a strict exhaust emission test?

mark one answer **ⓘ** p215

- **a** To recover the cost of expensive garage equipment
- **b** To help protect the environment against pollution
- **c** To discover which fuel supplier is used the most
- **d** To make sure diesel and petrol engines emit the same fumes

78 To reduce the damage your vehicle causes to the environment you should

mark three answers **ⓘ** p217

- **a** use narrow side streets
- **b** avoid harsh acceleration
- **c** brake in good time
- **d** anticipate well ahead
- **e** use busy routes

79 Your vehicle has a catalytic converter. Its purpose is to reduce

mark one answer **ⓘ** p216

- **a** exhaust noise
- **b** fuel consumption
- **c** exhaust emissions
- **d** engine noise

80 A properly serviced vehicle will give

mark two answers **ⓘ** p217

- **a** lower insurance premiums
- **b** you a refund on your road tax
- **c** better fuel economy
- **d** cleaner exhaust emissions

81 You enter a road where there are road humps. What should you do?

mark one answer **ⓘ** p113

- **a** Maintain a reduced speed throughout
- **b** Accelerate quickly between each one
- **c** Always keep to the maximum legal speed
- **d** Drive slowly at school times only

82 When should you especially check the engine oil level?

mark one answer **ⓘ** p207

- **a** Before a long journey
- **b** When the engine is hot
- **c** Early in the morning
- **d** Every 6000 miles

ANSWERS			
62 d	68 b	74 a,b	80 c,d
63 d	69 d	75 a	81 a
64 d	70 a	76 d	82 a
65 b	71 c	77 b	
66 c	72 a	78 b,c,d	
67 a	73 b	79 c	

83 You are having difficulty finding a parking space in a busy town. You can see there is space on the zigzag lines of a zebra crossing. Can you park there?

mark one answer *i* p180
- **a** No, unless you stay with your car
- **b** Yes, in order to drop off a passenger
- **c** Yes, if you do not block people from crossing
- **d** No, not in any circumstances

84 When leaving your car unattended for a few minutes you should

mark one answer *i* p179
- **a** leave the engine running
- **b** switch the engine off but leave the key in
- **c** lock it and remove the key
- **d** park near a traffic warden

85 When parking and leaving your car for a few minutes you should

mark one answer *i* p179
- **a** leave it unlocked
- **b** lock it and remove the key
- **c** leave the hazard warning lights on
- **d** leave the interior light on

86 When leaving your car to help keep it secure you should

mark one answer *i* p179
- **a** leave the hazard warning lights on
- **b** lock it and remove the key
- **c** park on a one way street
- **d** park in a residential area

87 When leaving your vehicle where should you park if possible?

mark one answer *i* p179
- **a** Opposite a traffic island
- **b** In a secure car park
- **c** On a bend
- **d** At or near a taxi rank

88 You are leaving your vehicle parked on a road. When may you leave the engine running?

mark one answer *i* p179
- **a** If you will be parking for less than five minutes
- **b** If the battery is flat
- **c** When in a 20 mph zone
- **d** Never on any occasion

89 In which THREE places would parking your vehicle cause danger or obstruction to other road users?

mark three answers *i* p49
- **a** In front of a property entrance
- **b** At or near a bus stop
- **c** On your driveway
- **d** In a marked parking space
- **e** On the approach to a level crossing

90 In which THREE places would parking cause an obstruction to others?

mark three answers *i* p49
- **a** Near the brow of a hill
- **b** In a lay-by
- **c** Where the kerb is raised
- **d** Where the kerb has been lowered for wheelchairs
- **e** At or near a bus stop

91 You are away from home and have to park your vehicle overnight. Where should you leave it?

mark one answer *i* p179
- **a** Opposite another parked vehicle
- **b** In a quiet road
- **c** Opposite a traffic island
- **d** In a secure car park

ANSWERS

83 d	86 b	89 a,b,e
84 c	87 b	90 a,d,e
85 b	88 d	91 d

SAFETY MARGINS

01 Braking distances on ice can be

mark one answer ⓘ p138

a twice the normal distance
b five times the normal distance
c seven times the normal distance
d ten times the normal distance

02 Freezing conditions will affect the distance it takes you to come to a stop. You should expect stopping distances to increase by up to

mark one answer ⓘ p138

a two times
b three times
c five times
d ten times

03 In very hot weather the road surface can become soft. Which TWO of the following will be most affected?

mark two answers ⓘ p191

a The suspension
b The grip of the tyres
c The braking
d The exhaust

04 Where are you most likely to be affected by a sidewind?

mark one answer ⓘ p191

a On a narrow country lane
b On an open stretch of road
c On a busy stretch of road
d On a long, straight road

05 In windy conditions you need to take extra care when

mark one answer ⓘ p191

a using the brakes
b making a hill start
c turning into a narrow road
d passing pedal cyclists

06 In good conditions, what is the typical stopping distance at 70 mph?

mark one answer ⓘ p138

a 53 metres (175 feet)
b 60 metres (197 feet)
c 73 metres (240 feet)
d 96 metres (315 feet)

07 What is the shortest overall stopping distance on a dry road at 60 mph?

mark one answer ⓘ p138

a 53 metres (175 feet)
b 58 metres (190 feet)
c 73 metres (240 feet)
d 96 metres (315 feet)

08 Your indicators may be difficult to see in bright sunlight. What should you do?

mark one answer ⓘ p60

a Put your indicator on earlier
b Give an arm signal as well as using your indicator
c Touch the brake several times to show the stop lights
d Turn as quickly as you can

09 In very hot weather the road surface can get soft. Which TWO of the following will be affected most?

mark two answers ⓘ p191

a The suspension
b The steering
c The braking
d The exhaust

ANSWERS

01 d	04 b	07 c
02 d	05 d	08 b
03 b,c	06 d	09 b,c

10 When approaching a right-hand bend you should keep well to the left. Why is this?

mark one answer *i* p109
- **a** To improve your view of the road
- **b** To overcome the effect of the road's slope
- **c** To let faster traffic from behind overtake
- **d** To be positioned safely if you skid

11 You should not overtake when

mark three answers *i* p83
- **a** intending to turn left shortly afterwards
- **b** in a one-way street
- **c** approaching a junction
- **d** going up a long hill
- **e** the view ahead is blocked

12 You have just gone through deep water. To dry off the brakes you should

mark one answer *i* p189
- **a** accelerate and keep to a high speed for a short time
- **b** go slowly while gently applying the brakes
- **c** avoid using the brakes at all for a few miles
- **d** stop for at least an hour to allow them time to dry

13 You are on a fast, open road in good conditions. For safety, the distance between you and the vehicle in front should be

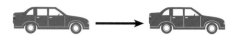

mark one answer *i* p77
- **a** a two-second time gap
- **b** one car length
- **c** 2 metres (6feet 6inches)
- **d** two car lengths

14 What is the most common cause of skidding?

mark one answer *i* p192
- **a** Worn tyres
- **b** Driver error
- **c** Other vehicles
- **d** Pedestrians

15 You are driving on an icy road. How can you avoid wheelspin?

mark one answer *i* p193
- **a** Drive at a slow speed in as high a gear as possible
- **b** Use the handbrake if the wheels start to slip
- **c** Brake gently and repeatedly
- **d** Drive in a low gear at all times

16 Skidding is mainly caused by

mark one answer *i* p192
- **a** the weather
- **b** the driver
- **c** the vehicle
- **d** the road

17 You are driving in freezing conditions. What should you do when approaching a sharp bend?

mark two answers *i* p193
- **a** Slow down before you reach the bend
- **b** Gently apply your handbrake
- **c** Firmly use your footbrake
- **d** Coast into the bend
- **e** Avoid sudden steering movements

18 You are turning left on a slippery road. The back of your vehicle slides to the right. You should

mark one answer *i* p194
- **a** brake firmly and not turn the steering wheel
- **b** steer carefully to the left
- **c** steer carefully to the right
- **d** brake firmly and steer to the left

19 You are braking on a wet road. Your vehicle begins to skid. It does not have anti-lock brakes. What is the FIRST thing you should do?

mark one answer **ⓘ** p194
a Quickly pull up the handbrake
b Release the footbrake fully
c Push harder on the brake pedal
d Gently use the accelerator

20 Coasting the vehicle

mark one answer **ⓘ** p31
a improves the driver's control
b makes steering easier
c reduces the driver's control
d uses more fuel

21 Before starting a journey in freezing weather you should clear ice and snow from your vehicle's

mark four answers **ⓘ** p187
a aerial
b windows
c bumper
d lights
e mirrors
f number plates

22 You are trying to move off on snow. You should use

mark one answer **ⓘ** p194
a the lowest gear you can
b the highest gear you can
c a high engine speed
d the handbrake and footbrake together

23 When driving in falling snow you should

mark one answer **ⓘ** p193
a brake firmly and quickly
b be ready to steer sharply
c use sidelights only
d brake gently in plenty of time

24 The MAIN benefit of having four-wheel drive is to improve

mark one answer **ⓘ** p195
a road holding
b fuel consumption
c stopping distances
d passenger comfort

25 You are about to go down a steep hill. To control the speed of your vehicle you should

mark one answer **ⓘ** p111
a select a high gear and use the brakes carefully
b select a high gear and use the brakes firmly
c select a low gear and use the brakes carefully
d select a low gear and avoid using the brakes

26 How can you use your vehicle's engine as a brake?

mark one answer **ⓘ** p47
a By changing to a lower gear
b By selecting reverse gear
c By changing to a higher gear
d By selecting neutral gear

27 You wish to park facing DOWNHILL. Which TWO of the following should you do?

mark two answers **ⓘ** p111
a Turn the steering wheel towards the kerb
b Park close to the bumper of another car
c Park with two wheels on the kerb
d Put the handbrake on firmly
e Turn the steering wheel away from the kerb

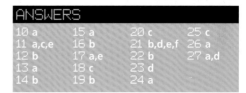

ANSWERS			
10 a	15 a	20 c	25 c
11 a,c,e	16 b	21 b,d,e,f	26 a
12 b	17 a,e	22 b	27 a,d
13 a	18 c	23 d	
14 b	19 b	24 a	

28 You are driving in a built-up area. You approach a speed hump. You should

mark one answer **ⓘ** p113
a move across to the left-hand side of the road
b wait for any pedestrians to cross
c slow your vehicle right down
d stop and check both pavements

29 You are on a long, downhill slope. What should you do to help control the speed of your vehicle?

mark one answer **ⓘ** p111
a Select neutral
b Select a lower gear
c Grip the handbrake firmly
d Apply the parking brake gently

30 Your vehicle is fitted with anti-lock brakes. To stop quickly in an emergency you should

mark one answer **ⓘ** p47
a brake firmly and pump the brake pedal on and off
b brake rapidly and firmly without releasing the brake pedal
c brake gently and pump the brake pedal on and off
d brake rapidly once, and immediately release the brake pedal

31 Anti-lock brakes prevent wheels from locking. This means the tyres are less likely to

mark one answer **ⓘ** p47
a aquaplane
b skid
c puncture
d wear

32 Anti-lock brakes reduce the chances of a skid occurring particularly when

mark one answer **ⓘ** p47
a driving down steep hills
b braking during normal driving
c braking in an emergency
d driving on good road surfaces

33 Anti-lock brakes are most effective when you

mark one answer **ⓘ** p47
a keep pumping the foot brake to prevent skidding
b brake normally, but grip the steering wheel tightly
c brake promptly and firmly until you have slowed down
d apply the handbrake to reduce the stopping distance

34 Your car is fitted with anti-lock brakes. You need to stop in an emergency. You should

mark one answer **ⓘ** p47
a brake normally and avoid turning the steering wheel
b press the brake pedal promptly and firmly until you have stopped
c keep pushing and releasing the foot brake quickly to prevent skidding
d apply the handbrake to reduce the stopping distance

35 Vehicles fitted with anti-lock brakes

mark one answer **ⓘ** p47
a are impossible to skid
b can be steered while you are braking
c accelerate much faster
d are not fitted with a handbrake

36 Anti-lock brakes may not work as effectively if the road surface is

mark two answers **ⓘ** p47
a dry
b loose
c wet
d good
e firm

37 Anti-lock brakes are of most use when you are

mark one answer 🛈 p47

a braking gently
b driving on worn tyres
c braking excessively
d driving normally

38 Driving a vehicle fitted with anti-lock brakes allows you to

mark one answer 🛈 p47

a brake harder because it is impossible to skid
b drive at higher speeds
c steer and brake at the same time
d pay less attention to the road ahead

39 Anti-lock brakes can greatly assist with

mark one answer 🛈 p47

a a higher cruising speed
b steering control when braking
c control when accelerating
d motorway driving

40 When would an anti-lock braking system start to work?

mark one answer 🛈 p47

a After the parking brake has been applied
b When ever pressure on the brake pedal is applied
c Just as the wheels are about to lock
d When the normal braking system fails to operate

41 You are driving a vehicle fitted with anti-lock brakes. You need to stop in an emergency. You should apply the footbrake

mark one answer 🛈 p47

a slowly and gently
b slowly but firmly
c rapidly and gently
d rapidly and firmly

42 Your vehicle has anti-lock brakes, but they may not always prevent skidding. This is most likely to happen when driving

mark two answers 🛈 p47

a in foggy conditions
b on surface water
c on loose road surfaces
d on dry tarmac
e at night on unlit roads

43 Anti-lock brakes will take effect when

mark one answer 🛈 p47

a you do not brake quickly enough
b maximum brake pressure has been applied
c you have not seen a hazard ahead
d speeding on slippery road surfaces

44 When driving in fog, which of the following are correct?

mark three answers 🛈 p190

a Use dipped headlights
b Use headlights on full beam
c Allow more time for your journey
d Keep close to the car in front
e Slow down
f Use side lights only

45 You are driving along a country road. You see this sign. AFTER dealing safely with the hazard you should always

mark one answer 🛈 p189

a check your tyre pressures
b switch on your hazard warning lights
c accelerate briskly
d test your brakes

ANSWERS			
28 c	33 c	38 c	43 b
29 b	34 b	39 b	44 a,c,e
30 b	35 b	40 c	45 d
31 b	36 b,c	41 d	
32 c	37 c	42 b,c	

46 You are driving in heavy rain. Your steering suddenly becomes very light. You should

mark one answer **ⓘ** p188

a steer towards the side of the road
b apply gentle acceleration
c brake firmly to reduce speed
d ease off the accelerator

47 How can you tell when you are driving over black ice?

mark one answer **ⓘ** p193

a It is easier to brake
b The noise from your tyres sounds louder
c You see black ice on the road
d Your steering feels light

48 The roads are icy. You should drive slowly

mark one answer **ⓘ** p193

a in the highest gear possible
b in the lowest gear possible
c with the handbrake partly on
d with your left foot on the brake

49 You are driving along a wet road. How can you tell if your vehicle is aquaplaning?

mark one answer **ⓘ** p188

a The engine will stall
b The engine noise will increase
c The steering will feel very heavy
d The steering will feel very light

50 How can you tell if you are driving on ice?

mark two answers **ⓘ** p193

a The tyres make a rumbling noise
b The tyres make hardly any noise
c The steering becomes heavier
d The steering becomes lighter

51 You are driving along a wet road. How can you tell if your vehicle's tyres are losing their grip on the surface?

mark one answer **ⓘ** p188

a The engine will stall
b The steering will feel very heavy
c The engine noise will increase
d The steering will feel very light

52 You are travelling at 50 mph on a good, dry road. What is your shortest overall stopping distance?

mark one answer **ⓘ** p138

a 36 metres (120 feet)
b 53 metres (175 feet)
c 75 metres (245 feet)
d 96 metres (315 feet)

53 Your overall stopping distance will be much longer when driving

mark one answer **ⓘ** p138

a in the rain
b in fog
c at night
d in strong winds

54 You have driven through a flood. What is the first thing you should do?

mark one answer **ⓘ** p189

a Stop and check the tyres
b Stop and dry the brakes
c Check your exhaust
d Test your brakes

55 You are on a good, dry road surface. Your vehicle has good brakes and tyres. What is the BRAKING distance at 50 mph?

mark one answer **ⓘ** p138

a 38 metres (125 feet)
b 14 metres (46 feet)
c 24 metres (79 feet)
d 55 metres (180 feet)

56 You are on a good, dry, road surface and your vehicle has good brakes and tyres. What is the typical overall stopping distance at 40 mph?

mark one answer **ⓘ** p138

a 23 metres (75 feet)
b 36 metres (120 feet)
c 53 metres (175 feet)
d 96 metres (315 feet)

ANSWERS

46 d	49 d	52 b	55 a
47 d	50 b,d	53 a	56 b
48 a	51 d	54 d	

HAZARD AWARENESS

01 You see this sign on the rear of a slow-moving lorry that you want to pass. It is travelling in the middle lane of a three lane motorway. You should

mark one answer ⓘp125
a cautiously approach the lorry then pass on either side
b follow the lorry until you can leave the motorway
c wait on the hard shoulder until the lorry has stopped
d approach with care and keep to the left of the lorry

02 Where would you expect to see these markers?

mark two answers ⓘp154
a On a motorway sign
b At the entrance to a narrow bridge
c On a large goods vehicle
d On a builder's skip placed on the road

03 What does this signal from a police officer, mean to oncoming traffic?

mark one answer ⓘp61
a Go ahead
b Stop
c Turn left
d Turn right

04 What is the main hazard shown in this picture?

mark one answer ⓘp128
a Vehicles turning right ⓘp151
b Vehicles doing U-turns
c The cyclist crossing the road
d Parked cars around the corner

05 Which road user has caused a hazard?

mark one answer ⓘp181
a The parked car (arrowed A)
b The pedestrian waiting to cross (arrowed B)
c The moving car (arrowed C)
d The car turning (arrowed D)

ANSWERS

01 d	03 b	05 a
02 c,d	04 c	

06 What should the driver of the car approaching the crossing do?

mark one answer   🛈 p144

- **a** Continue at the same speed
- **b** Sound the horn
- **c** Drive through quickly
- **d** Slow down and get ready to stop

07 What THREE things should the driver of the grey car (arrowed) be especially aware of?

mark three answers   🛈 p128

- **a** Pedestrians stepping out between cars
- **b** Other cars behind the grey car
- **c** Doors opening on parked cars
- **d** The bumpy road surface
- **e** Cars leaving parking spaces
- **f** Empty parking spaces

08 You think the driver of the vehicle in front has forgotten to cancel their right indicator. You should

mark one answer   🛈 p59

- **a** flash your lights to alert the driver
- **b** sound your horn before overtaking
- **c** overtake on the left if there is room
- **d** stay behind and not overtake

09 What is the main hazard the driver of the red car (arrowed) should be aware of?

mark one answer   🛈 p156

- **a** Glare from the sun may affect the driver's vision
- **b** The black car may stop suddenly
- **c** The bus may move out into the road
- **d** Oncoming vehicles will assume the driver is turning right

10 In heavy motorway traffic you are being followed closely by the vehicle behind. How can you lower the risk of an accident?

mark one answer   🛈 p78

- **a** Increase your distance from the vehicle in front
- **b** Tap your foot on the brake pedal sharply
- **c** Switch on your hazard lights
- **d** Move onto the hard shoulder and stop

11 You see this sign ahead. You should expect the road to

mark one answer *ⓘ* p109
a go steeply uphill
b go steeply downhill
c bend sharply to the left
d bend sharply to the right

12 You are approaching this cyclist. You should

mark one answer *ⓘ* p151
a overtake before the cyclist gets to the junction
b flash your headlights at the cyclist
c slow down and allow the cyclist to turn
d overtake the cyclist on the left-hand side

13 Why must you take extra care when turning right at this junction?

mark one answer *ⓘ* p94
a Road surface is poor
b Footpaths are narrow
c Road markings are faint
d There is reduced visibility

14 This yellow sign on a vehicle indicates this is

mark one answer *ⓘ* p157
a a broken-down vehicle
b a school bus
c an ice cream van
d a private ambulance

15 When approaching this bridge you should give way to

mark one answer *ⓘ* p155
a bicycles
b buses
c motorcycles
d cars

16 What type of vehicle could you expect to meet in the middle of the road?

mark one answer *ⓘ* p155
a Lorry
b Bicycle
c Car
d Motorcycle

ANSWERS

06 d	09 c	12 c	15 b
07 a,c,e	10 a	13 d	16 a
08 d	11 c	14 b	

17 At this blind junction you must stop

mark one answer **❶** p94
- **a** behind the line, then edge forward to see clearly
- **b** beyond the line at a point where you can see clearly
- **c** only if there is traffic on the main road
- **d** only if you are turning to the right

18 A driver pulls out of a side road in front of you. You have to brake hard. You should

mark one answer **❶** p228
- **a** ignore the error and stay calm
- **b** flash your lights to show your annoyance
- **c** sound your horn to show your annoyance
- **d** overtake as soon as possible

19 An elderly person's driving ability could be affected because they may be unable to

mark one answer **❶** p229
- **a** obtain car insurance
- **b** understand road signs
- **c** react very quickly
- **d** give signals correctly

20 You have just passed these warning lights. What hazard would you expect to see next?

mark one answer **❶** p145
- **a** A level crossing with no barrier
- **b** An ambulance station
- **c** A school crossing patrol
- **d** An opening bridge

21 Why should you be especially cautious when going past this bus?

mark two answers **❶** p157
- **a** There is traffic approaching in the distance
- **b** The driver may open the door
- **c** It may suddenly move off
- **d** People may cross the road in front of it
- **e** There are bicycles parked on the pavement

22 In areas where there are 'traffic calming measures you should

mark one answer **❶** p113
- **a** drive at a reduced speed
- **b** always travel at the speed limit
- **c** position in the centre of the road
- **d** only slow down if pedestrians are near

23 You are planning a long journey. Do you need to plan rest stops?

mark one answer *i* p135

a Yes, you should plan to stop every half an hour
b Yes, regular stops help concentration
c No, you will be less tired if you get there as soon as possible
d No, only fuel stops will be needed

24 A driver does something that upsets you. You should

mark one answer *i* p228

a try not to react
b let them know how you feel
c flash your headlights several times
d sound your horn

25 The red lights are flashing. What should you do when approaching this level crossing?

mark one answer *i* p161

a Go through quickly
b Go through carefully
c Stop before the barrier
d Switch on hazard warning lights

26 What TWO main hazards should you be aware of when going along this street?

mark two answers *i* p74

a Glare from the sun
b Car doors opening suddenly
c Lack of road markings
d The headlights on parked cars being switched on
e Large goods vehicles
f Children running out from between vehicles

27 What is the main hazard you should be aware of when following this cyclist?

mark one answer *i* p133
i p151

a The cyclist may move to the left and dismount
b The cyclist may swerve out into the road
c The contents of the cyclist's carrier may fall onto the road
d The cyclist may wish to turn right at the end of the road

ANSWERS

17 a	20 c	23 b	26 b,f
18 a	21 c,d	24 a	27 b
19 c	22 a	25 c	

28 When approaching this hazard why should you slow down?

mark two answers **𝒊** p108

a Because of the bend **𝒊** p160
b Because its hard to see to the right
c Because of approaching traffic
d Because of animals crossing
e Because of the level crossing

29 A driver's behaviour has upset you. It may help if you

mark one answer **𝒊** p228

a stop and take a break
b shout abusive language
c gesture to them with your hand
d follow their car, flashing your headlights

30 You are on a dual carriageway. Ahead you see a vehicle with an amber flashing light. What will this be?

mark one answer **𝒊** p143

a An ambulance
b A fire engine
c A doctor on call
d A disabled persons vehicle

31 You are approaching crossroads. The traffic lights have failed. What should you do?

mark one answer **𝒊** p69

a Brake and stop only for large vehicles
b Brake sharply to a stop before looking
c Be prepared to brake sharply to a stop
d Be prepared to stop for any traffic.

32 Why are place names painted on the road surface?

mark one answer **𝒊** p67

a To restrict the flow of traffic
b To warn you of oncoming traffic
c To enable you to change lanes early
d To prevent you changing lanes

33 What should the driver of the red car (arrowed) do?

mark one answer **𝒊** p143

a Wave the pedestrians who are waiting to cross
b Wait for the pedestrian in the road to cross
c Quickly drive behind the pedestrian in the roa
d Tell the pedestrian in the road she should not have crossed

34 You are following a slower-moving vehicle on a narrow country road. There is a junction just ahead on the right. What should you do?

mark one answer **𝒊** p84

a Overtake after checking your mirrors and signalling
b Stay behind until you are past the junction
c Accelerate quickly to pass before the junction
d Slow down and prepare to overtake on the le

35 What should you do as you approach this overhead bridge?

mark one answer   **ⓘ p155**

ⓐ Move out to the centre of the road before going through
ⓑ Find another route, this is only for high vehicles
ⓒ Be prepared to give way to large vehicles in the middle of the road
ⓓ Move across to the right hand side before going through

36 Why are mirrors often slightly curved (convex)?

mark one answer   **ⓘ p53**

ⓐ They give a wider field of vision
ⓑ They totally cover blind spots
ⓒ They make it easier to judge the speed of following traffic
ⓓ They make following traffic look bigger

37 What does the solid white line at the side of the road indicate?

mark one answer   **ⓘ p73**

ⓐ Traffic lights ahead
ⓑ Edge of the carriageway
ⓒ Footpath on the left
ⓓ Cycle path

38 You are driving towards this level crossing. What would be the first warning of an approaching train?

mark one answer   **ⓘ p161**

ⓐ Both half barriers down
ⓑ A steady amber light
ⓒ One half barrier down
ⓓ Twin flashing red lights

39 You are driving along this motorway. It is raining. When following this lorry you should

mark two answers   **ⓘ p188**

ⓐ allow at least a two-second gap
ⓑ move left and drive on the hard shoulder
ⓒ allow at least a four-second gap
ⓓ be aware of spray reducing your vision
ⓔ move right and stay in the right hand lane

ANSWERS			
28 a,e	31 d	34 b	37 b
29 a	32 c	35 c	38 b
30 d	33 b	36 a	39 c,d

40 You are behind this cyclist.
When the traffic lights change,
what should you do?

mark one answer　　　**ⓘ p154**

a Try to move off before the cyclist
b Allow the cyclist time and room
c Turn right but give the cyclist room
d Tap your horn and drive through first

41 You are driving towards this left hand
bend. What dangers should you be
aware of?

mark one answer　　　**ⓘ p115**

a A vehicle overtaking you
b No white lines in the centre of the
road
c No sign to warn you of the bend
d Pedestrians walking towards you

42 While driving, you see this sign ahead.
You should

mark one answer　　　**ⓘ p66**

a stop at the sign
b slow, but continue around the bend　**ⓘ p161**
c slow to a crawl and continue
d stop and look for open farm gates

43 Why should the junction on the left be
kept clear?

mark one answer　　　**ⓘ p79**

a To allow vehicles to enter and
emerge
b To allow the bus to reverse
c To allow vehicles to make a 'U' turn
d To allow vehicles to park

44 When the traffic lights change to green the white car should

mark one answer p154

a wait for the cyclist to pull away
b move off quickly and turn in front of the cyclist
c move close up to the cyclist to beat the lights
d sound the horn to warn the cyclist

45 You intend to turn left at the traffic lights. Just before turning you should

mark one answer p151

a check your right mirror
b move close up to the white car
c straddle the lanes
d check for bicycles on your left

46 You should reduce your speed when driving along this road because

mark one answer p94

a there is a staggered junction ahead
b there is a low bridge ahead
c there is a change in the road surface
d the road ahead narrows

47 You are driving at 60 mph. As you approach this hazard you should

mark one answer p94

a maintain your speed
b reduce your speed
c take the next right turn
d take the next left turn

ANSWERS

40 b	42 b	44 a	46 a
41 d	43 a	45 d	47 b

48 The traffic ahead of you in the left-hand lane is slowing. You should

mark two answers 🛈 p125

a be wary of cars on your right cutting in
b accelerate past the vehicles in the left-hand lane
c pull up on the left-hand verge
d move across and continue in the right-hand lane
e slow down, keeping a safe separation distance

49 What might you expect to happen in this situation?

mark one answer 🛈 p125

a Traffic will move into the right-hand lane
b Traffic speed will increase
c Traffic will move into the left-hand lane
d Traffic will not need to change position

50 You are driving on a road with several lanes. You see these signs above the lanes. What do they mean?

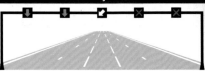

mark one answer 🛈 p123

a The two right lanes are open
b The two left lanes are open
c Traffic in the left lanes should stop
d Traffic in the right lanes should stop

51 As a provisional licence holder, you must not drive a motor car

mark two answers 🛈 p11

a at more than 40 mph
b on your own
c on the motorway
d under the age of 18 years at night
e with passengers in the rear seats

52 After passing your driving test, you suffer from ill health. This affects your driving. You MUST

mark one answer 🛈 p15

a inform your local police station
b get on as best you can
c not inform anyone as you hold a full licence
d inform the licensing authority

53 You are invited to a pub lunch. You know that you will have to drive in the evening. What is your best course of action?

mark one answer 🛈 p16

a Avoid mixing your alcoholic drinks
b Not drink any alcohol at all
c Have some milk before drinking alcohol
d Eat a hot meal with your alcoholic drinks

54 You have been convicted of driving whilst unfit through drink or drugs. You will find this is likely to cause the cost of one of the following to rise considerably. Which one?

mark one answer · p16
- Road fund licence
- Insurance premiums
- Vehicle test certificate
- Driving licence

55 What advice should you give to a driver who has had a few alcoholic drinks at a party?

mark one answer · p16
- Have a strong cup of coffee and then drive home
- Drive home carefully and slowly
- Go home by public transport
- Wait a short while and then drive home

56 You have been taking medicine for a few days which made you feel drowsy. Today you feel better but still need to take the medicine. You should only drive

mark one answer · p15
- if your journey is necessary
- at night on quiet roads
- if someone goes with you
- after checking with your doctor

57 You are about to return home from holiday when you become ill. A doctor prescribes drugs which are likely to affect your driving. You should

mark one answer · p15
- drive only if someone is with you
- avoid driving on motorways
- not drive yourself
- never drive at more than 30 mph

58 During periods of illness your ability to drive may be impaired. You MUST

mark two answers · p15
- see your doctor each time before you drive
- only take smaller doses of any medicines
- be medically fit to drive
- not drive after taking certain medicines
- take all your medicines with you when you drive

59 You feel drowsy when driving. You should

mark two answers · p135
- **a** stop and rest as soon as possible
- **b** turn the heater up to keep you warm and comfortable
- **c** make sure you have a good supply of fresh air
- **d** continue with your journey but drive more slowly
- **e** close the car windows to help you concentrate

60 You are driving along a motorway and become tired. You should

mark two answers · p135
- **a** stop at the next service area and rest
- **b** leave the motorway at the next exit and rest
- **c** increase your speed and turn up the radio volume
- **d** close all your windows and set heating to warm
- **e** pull up on the hard shoulder and change drivers

61 You are taking drugs that are likely to affect your driving. What should you do?

mark one answer · p15
- **a** Seek medical advice before driving
- **b** Limit your driving to essential journeys
- **c** Only drive if accompanied by a full licence-holder
- **d** Drive only for short distances

62 You are about to drive home. You feel very tired and have a severe headache. You should

mark one answer · p15
- **a** wait until you are fit and well before driving
- **b** drive home, but take a tablet for headaches
- **c** drive home if you can stay awake for the journey
- **d** wait for a short time, then drive home slowly

ANSWERS

48 a,e	52 d	56 d	60 a,b
49 c	53 b	57 c	61 a
50 b	54 b	58 c,d	62 a
51 b,c	55 c	59 a,c	

63 If you are feeling tired it is best to stop as soon as you can. Until then you should

mark one answer ⓘ p135
- **a** increase your speed to find a stopping place quickly
- **b** ensure a supply of fresh air
- **c** gently tap the steering wheel
- **d** keep changing speed to improve concentration

64 If your motorway journey seems boring and you feel drowsy whilst driving you should

mark one answer ⓘ p135
- **a** open a window and drive to the next service area
- **b** stop on the hard shoulder for a sleep
- **c** speed up to arrive at your destination sooner
- **d** slow down and let other drivers overtake

65 Driving long distances can be tiring. You can prevent this by

mark three answers ⓘ p135
- **a** stopping every so often for a walk
- **b** opening a window for some fresh air
- **c** ensuring plenty of refreshment breaks
- **d** completing the journey without stopping
- **e** eating a large meal before driving

66 You go to a social event and need to drive a short time after. What precaution should you take?

mark one answer ⓘ p16
- **a** Avoid drinking alcohol on an empty stomach
- **b** Drink plenty of coffee after drinking alcohol
- **c** Avoid drinking alcohol completely
- **d** Drink plenty of milk before drinking alcohol

67 You take some cough medicine given to you by a friend. What should you do before driving?

mark one answer ⓘ p15
- **a** Ask your friend if taking the medicine affected their driving
- **b** Drink some strong coffee one hour before driving
- **c** Check the label to see if the medicine will affect your driving
- **d** Drive a short distance to see if the medicine is affecting your driving

68 You take the wrong route and find you are on a one-way street. You should

mark one answer ⓘ p75
- **a** reverse out of the road
- **b** turn round in a side road
- **c** continue to the end of the road
- **d** reverse into a driveway

69 Which THREE are likely to make you lose concentration while driving?

mark three answers ⓘ p135
- **a** Looking at road maps
- **b** Listening to loud music
- **c** Using your windscreen washers
- **d** Looking in your wing mirror
- **e** Using a mobile phone

70 You are driving along this road. The driver on the left is reversing from a driveway. You should

mark one answer ⓘ p59
- **a** move to the opposite side of the road
- **b** drive through as you have priority
- **c** sound your horn and be prepared to stop
- **d** speed up and drive through quickly

71 You have been involved in an argument before starting your journey. This has made you feel angry. You should

mark one answer ***i*** p135

- start to drive, but open a window
- drive slower than normal and turn your radio on
- have an alcoholic drink to help you relax before driving
- calm down before you start to drive

72 You start to feel tired while driving. What should you do?

mark one answer ***i*** p135

- Increase your speed slightly
- Decrease your speed slightly
- Find a less busy route
- Pull over at a safe place to rest

73 You are driving on this dual carriageway. Why may you need to slow down?

mark one answer ***i*** p125

- There is a broken white line in the centre
- There are solid white lines either side
- There are roadworks ahead of you
- There are no footpaths

74 You have just been overtaken by this motorcyclist who is cutting in sharply. You should

mark one answer ***i*** p78

- **a** sound the horn
- **b** brake firmly
- **c** keep a safe gap
- **d** flash your lights

75 You are about to drive home. You cannot find the glasses you need to wear. You should

mark one answer ***i*** p17

- **a** drive home slowly, keeping to quiet roads
- **b** borrow a friend's glasses and use those
- **c** drive home at night, so that the lights will help you
- **d** find a way of getting home without driving

76 Which THREE result from drinking alcohol?

mark three answers ***i*** p16

- **a** Less control
- **b** A false sense of confidence
- **c** Faster reactions
- **d** Poor judgement of speed
- **e** Greater awareness of danger

77 Which THREE of these are likely effects of drinking alcohol?

mark three answers ⓘ p16
- **a** Reduced co-ordination
- **b** Increased confidence
- **c** Poor judgement
- **d** Increased concentration
- **e** Faster reactions
- **f** Colour blindness

78 How does alcohol affect you?

mark one answer ⓘ p16
- **a** It speeds up your reactions
- **b** It increases your awareness
- **c** It improves your co-ordination
- **d** It reduces your concentration

79 Your doctor has given you a course of medicine. Why should you ask how it will affect you?

mark one answer ⓘ p15
- **a** Drugs make you a better driver by quickening your reactions
- **b** You will have to let your insurance company know about the medicine
- **c** Some types of medicine can cause your reactions to slow down
- **d** The medicine you take may affect your hearing

80 You are not sure if your cough medicine will affect you. What TWO things should you do?

mark two answers ⓘ p15
- **a** Ask your doctor
- **b** Check the medicine label
- **c** Drive if you feel alright
- **d** Ask a friend or relative for advice

81 You are on a motorway. You feel tired. You should

mark one answer ⓘ p135
- **a** carry on but go slowly
- **b** leave the motorway at the next exit
- **c** complete your journey as quickly as possible
- **d** stop on the hard shoulder

82 You find that you need glasses to read vehicle number plates at the required distance. When MUST you wear them?

mark one answer ⓘ p17
- **a** Only in bad weather conditions
- **b** At all times when driving
- **c** Only when you think it necessary
- **d** Only in bad light or at night time

83 Which TWO things would help to keep you alert during a long journey?

mark two answers ⓘ p135
- **a** Finishing your journey as fast as you can
- **b** Keeping off the motorways and using country roads
- **c** Making sure that you get plenty of fresh air
- **d** Making regular stops for refreshments

84 Which of the following types of glasses should NOT be worn when driving at night?

mark one answer ⓘ p185
- **a** Half-moon
- **b** Round
- **c** Bi-focal
- **d** Tinted

85 Drinking any amount of alcohol is likely to

mark three answers ⓘ p16
- **a** slow down your reactions to hazards
- **b** increase the speed of your reactions
- **c** worsen your judgement of speed
- **d** improve your awareness of danger
- **e** give a false sense of confidence

86 What else can seriously affect your concentration, other than alcoholic drinks?

mark three answers ⓘ p13
- **a** Drugs
- **b** Tiredness
- **c** Tinted windows
- **d** Contact lenses
- **e** Loud music

7 As a driver you find that your eyesight has become very poor. Your optician says they cannot help you. The law says that you should tell

mark one answer   *i* p15

- the licensing authority
- your own doctor
- the local police station
- another optician

8 For which of these may you use hazard warning lights?

mark one answer   *i* p58

- When driving on a motorway to warn traffic behind of a hazard ahead
- When you are double-parked on a two way road
- When your direction indicators are not working
- When warning oncoming traffic that you intend to stop

9 When should you use hazard warning lights?

mark one answer   *i* p58

- When you are double-parked on a two way road
- When your direction indicators are not working
- When warning oncoming traffic that you intend to stop
- When your vehicle has broken down and is causing an obstruction

0 You want to turn left at this junction. The view of the main road is restricted. What should you do?

mark one answer   *i* p94

- Stay well back and wait to see if something comes
- Build up your speed so that you can emerge quickly
- Stop and apply the handbrake even if the road is clear
- Approach slowly and edge out until you can see more clearly

91 You are driving on a motorway. The traffic ahead is braking sharply because of an accident. How could you warn traffic behind you?

mark one answer   *i* p58

- **a** Briefly use the hazard warning lights
- **b** Switch on the hazard warning lights continuously
- **c** Briefly use the rear fog lights
- **d** Switch on the headlights continuously

92 When may you use hazard warning lights?

mark one answer   *i* p58

- **a** To park alongside another car
- **b** To park on double yellow lines
- **c** When you are being towed
- **d** When you have broken down

93 Hazard warning lights should be used when vehicles are

mark one answer   *i* p58

- **a** broken down and causing an obstruction
- **b** faulty and moving slowly
- **c** being towed along a road
- **d** reversing into a side road

94 When driving a car fitted with automatic transmission what would you use 'kick down' for?

mark one answer   *i* p43

- **a** Cruise control
- **b** Quick acceleration
- **c** Slow braking
- **d** Fuel economy

ANSWERS

77 a,b,c	82 b	87 a	92 d
78 d	83 c,d	88 a	93 a
79 c	84 d	89 d	94 b
80 a,b	85 a,c,e	90 d	
81 b	86 a,b,e	91 a	

01 Which sign means that there may be people walking along the road?

mark one answer 🛈 p145

a

b

c

d

02 You are turning left at a junction. Pedestrians have started to cross the road. You should

mark one answer 🛈 p89

a go on, giving them plenty of room
b stop and wave at them to cross
c blow your horn and proceed
d give way to them

03 You are turning left from a main road into a side road. People are already crossing the road into which you are turning. You should

mark one answer 🛈 p89

a continue, as it is your right of way
b signal to them to continue crossing
c wait and allow them to cross
d sound your horn to warn them of your presence

04 You are at a road junction, turning into minor road. There are pedestrians crossing the minor road. You should

mark one answer 🛈 p89

a stop and wave the pedestrians across
b sound your horn to let the pedestrians know that you are there
c give way to the pedestrians who are already crossing
d carry on; the pedestrians should give way to you

5 You are turning left into a side road. What hazards should you be especially aware of?

ark one answer p97

- One way street
- Pedestrians
- Traffic congestion
- Parked vehicles

6 You intend to turn right into a side road. Just before turning you should check for motorcyclists who might be

ark one answer p98

- overtaking on your left
- following you closely
- emerging from the side road
- overtaking on your right

7 A toucan crossing is different from other crossings because

ark one answer p145

- moped riders can use it
- it is controlled by a traffic warden
- it is controlled by two flashing lights
- cyclists can use it

8 At toucan crossings

ark two answers p145

- there is no flashing amber light
- cyclists are not permitted
- there is a continuously flashing amber beacon
- pedestrians and cyclists may cross
- you only stop if someone is waiting to cross

9 What does this sign tell you?

ark one answer p151

- No cycling
- Cycle route ahead
- Route for cycles only
- End of cycle route

10 How will a school crossing patrol signal you to stop?

mark one answer p145

- a By pointing to children on the opposite pavement
- b By displaying a red light
- c By displaying a stop sign
- d By giving you an arm signal

11 Where would you see this sign?

mark one answer p156

- a In the window of a car taking children to school
- b At the side of the road
- c At playground areas
- d On the rear of a school bus or coach

12 Which sign tells you that pedestrians may be walking in the road as there is no pavement?

mark one answer p145

a

b

c

d

ANSWERS			
01 d	04 c	07 d	10 c
02 d	05 b	08 a,d	11 d
03 c	06 d	09 b	12 a

13 What does this sign mean?

mark one answer   *i* p151

a No route for pedestrians and cyclists
b A route for pedestrians only
c A route for cyclists only
d A route for pedestrians and cyclists

14 You see a pedestrian with a white stick and red band. This means that the person is

mark one answer   *i* p143

a physically disabled
b deaf only
c blind only
d deaf and blind

15 What action would you take when elderly people are crossing the road?

mark one answer   *i* p143

a Wave them across so they know that you have seen them
b Be patient and allow them to cross in their own time
c Rev the engine to let them know that you are waiting
d Tap the horn in case they are hard of hearing

16 You see two elderly pedestrians about to cross the road ahead. You should

mark one answer   *i* p143

a expect them to wait for you to pass
b speed up to get past them quickly
c stop and wave them across the road
d be careful, they may misjudge your speed

17 What does this sign mean?

mark one answer   *i* p151

a Contra-flow pedal cycle lane
b With-flow pedal cycle lane
c Pedal cycles and buses only
d No pedal cycles or buses

18 You are coming up to a roundabout. A cyclist is signalling to turn right. What should you do?

mark one answer   *i* p151

a Overtake on the right
b Give a horn warning
c Signal the cyclist to move across
d Give the cyclist plenty of room

19 You are approaching this roundabout and see the cyclist signal right. Why is the cyclist keeping to the left?

mark one answer   *i* p151

a It is a quicker route for the cyclist
b The cyclist is going to turn left instead
c The cyclist thinks The Highway Code does not apply to bicycles
d The cyclist is slower and more vulnerable

20 When you are overtaking a cyclist you should leave as much room as you would give to a car. What is the main reason for this?

mark one answer   *i* p151

a The cyclist might change lanes
b The cyclist might get off the bike
c The cyclist might swerve
d The cyclist might have to make a right turn

21 Which TWO should you allow extra room when overtaking?

mark two answers ⓘ p151 ⓘ p153
a Motorcycles
b Tractors
c Bicycles
d Road-sweeping vehicles

22 Why should you look particularly for motorcyclists and cyclists at junctions?

mark one answer ⓘ p94
a They may want to turn into the side road
b They may slow down to let you turn
c They are harder to see
d They might not see you turn

23 You are waiting to come out of a side road. Why should you watch carefully for motorcycles?

mark one answer ⓘ p94
a Motorcycles are usually faster than cars
b Police patrols often use motorcycles
c Motorcycles are small and hard to see
d Motorcycles have right of way

24 In daylight, an approaching motorcyclist is using a dipped headlight. Why?

mark one answer ⓘ p153
a So that the rider can be seen more easily
b To stop the battery overcharging
c To improve the rider's vision
d The rider is inviting you to proceed

25 Motorcyclists should wear bright clothing mainly because

mark one answer ⓘ p153
a they must do so by law
b it helps keep them cool in summer
c the colours are popular
d drivers often do not see them

26 There is a slow-moving motorcyclist ahead of you. You are unsure what the rider is going to do. You should

mark one answer ⓘ p153
a pass on the left
b pass on the right
c stay behind
d move closer

27 Motorcyclists will often look round over their right shoulder just before turning right. This is because

mark one answer ⓘ p153
a they need to listen for following traffic
b motorcycles do not have mirrors
c looking around helps them balance as they turn
d they need to check for traffic in their blind area

28 At road junctions which of the following are most vulnerable?

mark three answers ⓘ p89
a Cyclists
b Motorcyclists
c Pedestrians
d Car drivers
e Lorry drivers

29 Motorcyclists are particularly vulnerable

mark one answer ⓘ p94
a when moving off
b on dual carriageways
c when approaching junctions
d on motorways

30 An injured motorcyclist is lying unconscious in the road. You should

mark one answer ⓘ p240
a remove the safety helmet
b seek medical assistance
c move the person off the road
d remove the leather jacket

ANSWERS

13 d	18 d	23 c	28 a,b,c
14 d	19 d	24 a	29 c
15 b	20 c	25 d	30 b
16 d	21 a,c	26 c	
17 b	22 c	27 d	

31 You notice horse riders in front. What should you do FIRST?

mark one answer **ⓘ** p147
- **a** Pull out to the middle of the road
- **b** Slow down and be ready to stop
- **c** Accelerate around them
- **d** Signal right

32 You are approaching a roundabout. There are horses just ahead of you. You should

mark two answers **ⓘ** p147
- **a** be prepared to stop
- **b** treat them like any other vehicle
- **c** give them plenty of room
- **d** accelerate past as quickly as possible
- **e** sound your horn as a warning

33 Which THREE should you do when passing sheep on a road?

mark three answers **ⓘ** p149
- **a** Allow plenty of room
- **b** Go very slowly
- **c** Pass quickly but quietly
- **d** Be ready to stop
- **e** Briefly sound your horn

34 At night you see a pedestrian wearing reflective clothing and carrying a bright red light. What does this mean?

mark one answer **ⓘ** p143
- **a** You are approaching roadworks
- **b** You are approaching an organised walk
- **c** You are approaching a slow-moving vehicle
- **d** You are approaching an accident black spot

35 As you approach a pelican crossing the lights change to green. Elderly people are halfway across. You should

mark one answer **ⓘ** p143
- **a** wave them to cross as quickly as they can
- **b** rev your engine to make them hurry
- **c** flash your lights in case they have not heard you
- **d** wait because they will take longer to cross

36 There are flashing amber lights under a school warning sign. What action should you take?

mark one answer **ⓘ** p145
- **a** Reduce speed until you are clear of the area
- **b** Keep up your speed and sound the horn
- **c** Increase your speed to clear the area quickly
- **d** Wait at the lights until they change to green

37 Which of the following types of crossing can detect when people are on them?

mark one answer **ⓘ** p145
- **a** Pelican
- **b** Toucan
- **c** Zebra
- **d** Puffin

38 You are approaching this crossing. You should

mark one answer **ⓘ** p144
- **a** prepare to slow down and stop
- **b** stop and wave the pedestrians across
- **c** speed up and pass by quickly
- **d** drive on unless the pedestrians step out

39 You see a pedestrian with a dog that has a yellow or burgundy coat. This especially warns you that the pedestrian is

mark one answer p143
a elderly
b dog training
c colour blind
d deaf

40 These road markings must be kept clear to allow

⋀-SCHOOL KEEP CLEAR-⋀

mark one answer p113
a school children to be dropped off
b for teachers to park
c school children to be picked up
d a clear view of the crossing area

41 You must not stop on these road markings because you may obstruct

⋀-SCHOOL KEEP CLEAR-⋀

mark one answer p113
a children's view of the crossing area
b teachers' access to the school
c delivery vehicles' access to the school
d emergency vehicles' access to the school

42 The left-hand pavement is closed due to street repairs. What should you do?

mark one answer p125
a Watch out for pedestrians walking in the road
b Use your right-hand mirror more often
c Speed up to get past the roadworks quicker
d Position close to the left-hand kerb

43 Where would you see this sign?

mark one answer p157
a Near a school crossing
b At a playground entrance
c On a school bus
d At a 'pedestrians only' area

44 You are following a motorcyclist on an uneven road. You should

mark one answer p153
a allow less room so you can be seen in their mirrors
b overtake immediately
c allow extra room in case they swerve to avoid pot-holes
d allow the same room as normal because road surfaces do not affect motorcyclists

45 You are following two cyclists. They approach a roundabout in the left-hand lane. In which direction should you expect the cyclists to go?

mark one answer p151
a Left
b Right
c Any direction
d Straight ahead

46 You are travelling behind a moped. You want to turn left just ahead. You should

mark one answer p97
a overtake the moped before the junction
b pull alongside the moped and stay level until just before the junction
c sound your horn as a warning and pull in front of the moped
d stay behind until the moped has passed the junction

ANSWERS

31 b	35 d	39 d	43 c
32 a,c	36 a	40 d	44 c
33 a,b,d	37 d	41 a	45 c
34 b	38 a	42 a	46 d

47 Which THREE of the following are hazards motorcyclists present in queues of traffic?

mark three answers ⓘ p153

- **a** Cutting in just in front of you
- **b** Riding in single file
- **c** Passing very close to you
- **d** Riding with their headlight on dipped beam
- **e** Filtering between the lanes

48 You see a horse rider as you approach a roundabout. They are signalling right but keeping well to the left. You should

mark one answer ⓘ p147

- **a** proceed as normal
- **b** keep close to them
- **c** cut in front of them
- **d** stay well back

49 How would you react to drivers who appear to be inexperienced?

mark one answer ⓘ p229

- **a** Sound your horn to warn them of your presence
- **b** Be patient and prepare for them to react more slowly
- **c** Flash your headlights to indicate that it is safe for them to proceed
- **d** Overtake them as soon as possible

50 You are following a learner driver who stalls at a junction. You should

mark one answer ⓘ p229

- **a** be patient as you expect them to make mistakes
- **b** stay very close behind and flash your headlight
- **c** start to rev your engine if they take too long to restart
- **d** immediately steer around them and drive on

51 You are on a country road. What should you expect to see coming towards you on YOUR side of the road?

mark one answer ⓘ p115

- **a** Motorcycles
- **b** Bicycles
- **c** Pedestrians
- **d** Horse riders

52 You are turning left into a side road. Pedestrians are crossing the road near the junction. You must

mark one answer ⓘ p89

- **a** wave them on
- **b** sound your horn
- **c** switch on your hazard lights
- **d** wait for them to cross

53 You are following a car driven by an elderly driver. You should

mark one answer ⓘ p229

- **a** expect the driver to drive badly
- **b** flash your lights and overtake
- **c** be aware that the driver's reactions may not be as fast as yours
- **d** stay very close behind but be careful

54 You are following a cyclist. You wish to turn left just ahead. You should

mark one answer *i* p151
a overtake the cyclist before the junction
b pull alongside the cyclist and stay level until after the junction
c hold back until the cyclist has passed the junction
d go around the cyclist on the junction

55 A horse rider is in the left-hand lane approaching a roundabout. You should expect the rider to

mark one answer *i* p147
a go in any direction
b turn right
c turn left
d go ahead

56 You have just passed your test. How can you decrease your risk of accidents on the motorway?

mark one answer *i* p253
a By keeping up with the car in front
b By never going over 40 mph
c By staying only in the left hand lane
d By taking further training

57 Powered vehicles used by disabled people are small and hard to see. How do they give early warning when on a dual carriageway?

mark one answer *i* p143
a They will have a flashing red light
b They will have a flashing green light
c They will have a flashing blue light
d They will have a flashing amber light.

58 You should never attempt to overtake a cyclist

mark one answer *i* p151
a just before you turn left
b on a left hand bend
c on a one-way street
d on a dual carriageway

59 Ahead of you there is a moving vehicle with a flashing amber beacon. This means it is

mark one answer *i* p163
a slow moving
b broken down
c a doctor's car
d a school crossing patrol

60 You want to reverse into a side road. You are not sure that the area behind your car is clear. What should you do?

mark one answer *i* p168
a Look through the rear window only
b Get out and check
c Check the mirrors only
d Carry on, assuming it is clear

61 You are about to reverse into a side road. A pedestrian wishes to cross behind you. You should

mark one answer *i* p168
a wave to the pedestrian to stop
b give way to the pedestrian
c wave to the pedestrian to cross
d reverse before the pedestrian starts to cross

62 Who is especially in danger of not being seen as you reverse your car?

mark one answer *i* p168
a Motorcyclists
b Car drivers
c Cyclists
d Children

ANSWERS

47 a,c,e	51 c	55 a	59 a
48 d	52 d	56 d	60 b
49 b	53 c	57 d	61 b
50 a	54 c	58 a	62 d

63 You are reversing around a corner when you notice a pedestrian walking behind you. What should you do?

mark one answer p168

- **a** Slow down and wave the pedestrian across
- **b** Continue reversing and steer round the pedestrian
- **c** Stop and give way
- **d** Continue reversing and sound your horn

64 You want to turn right from a junction but your view is restricted by parked vehicles. What should you do?

mark one answer **i** p94

- **a** Move out quickly, but be prepared to stop
- **b** Sound your horn and pull out if there is no reply
- **c** Stop, then move slowly forward until you have a clear view
- **d** Stop, get out and look along the main road to check

65 You are at the front of a queue of traffic waiting to turn right into a side road. Why is it important to check your right mirror just before turning?

mark one answer **i** p98

- **a** To look for pedestrians about to cross
- **b** To check for overtaking vehicles
- **c** To make sure the side road is clear
- **d** To check for emerging traffic

66 What must a driver do at a pelican crossing when the amber light is flashing?

mark one answer **i** p144

- **a** Signal the pedestrian to cross
- **b** Always wait for the green light before proceeding
- **c** Give way to any pedestrians on the crossing
- **d** Wait for the red-and-amber light before proceeding

67 You have stopped at a pelican crossing. A disabled person is crossing slowly in front of you. The lights have now changed to green. You should

mark two answers **i** p144

- **a** allow the person to cross
- **b** drive in front of the person
- **c** drive behind the person
- **d** sound your horn
- **e** be patient
- **f** edge forward slowly

68 You are driving past parked cars. You notice a bicycle wheel sticking out between them. What should you do?

mark one answer **i** p151

- **a** Accelerate past quickly and sound your horn
- **b** Slow down and wave the cyclist across
- **c** Brake sharply and flash your headlights
- **d** Slow down and be prepared to stop for a cyclist

69 You are driving past a line of parked cars. You notice a ball bouncing out into the road ahead. What should you do?

mark one answer **i** p143

- **a** Continue driving at the same speed and sound your horn
- **b** Continue driving at the same speed and flash your headlights
- **c** Slow down and be prepared to stop for children
- **d** Stop and wave the children across to fetch their ball

70 You want to turn right from a main road into a side road. Just before turning you should

mark one answer   *i* p98

a cancel your right-turn signal
b select first gear
c check for traffic overtaking on your right
d stop and set the handbrake

71 You are driving in slow-moving queues of traffic. Just before changing lane you should

mark one answer   *i* p153

a sound the horn
b look for motorcyclists filtering through the traffic
c give a 'slowing down' arm signal
d change down to first gear

72 You are driving in town. There is a bus at the bus stop on the other side of the road. Why should you be careful?

mark one answer   *i* p157

a The bus may have broken down
b Pedestrians may come from behind the bus
c The bus may move off suddenly
d The bus may remain stationary

73 How should you overtake horse riders?

mark one answer   *i* p147

a Drive up close and overtake as soon as possible
b Speed is not important but allow plenty of room
c Use your horn just once to warn them
d Drive slowly and leave plenty of room

74 A friend wants to help you learn to drive. They must be

mark one answer   *i* p13

a over 21 and have held a full licence for at least two years
b over 18 and hold an advanced driver's certificate
c over 18 and have fully comprehensive insurance
d over 21 and have held a full licence for at least three years

75 You are dazzled at night by a vehicle behind you. You should

mark one answer   *i* p185

a set your mirror to anti dazzle
b set your mirror to dazzle the other driver
c brake sharply to a stop
d switch your rear lights on and off

76 You have a collision whilst your car is moving. What is the first thing you must do?

mark one answer   *i* p239

a Stop only if there are injured people
b Call the emergency services
c Stop at the scene of the accident
d Call your insurance company

77 Yellow zig zag lines on the road outside schools mean

SCHOOL KEEP CLEAR

mark one answer   *i* p113

a sound your horn to alert other road users
b stop to allow children to cross
c you must not wait or park on these lines
d you must not drive over these lines

78 What do these road markings outside a school mean?

SCHOOL KEEP CLEAR

mark one answer   *i* p113

a You may park here if you are a teacher
b Sound your horn before parking
c When parking use your hazard warning lights
d You must not wait or park your vehicle here

ANSWERS			
63 c	67 a,e	71 b	75 a
64 c	68 d	72 b	76 c
65 b	69 c	73 d	77 c
66 c	70 c	74 d	78 d

79 You are driving on a main road. You intend to turn right into a side road. Just before turning you should

mark one answer   p98
- **a** adjust your interior mirror
- **b** flash your headlamps
- **c** steer over to the left
- **d** check for traffic overtaking on your right

80 Why should you allow extra room when overtaking a motorcyclist on a windy day?

mark one answer   p191
- **a** The rider may turn off suddenly to get out of the wind
- **b** The rider may be blown across in front of you
- **c** The rider may stop suddenly
- **d** The rider may be travelling faster than normal

81 Which age group of drivers is most likely to be involved in a road accident?

mark one answer   p225
- **a** 17 to 25-year-olds
- **b** 36 to 45-year-olds
- **c** 46 to 55-year-olds
- **d** 55-year-olds and over

82 You are driving towards a zebra crossing. A person in a wheelchair is waiting to cross. What should you do?

mark one answer ⓘ p143
- **a** continue on your way
- **b** wave to the person to cross
- **c** wave to the person to wait
- **d** be prepared to stop

83 Where in particular should you look out for motorcyclists?

mark one answer   p153
- **a** In a filling station
- **b** At a road junction
- **c** Near a service area
- **d** When entering a car park

84 Where should you take particular care to look out for motorcyclists and cyclists?

mark one answer ⓘ p94
- **a** On dual carriageways
- **b** At junctions
- **c** At zebra crossings
- **d** On one-way streets

85 The road outside this school is marked with yellow zigzag lines. What do these lines mean?

mark one answer ⓘ p113
- **a** You may park on the lines when dropping off schoolchildren
- **b** You may park on the lines when picking schoolchildren up
- **c** You must not wait or park your vehicle here at all
- **d** You must stay with your vehicle if you park here

ANSWERS

79 d	81 a	83 b	85 c
80 b	82 d	84 b	

15

OTHER TYPES OF VEHICLE

Ø1 The road is wet. Why might a motorcyclist steer round drain covers on a bend?

mark one answer   ⓘ p151

a To avoid puncturing the tyres on the edge of the drain covers

b To prevent the motorcycle sliding on the metal drain covers

c To help judge the bend using the drain covers as marker points

d To avoid splashing pedestrians on the pavement

Ø2 You are about to overtake a slow-moving motorcyclist. Which one of these signs would make you take special care?

mark one answer   ⓘ p85

a

b

c

d

Ø3 You are waiting to emerge left from a minor road. A large vehicle is approaching from the right. You have time to turn, but you should wait. Why?

mark one answer   ⓘ p94

a The large vehicle can easily hide an overtaking vehicle

b The large vehicle can turn suddenly

c The large vehicle is difficult to steer in a straight line

d The large vehicle can easily hide vehicles from the left

Ø4 You are following a long vehicle. It approaches a crossroads and signals left, but moves out to the right. You should

mark one answer   ⓘ p155

a get closer in order to pass it quickly

b stay well back and give it room

c assume the signal is wrong and it is really turning right

d overtake as it starts to slow down

Ø5 You are following a long vehicle approaching a crossroads. The driver signals right but moves close to the left-hand kerb. What should you do?

mark one answer   ⓘ p155

a Warn the driver of the wrong signal

b Wait behind the long vehicle

c Report the driver to the police

d Overtake on the right-hand side

Ø6 You are approaching a mini-roundabout. The long vehicle in front is signalling left but positioned over to the right. You should

mark one answer   ⓘ p155

a sound your horn

b overtake on the left

c follow the same course as the lorry

d keep well back

ANSWERS

Ø1 b	Ø3 a	Ø5 b
Ø2 a	Ø4 b	Ø6 d

07 Before overtaking a large vehicle you should keep well back. Why is this?

mark one answer   *p155*

- **a** To give acceleration space to overtake quickly on blind bends
- **b** To get the best view of the road ahead
- **c** To leave a gap in case the vehicle stops and rolls back
- **d** To offer other drivers a safe gap if they want to overtake you

08 Why is passing a lorry more risky than passing a car?

mark one answer   *p155*

- **a** Lorries are longer than cars
- **b** Lorries may suddenly pull up
- **c** The brakes of lorries are not as good
- **d** Lorries climb hills more slowly

09 You are travelling behind a bus that pulls up at a bus stop. What should you do?

mark two answers   *p157*

- **a** Accelerate past the bus sounding your horn
- **b** Watch carefully for pedestrians
- **c** Be ready to give way to the bus
- **d** Pull in closely behind the bus

10 When you approach a bus signalling to move off from a bus stop you should

mark one answer   *p157*

- **a** get past before it moves
- **b** allow it to pull away, if it is safe to do so
- **c** flash your headlights as you approach
- **d** signal left and wave the bus on

11 Which of these is LEAST likely to be affected by crosswinds?

mark one answer   *p191*

- **a** Cyclists
- **b** Motorcyclists
- **c** High-sided vehicles
- **d** Cars

12 You are following a large lorry on a wet road. Spray makes it difficult to see. You should

mark one answer   *p188*

- **a** drop back until you can see better
- **b** put your headlights on full beam
- **c** keep close to the lorry, away from the spray
- **d** speed up and overtake quickly

13 Some two way roads are divided into three lanes. Why are these particularly dangerous?

mark one answer   *p85*

- **a** Traffic in both directions can use the middle lane to overtake
- **b** Traffic can travel faster in poor weather conditions
- **c** Traffic can overtake on the left
- **d** Traffic uses the middle lane for emergencies only

14 What should you do as you approach this lorry?

mark one answer   *p155*

- **a** Slow down and be prepared to wait
- **b** Make the lorry wait for you
- **c** Flash your lights at the lorry
- **d** Move to the right hand side of the road

15 You are following a large articulated vehicle. It is going to turn left into a narrow road. What action should you take?

mark one answer **ⓘ** p151
a Move out and overtake on the right
b Pass on the left as the vehicle moves out
c Be prepared to stop behind
d Overtake quickly before the lorry moves out

16 You keep well back while waiting to overtake a large vehicle. A car fills the gap. You should

mark one answer **ⓘ** p79
a sound your horn
b drop back further
c flash your headlights
d start to overtake

17 At a junction you see this signal. It means

mark one answer **ⓘ** p159
a cars must stop
b trams must stop
c both trams and cars must stop
d both trams and cars can continue

18 You are following a large vehicle approaching crossroads. The driver signals to turn left. What should you do?

mark one answer **ⓘ** p151
a Overtake if you can leave plenty of room
b Overtake only if there are no oncoming vehicles
c Do not overtake until the vehicle begins to turn.
d Do not overtake when at or approaching a junction.

19 You are following a long lorry. The driver signals to turn left into a narrow road. What should you do?

mark one answer **ⓘ** p151
a Overtake on the left before the lorry reaches the junction
b Overtake on the right as soon as the lorry slows down
c Do not overtake unless you can see there is no oncoming traffic
d Do not overtake, stay well back and be prepared to stop.

20 You wish to overtake a long, slow moving vehicle on a busy road. You should

mark one answer **ⓘ** p151
a follow it closely and keep moving out to see the road ahead
b flash your headlights for the oncoming traffic to give way
c stay behind until the driver waves you past
d keep well back until you can see that it is clear

21 It is very windy. You are behind a motorcyclist who is overtaking a high-sided vehicle. What should you do?

mark one answer **ⓘ** p191
a Overtake the motorcyclist immediately
b Keep well back
c Stay level with the motorcyclist
d Keep close to the motorcyclist

22 It is very windy. You are about to overtake a motorcyclist. You should

mark one answer **ⓘ** p191
a overtake slowly
b allow extra room
c sound your horn
d keep close as you pass

ANSWERS			
07 b	11 d	15 c	19 d
08 a	12 a	16 b	20 d
09 b,c	13 a	17 b	21 b
10 b	14 a	18 d	22 b

23 You are towing a caravan. Which is the safest type of rear-view mirror to use?

mark one answer ⓘ p212
- **a** Interior wide-angle mirror
- **b** Extended-arm side mirrors
- **c** Ordinary door mirrors
- **d** Ordinary interior mirror

24 You are driving downhill. There is a car parked on the other side of the road. Large, slow lorries are coming towards you. You should

mark one answer ⓘ p81
- **a** keep going because you have the right of way
- **b** slow down and give way
- **c** speed up and get past quickly
- **d** pull over on the right behind the parked car

25 You are driving in town. Ahead of you a bus is at a bus stop. Which TWO of the following should you do?

mark two answers ⓘ p157
- **a** Be prepared to give way if the bus suddenly moves off
- **b** Continue at the same speed but sound your horn as a warning
- **c** Watch carefully for the sudden appearance of pedestrians
- **d** Pass the bus as quickly as you possibly can

26 You are driving in heavy traffic on a wet road. Spray makes it difficult to be seen. You should use your

mark two answers ⓘ p188
- **a** full beam headlights
- **b** rear fog lights if visibility is less than 100 metres (328 feet)
- **c** rear fog lights if visibility is more than 100 metres (328 feet)
- **d** dipped headlights
- **e** side lights only

27 You are driving along this road. What should you be prepared to do?

mark one answer ⓘ p155
- **a** Sound your horn and continue
- **b** Slow down and give way
- **c** Report the driver to the police
- **d** Squeeze through the gap

28 You are on a wet motorway with surface spray. You should use

mark one answer ⓘ p188
- **a** hazard flashers
- **b** dipped headlights
- **c** rear fog lights
- **d** sidelights

29 As a driver why should you be more careful where trams operate?

mark one answer ⓘ p158
- **a** Because they do not have a horn
- **b** Because they do not stop for cars
- **c** Because they do not have lights
- **d** Because they cannot steer to avoid you

ANSWERS

23 b	25 a,c	27 b	29 d
24 b	26 b,d	28 b	

01 You are following a vehicle at a safe distance on a wet road. Another driver overtakes you and pulls into the gap you have left. What should you do?

mark one answer ⓘ p79

a Flash your headlights as a warning

b Try to overtake safely as soon as you can

c Drop back to regain a safe distance

d Stay close to the other vehicle until it moves on

02 In which THREE of these situations may you overtake another vehicle on the left?

mark three answers ⓘ p85

a When you are in a one-way street

b When approaching a motorway slip road where you will be turning off

c When the vehicle in front is signalling to turn right

d When a slower vehicle is travelling in the right-hand lane of a dual carriageway

e In slow-moving traffic queues when traffic in the right-hand lane is moving more slowly

03 You are travelling in very heavy rain. Your overall stopping distance is likely to be

mark one answer ⓘ p138

a doubled

b halved

c up to ten times greater

d no different

04 Which TWO of the following are correct? When overtaking at night you should

mark two answers ⓘ p185

a wait until a bend so that you can see the oncoming headlights

b sound your horn twice before moving out

c be careful because you can see less

d beware of bends in the road ahead

e put headlights on full beam

05 When may you wait in a box junction?

mark one answer ⓘ p90

a When you are stationary in a queue of traffic

b When approaching a pelican crossing

c When approaching a zebra crossing

d When oncoming traffic prevents you turning right

06 Which of these plates normally appear with this road sign?

mark one answer ⓘ p113

a Humps for ½ mile

b Hump Bridge

c Low Bridge

d Soft Verge

07 Areas reserved for trams may have

mark three answers ⓘ p159

a metal studs around them

b white line markings

c zig zag markings

d a different coloured surface

e yellow hatch markings

f a different surface texture

ANSWERS

01 c	03 a	05 d	07 b,d,f
02 a,c,e	04 c,d	06 a	

08 Traffic calming measures are used to

mark one answer *i* p113
- **a** stop road rage
- **b** help overtaking
- **c** slow traffic down
- **d** help parking

09 Why should you always reduce your speed when travelling in fog?

mark one answer *i* p190
- **a** Because the brakes do not work as well
- **b** Because you could be dazzled by other people's fog lights
- **c** Because the engine is colder
- **d** Because it is more difficult to see events ahead

10 You are on a motorway in fog. The left-hand edge of the motorway can be identified by reflective studs. What colour are they?

mark one answer *i* p190
- **a** Green
- **b** Amber
- **c** Red
- **d** White

11 A rumble device is designed to

mark two answers *i* p67
- **a** give directions
- **b** prevent cattle escaping
- **c** alert you to low tyre pressure
- **d** alert you to a hazard
- **e** encourage you to reduce speed

12 You are on a narrow road at night. A slower-moving vehicle ahead has been signalling right for some time. What should you do?

mark one answer *i* p59
- **a** Overtake on the left
- **b** Flash your headlights before overtaking
- **c** Signal right and sound your horn
- **d** Wait for the signal to be cancelled before overtaking

13 Why should you test your brakes after this hazard?

mark one answer *i* p189
- **a** Because you will be on a slippery road
- **b** Because your brakes will be soaking wet
- **c** Because you will have gone down a long hill
- **d** Because you will have just crossed a long bridge

14 You have to make a journey in foggy conditions. You should

mark one answer *i* p190
- **a** follow other vehicles' tail lights closely
- **b** avoid using dipped headlights
- **c** leave plenty of time for your journey
- **d** keep two seconds behind other vehicles

15 You are overtaking a car at night. You must be sure that

mark one answer *i* p185
- **a** you flash your headlights before overtaking
- **b** you select a higher gear
- **c** you have switched your lights to full beam before overtaking
- **d** you do not dazzle other road users

16 You see a vehicle coming towards you on a single track road. You should

mark one answer ⓘ p81

a go back to the main road
b do an emergency stop
c stop at a passing place
d put on your hazard warning lights

17 You are on a road which has speed humps. A driver in front is travelling slower than you. You should

mark one answer ⓘ p113

a sound your horn
b overtake as soon as you can
c flash your headlights
d slow down and stay behind

18 You are following other vehicles in fog with your lights on. How else can you reduce the chances of being involved in an accident?

mark one answer ⓘ p190

a Keep close to the vehicle in front
b Use your main beam instead of dipped headlights
c Keep together with the faster vehicles
d Reduce your speed and increase the gap

19 You see these markings on the road. Why are they there?

mark one answer ⓘ p67

a To show a safe distance between vehicles
b To keep the area clear of traffic
c To make you aware of your speed
d To warn you to change direction

20 When MUST you use dipped headlights during the day?

mark one answer ⓘ p185

a All the time
b Along narrow streets
c In poor visibility
d When parking

21 What are TWO main reasons why coasting downhill is wrong?

mark two answers ⓘ p31

a Fuel consumption will be higher
b The vehicle will pick up speed
c It puts more wear and tear on the tyres
d You have less braking and steering control
f It damages the engine

22 Hills can affect the performance of your vehicle. Which TWO apply when driving up steep hills?

mark two answers ⓘ p111

a Higher gears will pull better
b You will slow down sooner
c Overtaking will be easier
d The engine will work harder
f The steering will feel heavier

23 Why is coasting wrong?

mark one answer ⓘ p31

a It will cause the car to skid
b It will make the engine stall
c The engine will run faster
d There is no engine braking

24 You are driving on the motorway in windy conditions. When passing high-sided vehicles you should

mark one answer ⓘ p190

a increase your speed
b be wary of a sudden gust
c drive alongside very closely
d expect normal conditions

25 To correct a rear-wheel skid you should

mark one answer ⓘ p195

a not steer at all
b steer away from it
c steer into it
d apply your handbrake

ANSWERS

08 c	13 b	18 d	23 d
09 d	14 c	19 c	24 b
10 c	15 d	20 c	25 c
11 d,e	16 c	21 b,d	
12 d	17 d	22 b,d	

26 You have to make a journey in fog. What are the TWO most important things you should do before you set out?

mark two answers 🛈 p190

- **a** Top up the radiator with antifreeze
- **b** Make sure that you have a warning triangle in the vehicle
- **c** Check that your lights are working
- **d** Check the battery
- **e** Make sure that the windows are clean

27 You are driving in fog. Why should you keep well back from the vehicle in front?

mark one answer 🛈 p190

- **a** In case it changes direction suddenly
- **b** In case its fog lights dazzle you
- **c** In case it stops suddenly
- **d** In case its brake lights dazzle you

28 You should switch your rear fog lights on when visibility drops below

mark one answer 🛈 p190

- **a** your overall stopping distance
- **b** ten car lengths
- **c** 200 metres (656 feet)
- **d** 100 metres (328 feet)

29 Whilst driving, the fog clears and you can see more clearly. You must remember to

mark one answer 🛈 p190

- **a** switch off the fog lights
- **b** reduce your speed
- **c** switch off the demister
- **d** close any open windows

30 You have to park on the road in fog. You should

mark one answer 🛈 p190

- **a** leave sidelights on
- **b** leave dipped headlights and fog lights on
- **c** leave dipped headlights on
- **d** leave main beam headlights on

31 On a foggy day you unavoidably have to park your car on the road. You should

mark one answer 🛈 p190

- **a** leave your headlights on
- **b** leave your fog lights on
- **c** leave your sidelights on
- **d** leave your hazard lights on

32 You are travelling at night. You are dazzled by headlights coming towards you. You should

mark one answer 🛈 p185

- **a** pull down your sun visor
- **b** slow down or stop
- **c** switch on your main beam headlights
- **d** put your hand over your eyes

33 Which of the following may apply when dealing with this hazard?

mark four answers 🛈 p189

- **a** It could be more difficult in winter
- **b** Use a low gear and drive slowly
- **c** Use a high gear to prevent wheelspin
- **d** Test your brakes afterwards
- **e** Always switch on fog lamps
- **f** There may be a depth gauge

34 Front fog lights may be used ONLY if

mark one answer 🛈 p190

- **a** visibility is seriously reduced
- **b** they are fitted above the bumper
- **c** they are not as bright as the headlights
- **d** an audible warning device is used

35 Front fog lights may be used ONLY if

mark one answer 🛈 p190

- **a** your headlights are not working
- **b** they are operated with rear fog lights
- **c** they were fitted by the vehicle manufacturer
- **d** visibility is seriously reduced

36 You are driving with your front fog lights switched on. Earlier fog has now cleared. What should you do?

N 512 CTW

mark one answer   *i* p190

a Leave them on if other drivers have their lights on
b Switch them off as long as visibility remains good
c Flash them to warn oncoming traffic that it is foggy
d Drive with them on instead of your headlights

37 Front fog lights should be used ONLY when

mark one answer   *i* p190

a travelling in very light rain
b visibility is seriously reduced
c daylight is fading
d driving after midnight

38 Why is it dangerous to leave rear fog lights on when they are not needed?

mark two answers   *i* p190

a Brake lights are less clear
b Following drivers can be dazzled
c Electrical systems could be overloaded
d Direction indicators may not work properly
e The battery could fail

39 You are driving on a clear dry night with your rear fog lights switched on. This may

mark two answers   *i* p190

a reduce glare from the road surface
b make other drivers think you are braking
c give a better view of the road ahead
d dazzle following drivers
e help your indicators to be seen more clearly

40 You have just driven out of fog. Visibility is now good. You MUST

mark one answer   *i* p190

a switch off all your fog lights
b keep your rear fog lights on
c keep your front fog lights on
d leave fog lights on in case fog returns

41 You forget to switch off your rear fog lights when the fog has cleared. This may

mark three answers   *i* p190

a dazzle other road users
b reduce battery life
c cause brake lights to be less clear
d be breaking the law
e seriously affect engine power

42 You have been driving in thick fog which has now cleared. You must switch OFF your rear fog lights because

mark one answer   *i* p190

a they use a lot of power from the battery
b they make your brake lights less clear
c they will cause dazzle in your rear view mirrors
d they may not be properly adjusted

43 Front fog lights should be used

mark one answer   *i* p190

a when visibility is reduced to 100 metres (328 feet)
b as a warning to oncoming traffic
c when driving during the hours of darkness
d in any conditions and at any time

44 Using rear fog lights in clear daylight will

mark one answer   *i* p190

a be useful when towing a trailer
b give extra protection
c dazzle other drivers
d make following drivers keep back

ANSWERS

26 c,e	31 c	36 b	41 a,c,d
27 c	32 b	37 b	42 b
28 d	33 a,b,d,f	38 a,b	43 a
29 a	34 a	39 b,d	44 c
30 a	35 d	40 a	

315

45 Using front fog lights in clear daylight will

mark one answer *i* p190
a flatten the battery
b dazzle other drivers
c improve your visibility
d increase your awareness

46 You may use front fog lights with headlights ONLY when visibility is reduced to less than

mark one answer *i* p190
a 100 metres (328 feet)
b 200 metres (656 feet)
c 300 metres (984 feet)
d 400 metres (1312 feet)

47 You may drive with front fog lights switched-on

N 512 CTW

mark one answer *i* p190
a when visibility is less than 100 metres (328 feet)
b at any time to be noticed
c instead of headlights on high speed roads
d when dazzled by the lights of oncoming vehicles

48 Chains can be fitted to your wheels to help prevent

mark one answer *i* p187
a damage to the road surface
b wear to the tyres
c skidding in deep snow
d the brakes locking

49 Holding the clutch pedal down or rolling in neutral for too long while driving will

mark one answer *i* p31
a use more fuel
b cause the engine to overheat
c reduce your control
d improve tyre wear

50 How can you use the engine of your vehicle to control your speed?

mark one answer *i* p47
a By changing to a lower gear
b By selecting reverse gear
c By changing to a higher gear
d By selecting neutral

51 You are driving down a steep hill. Why could keeping the clutch down or rolling in neutral for too long be dangerous?

mark one answer *i* p31
a Fuel consumption will be higher
b Your vehicle will pick up speed
c It will damage the engine
d It will wear tyres out more quickly

52 Why could keeping the clutch down or selecting neutral for long periods of time be dangerous?

mark one answer *i* p31
a Fuel spillage will occur
b Engine damage may be caused
c You will have less steering and braking control
d It will wear tyres out more quickly

53 You are driving on an icy road. What distance should you drive from the car in front?

mark one answer *i* p77
a four times the normal distance
b six times the normal distance
c eight times the normal distance
d ten times the normal distance

54 You are on a well-lit motorway at night. You must

mark one answer *i* p123
a use only your sidelights
b always use your headlights
c always use rear fog lights
d use headlights only in bad weather

55 You are on a motorway at night with other vehicles just ahead of you. Which lights should you have on?

mark one answer *i* p123
a Front fog lights
b Main beam headlights
c Sidelights only
d Dipped headlights

56 Which THREE of the following will affect your stopping distance?

mark three answers ⓘ p138

a How fast you are going
b The tyres on your vehicle
c The time of day
d The weather
e The street lighting

57 You are on a motorway at night. You MUST have your headlights switched on unless

mark one answer ⓘ p236

a there are vehicles close in front of you
b you are travelling below 50 mph
c the motorway is lit
d your vehicle is broken down on the hard shoulder

58 You will feel the effects of engine braking when you

mark one answer ⓘ p47

a only use the handbrake
b only use neutral
c change to a lower gear
d change to a higher gear

59 Daytime visibility is poor but not seriously reduced. You should switch on

mark one answer ⓘ p185

a headlights and fog lights
b front fog lights
c dipped headlights
d rear fog lights

60 Why are vehicles fitted with rear fog lights?

mark one answer ⓘ p190

a To be seen when driving at high speed
b To use if broken down in a dangerous position
c To make them more visible in thick fog
d To warn drivers following closely to drop back

61 While you are driving in fog, it becomes necessary to use front fog lights. You should

mark one answer ⓘ p190

a only turn them on in heavy traffic conditions
b remember not to use them on motorways
c only use them on dual carriageways
d remember to switch them off as visibility improves

62 When snow is falling heavily you should

mark one answer ⓘ p186

a only drive with your hazard lights on
b not drive unless you have a mobile phone
c only drive when your journey is short
d not drive unless it is essential

63 You are driving down a long steep hill. You suddenly notice your brakes are not working as well as normal. What is the usual cause of this?

mark one answer ⓘ p46

a The brakes overheating
b Air in the brake fluid
c Oil on the brakes
d Badly adjusted brakes

ANSWERS			
45 b	50 a	55 d	60 c
46 a	51 b	56 a,b,d	61 d
47 a	52 c	57 d	62 d
48 c	53 d	58 c	63 a
49 c	54 b	59 c	

01 Which FOUR of these must NOT use motorways?

mark four answers **ⓘ p121**

- **a** Learner car drivers
- **b** Motorcycles over 50cc
- **c** Double deck buses
- **d** Farm tractors
- **e** Horse riders
- **f** Cyclists

02 Which FOUR of these must NOT use motorways?

mark four answers **ⓘ p121**

- **a** Learner car drivers
- **b** Motorcycles over 50cc
- **c** Double-decker buses
- **d** Farm tractors
- **e** Learner motorcyclists
- **f** Cyclists

03 Immediately after joining a motorway you should normally

mark one answer **ⓘ p122**

- **a** try to overtake
- **b** re-adjust your mirrors
- **c** position your vehicle in the centre lane
- **d** keep in the left-hand lane

04 When joining a motorway you must always

mark one answer **ⓘ p122**

- **a** use the hard shoulder
- **b** stop at the end of the acceleration lane
- **c** come to a stop before joining the motorway
- **d** give way to traffic already on the motorway

05 What is the national speed limit for cars and motorcycles in the centre lane of a three-lane motorway?

mark one answer **ⓘ p136**

- **a** 40 mph
- **b** 50 mph
- **c** 60 mph
- **d** 70 mph

06 What is the national speed limit on motorways for cars and motorcycles?

mark one answer **ⓘ p136**

- **a** 30 mph
- **b** 50 mph
- **c** 60 mph
- **d** 70 mph

07 The left-hand lane on a three-lane motorway is for use by

mark one answer **ⓘ p121**

- **a** any vehicle
- **b** large vehicles only
- **c** emergency vehicles only
- **d** slow vehicles only

08 What is the right hand lane used for on three lane motorway?

mark one answer **ⓘ p121**

- **a** Emergency vehicles only
- **b** Overtaking
- **c** Vehicles towing trailers
- **d** Coaches only

09 Which of these IS NOT allowed to travel in the right-hand lane of a three-lane motorway?

mark one answer **ⓘ p121**

- **a** A small delivery van
- **b** A motorcycle
- **c** A vehicle towing a trailer
- **d** A motorcycle and side-car

10 You are travelling on a motorway. You decide you need a rest. You should

mark two answers **ⓘ p121**

- **a** stop on the hard shoulder
- **b** go to a service area
- **c** park on the slip road
- **d** park on the central reservation
- **e** leave at the next exit

1 You break down on a motorway. You need to call for help. Why may it be better to use an emergency roadside telephone rather than a mobile phone?

mark one answer **🛈 p236**
- It connects you to a local garage
- Using a mobile phone will distract other drivers
- It allows easy location by the emergency services
- Mobile phones do not work on motorways

2 What should you use the hard shoulder of a motorway for?

mark one answer **🛈 p121**
- Stopping in an emergency
- Leaving the motorway
- Stopping when you are tired
- Joining the motorway

3 After a breakdown you need to rejoin the main carriageway of a motorway from the hard shoulder. You should

mark one answer **🛈 p237**
- move out onto the carriageway then build up your speed
- move out onto the carriageway using your hazard lights
- gain speed on the hard shoulder before moving out onto the carriageway
- wait on the hard shoulder until someone flashes their headlights at you

4 A crawler lane on a motorway is found

mark one answer **🛈 p111**
- on a steep gradient
- before a service area
- before a junction
- along the hard shoulder

15 You are driving on a motorway. There are red flashing lights above every lane. You must

mark one answer **🛈 p123**
- **a** pull onto the hard shoulder
- **b** slow down and watch for further signals
- **c** leave at the next exit
- **d** stop and wait

16 You are in the right-hand lane on a motorway. You see these overhead signs. This means

mark one answer **🛈 p123**
- **a** move to the left and reduce your speed to 50 mph
- **b** there are roadworks 50 metres (55 yards) ahead
- **c** use the hard shoulder until you have passed the hazard
- **d** leave the motorway at the next exit

17 What do these motorway signs show?

mark one answer **🛈 p123**
- **a** They are countdown markers to a bridge
- **b** They are distance markers to the next telephone
- **c** They are countdown markers to the next exit
- **d** They warn of a police control ahead

ANSWERS

01 a,d,e,f	06 d	11 c	16 a
02 a,d,e,f	07 a	12 a	17 c
03 d	08 b	13 c	
04 d	09 c	14 a	
05 d	10 b,e	15 d	

18 On a motorway the amber reflective studs can be found between

mark one answer　　*i* p67
- **a** the hard shoulder and the carriageway
- **b** the acceleration lane and the carriageway
- **c** the central reservation and the carriageway
- **d** each pair of the lanes

19 What colour are the reflective studs between the lanes on a motorway?

mark one answer　　*i* p67
- **a** Green
- **b** Amber
- **c** White
- **d** Red

20 What colour are the reflective studs between a motorway and its slip road?

mark one answer　　*i* p67
- **a** Amber
- **b** White
- **c** Green
- **d** Red

21 You are allowed to stop on a motorway when you

mark one answer　　*i* p121
- **a** need to walk and get fresh air
- **b** wish to pick up hitch hikers
- **c** are told to do so by flashing red lights
- **d** need to use a mobile telephone

22 You have broken down on a motorway. To find the nearest emergency telephone you should always walk

mark one answer　　*i* p236
- **a** with the traffic flow
- **b** facing oncoming traffic
- **c** in the direction shown on the marker posts
- **d** in the direction of the nearest exit

23 You are travelling along the left-hand lane of a three-lane motorway. Traffic is joining from a slip road. You should

mark one answer　　*i* p121
- **a** race the other vehicles
- **b** move to another lane
- **c** maintain a steady speed
- **d** switch on your hazard flashers

24 You are joining a motorway. Why is it important to make full use of the slip road?

mark one answer　　*i* p122
- **a** Because there is space available to turn round if you need to
- **b** To allow you direct access to the overtaking lan
- **c** To build up a speed similar to traffic on the motorway
- **d** Because you can continue on the hard should

25 How should you use the emergency telephone on a motorway?

mark one answer　　*i* p236
- **a** Stay close to the carriageway
- **b** Face the oncoming traffic
- **c** Keep your back to the traffic
- **d** Stand on the hard shoulder

26 You are on a motorway. What colour ar the reflective studs on the left of the carriageway?

mark one answer　　*i* p67
- **a** Green
- **b** Red
- **c** White
- **d** Amber

27 On a three-lane motorway which lane should you normally use?

mark one answer　　*i* p12
- **a** Left
- **b** Right
- **c** Centre
- **d** Either the right or centre

28 A basic rule when on motorways is

mark one answer　　*i* p12
- **a** use the lane that has least traffic
- **b** keep to the left lane unless overtaking
- **c** overtake on the side that is clearest
- **d** try to keep above 50 mph to prevent congesti

29 When going through a contraflow system on a motorway you should

mark one answer 🛈 p125

a ensure that you do not exceed 30 mph
b keep a good distance from the vehicle ahead
c switch lanes to keep the traffic flowing
d stay close to the vehicle ahead to reduce queues

30 You are on a three-lane motorway. There are red reflective studs on your left and white ones to your right. Where are you?

mark one answer 🛈 p67

a In the right-hand lane
b In the middle lane
c On the hard shoulder
d In the left-hand lane

31 When may you stop on a motorway?

mark three answers 🛈 p121

a If you have to read a map
b When you are tired and need a rest
c If red lights show above every lane
d When told to by the police
e If your mobile phone rings
f In an emergency or a breakdown

32 You are approaching roadworks on a motorway. What should you do?

mark one answer 🛈 p125

a Speed up to clear the area quickly
b Always use the hard shoulder
c Obey all speed limits
d Stay very close to the vehicle in front

33 On motorways you should never overtake on the left UNLESS

mark one answer 🛈 p85

a you can see well ahead that the hard shoulder is clear
b the traffic in the right-hand lane is signalling right
c you warn drivers behind by signalling left
d there is a queue of slow moving traffic to your right that is moving slower than you are

34 You are towing a trailer on a motorway. What is your maximum speed limit?

mark one answer 🛈 p210

a 40 mph
b 50 mph
c 60 mph
d 70 mph

35 The left-hand lane of a motorway should be used for

mark one answer 🛈 p121

a breakdowns and emergencies only
b overtaking slower traffic in the other lanes
c slow vehicles only
d normal driving

36 You are driving on a motorway. You have to slow down quickly due to a hazard. You should

mark one answer 🛈 p122

a switch on your hazard lights
b switch on your headlights
c sound your horn
d flash your headlights

ANSWERS

18 c	23 b	28 b	33 d
19 c	24 c	29 b	34 c
20 c	25 b	30 d	35 d
21 c	26 b	31 c,d,f	36 a
22 c	27 a	32 c	

37 You get a puncture on the motorway. You manage to get your vehicle onto the hard shoulder. You should

mark one answer   *i* p236

a change the wheel yourself immediately
b use the emergency telephone and call for assistance
c try to wave down another vehicle for help
d only change the wheel if you have a passenger to help you

38 You are driving on a motorway. By mistake, you go past the exit that you wanted to take. You should

mark one answer   *i* p122

a carefully reverse on the hard shoulder
b carry on to the next exit
c carefully reverse in the left-hand lane
d make a U-turn at the next gap in the central reservation

39 Your vehicle breaks down on the hard shoulder of a motorway. You decide to use your mobile phone to call for help. You should

mark one answer   *i* p236

a stand at the rear of the vehicle while making the call
b try to repair the vehicle yourself
c get out of the vehicle by the right hand door
d check your location from the marker posts on the left

40 You are driving a car on a motorway. Unless signs show otherwise you must NOT exceed

mark one answer   *i* p137

a 50 mph
b 60 mph
c 70 mph
d 80 mph

41 You are on a three lane motorway a towing trailer. You may use the right hand lane when

mark one answer   *i* p213

a there are lane closures
b there is slow moving traffic
c you can maintain a high speed
d large vehicles are in the left and centre lanes

42 You are on a motorway. There is a contra flow system ahead. What would you expect to find?

mark one answer   *i* p125

a Temporary traffic lights
b Lower speed limits
c Wider lanes than normal
d Speed humps

43 You are driving at 70 mph on a three-lane motorway. There is no traffic ahead. Which lane should you use?

mark one answer   *i* p121

a Any lane
b Middle lane
c Right lane
d Left lane

44 Your vehicle has broken down on a motorway. You are not able to stop on the hard shoulder. What should you do?

mark one answer   *i* p236

a Switch on your hazard warning lights
b Stop following traffic and ask for help
c Attempt to repair your vehicle quickly
d Stand behind your vehicle to warn others

45 Why is it particularly important to carry out a check on your vehicle before making a long motorway journey?

mark one answer   *i* p121

a You will have to do more harsh braking on motorways
b Motorway service stations do not deal with breakdowns
c The road surface will wear down the tyres faster
d Continuous high speeds may increase the risk of your vehicle breaking down

46 For what reason may you use the right-hand lane of a motorway?

mark one answer *p121*
a For keeping out of the way of lorries
b For driving at more than 70 mph
c For turning right
d For overtaking other vehicles

47 On a motorway you may ONLY stop on the hard shoulder

mark one answer *p121*
a in an emergency
b if you feel tired and need to rest
c if you accidentally go past the exit that you wanted to take
d to pick up a hitchhiker

48 You are driving on a motorway. The car ahead shows its hazard lights for a short time. This tells you that

mark one answer *p122*
a the driver wants you to overtake
b the other car is going to change lanes
c traffic ahead is slowing or stopping suddenly
d there is a police speed check ahead

49 The emergency telephones on a motorway are connected to the

mark one answer *p236*
a ambulance service
b police control
c fire brigade
d breakdown service

50 You are intending to leave the motorway at the next exit. Before you reach the exit you should normally position your vehicle

mark one answer *p122*
a in the middle lane
b in the left-hand lane
c on the hard shoulder
d in any lane

51 As a provisional licence holder you should not drive a car

mark one answer *p121*
a over 30 mph
b at night
c on the motorway
d with passengers in rear seats

ANSWERS

37 b	41 a	45 d	49 b
38 b	42 b	46 d	50 b
39 d	43 d	47 a	51 c
40 c	44 a	48 c	

01 What is the meaning of this sign?

mark one answer 🛈 p139
- **a** Local speed limit applies
- **b** No waiting on the carriageway
- **c** National speed limit applies
- **d** No entry to vehicular traffic

02 What is the national speed limit on a single carriageway road for cars and motorcycles?

mark one answer 🛈 p137
- **a** 70 mph
- **b** 60 mph
- **c** 50 mph
- **d** 30 mph

03 What is the national speed limit for cars and motorcycles on a dual carriageway?

mark one answer 🛈 p137
- **a** 30 mph
- **b** 50 mph
- **c** 60 mph
- **d** 70 mph

04 There are no speed limit signs on the road. How is a 30 mph limit indicated?

mark one answer 🛈 p137
- **a** By hazard warning lines
- **b** By street lighting
- **c** By pedestrian islands
- **d** By double or single yellow lines

05 Where you see street lights but no speed limit signs the limit is usually

mark one answer 🛈 p137
- **a** 30 mph
- **b** 40 mph
- **c** 50 mph
- **d** 60 mph

06 What does this sign mean?

mark one answer 🛈 p139
- **a** Minimum speed 30 mph
- **b** End of maximum speed
- **c** End of minimum speed
- **d** Maximum speed 30 mph

07 There is a tractor ahead of you. You wish to overtake but you are NOT sure if it is safe to do so. You should

mark one answer 🛈 p82
- **a** follow another overtaking vehicle through
- **b** sound your horn to the slow vehicle to pull over
- **c** speed through but flash your lights to oncoming traffic
- **d** not overtake if you are in doubt

08 Which three of the following are most likely to take an unusual course at roundabouts?

mark three answers 🛈 p103
- **a** Horse riders
- **b** Milk floats
- **c** Delivery vans
- **d** Long vehicles
- **e** Estate cars
- **f** Cyclists

09 In which FOUR places must you NOT park or wait?

mark four answers 🛈 p49
- **a** On a dual carriageway
- **b** At a bus stop
- **c** On the slope of a hill
- **d** Opposite a traffic island
- **e** In front of someone else's drive
- **f** On the brow of a hill

In which TWO places should you NOT park?

mark two answers   *i* p49

- Near a school entrance
- Near a police station
- In a side road
- At a bus stop
- In a one-way street

On a clearway you must not stop

mark one answer   *i* p180

- at any time
- when it is busy
- in the rush hour
- during daylight hours

What is the meaning of this sign?

mark one answer   *i* p181

- No entry
- Waiting restrictions
- National speed limit
- School crossing patrol

You can park on the right-hand side of a road at night

mark one answer   *i* p179

- in a one-way street
- with your sidelights on
- more than 10 metres (32 feet) from a junction
- under a lamp-post

On a three-lane dual carriageway the right-hand lane can be used for

mark one answer   *i* p118

- overtaking only, never turning right
- overtaking or turning right
- fast-moving traffic only
- turning right only, never overtaking

---

15 You are approaching a busy junction. There are several lanes with road markings. At the last moment you realise that you are in the wrong lane. You should

mark one answer   *i* p73

- **a** continue in that lane
- **b** force your way across
- **c** stop until the area has cleared
- **d** use clear arm signals to cut across

---

16 Where may you overtake on a one-way street?

mark one answer   *i* p75

- **a** Only on the left-hand side
- **b** Overtaking is not allowed
- **c** Only on the right-hand side
- **d** Either on the right or the left

---

17 When going straight ahead at a roundabout you should

mark one answer   *i* p104

- **a** indicate left before leaving the roundabout
- **b** not indicate at any time
- **c** indicate right when approaching the roundabout
- **d** indicate left when approaching the roundabout

---

18 Which vehicle might have to use a different course to normal at roundabouts?

mark one answer   *i* p102

- **a** Sports car
- **b** Van
- **c** Estate car
- **d** Long vehicle

---

19 You are going straight ahead at a roundabout. How should you signal?

mark one answer   *i* p104

- **a** Signal right on the approach and then left to leave the roundabout
- **b** Signal left as you leave the roundabout
- **c** Signal left on the approach to the roundabout and keep the signal on until you leave
- **d** Signal left just after you pass the exit before the one you will take

---

ANSWERS

01 c	06 c	11 a	16 d
02 b	07 d	12 b	17 a
03 d	08 a,d,f	13 a	18 d
04 b	09 b,d,e,f	14 b	19 d
05 a	10 a,d	15 a	

20 You may only enter a box junction when

mark one answer ⓘ p90
- **a** there are less than two vehicles in front of you
- **b** the traffic lights show green
- **c** your exit road is clear
- **d** you need to turn left

21 You may wait in a yellow box junction when

mark one answer ⓘ p90
- **a** oncoming traffic is preventing you from turning right
- **b** you are in a queue of traffic turning left
- **c** you are in a queue of traffic to go ahead
- **d** you are on a roundabout

22 You MUST stop when signalled to do so by which THREE of these?

mark three answers ⓘ p61
- **a** A police officer
- **b** A pedestrian
- **c** A school crossing patrol
- **d** A bus driver
- **e** A red traffic light

23 You will see these markers when approaching

mark one answer ⓘ p161
- **a** the end of a motorway
- **b** a concealed level crossing
- **c** a concealed speed limit sign
- **d** the end of a dual carriageway

24 Someone is waiting to cross at a zebra crossing. They are standing on the pavement. You should normally

mark one answer ⓘ p144
- **a** go on quickly before they step onto the crossing
- **b** stop before you reach the zigzag lines and let them cross
- **c** stop, let them cross, wait patiently
- **d** ignore them as they are still on the pavement

25 At toucan crossings, apart from pedestrians you should be aware of

mark one answer ⓘ p145
- **a** emergency vehicles emerging
- **b** buses pulling out
- **c** trams crossing in front
- **d** cyclists riding across

26 Who can use a toucan crossing?

mark two answers ⓘ p145
- **a** Trains
- **b** Cyclists
- **c** Buses
- **d** Pedestrians
- **e** Trams

27 At a pelican crossing, what does a flashing amber light mean?

mark one answer ⓘ p144
- **a** You must not move off until the lights stop flashing
- **b** You must give way to pedestrians still on the crossing
- **c** You can move off, even if pedestrians are still on the crossing
- **d** You must stop because the lights are about to change to red

28 You are waiting at a pelican crossing. The red light changes to flashing amber. This means you must

mark one answer ⓘ p144
- **a** wait for pedestrians on the crossing to clear
- **b** move off immediately without any hesitation
- **c** wait for the green light before moving off
- **d** get ready and go when the continuous amber light shows

29 You are travelling on a well lit road at night in a built up area. By using dipped headlights you will be able to

mark one answer   *i* p185

a see further along the road
b go at a much faster speed
c switch to main beam quickly
d be easily seen by others

30 When can you park on the left opposite these road markings?

mark one answer   *i* p180

a If the line nearest to you is broken
b When there are no yellow lines
c To pick up or set down passengers
d During daylight hours only

31 You are intending to turn right at a crossroads. An oncoming driver is also turning right. It will normally be safer to

mark one answer   *i* p101

a keep the other vehicle to your RIGHT and turn behind it (offside to offside)
b keep the other vehicle to your LEFT and turn in front of it (nearside to nearside)
c carry on and turn at the next junction instead
d hold back and wait for the other driver to turn first

32 You are on a road that has no traffic signs. There are street lights. What is the speed limit?

mark one answer   *i* p137

a 20 mph
b 30 mph
c 40 mph
d 60 mph

33 You are going along a street with parked vehicles on the left-hand side. For which THREE reasons should you keep your speed down?

mark three answers   *i* p74

a So that oncoming traffic can see you more clearly
b You may set off car alarms
c Vehicles may be pulling out
d Drivers' doors may open
e Children may run out from between the vehicles

34 You meet an obstruction on your side of the road. You should

mark one answer   *i* p81

a carry on, you have priority
b give way to oncoming traffic
c wave oncoming vehicles through
d accelerate to get past first

35 You are on a two-lane dual carriageway. For which TWO of the following would you use the right-hand lane?

mark two answers   *i* p118

a Turning right
b Normal progress
c Staying at the minimum allowed speed
d Constant high speed
e Overtaking slower traffic
f Mending punctures

36 Who has priority at an unmarked crossroads?

mark one answer   *i* p90

a The larger vehicle
b No one has priority
c The faster vehicle
d The smaller vehicle

37 What is the nearest you may park to a junction?

mark one answer   *i* p49

a 10 metres (32 feet)
b 12 metres (39 feet)
c 15 metres (49 feet)
d 20 metres (66 feet)

38 In which THREE places must you NOT park?

mark three answers   *i* p49

a Near the brow of a hill
b At or near a bus stop
c Where there is no pavement
d Within 10 metres (32 feet) of a junction
e On a 40 mph road

ANSWERS

20 c	25 d	30 c	35 a,e
21 a	26 b,d	31 a	36 b
22 a,c,e	27 b	32 b	37 a
23 b	28 a	33 c,d,e	38 a,b,d
24 c	29 d	34 b	

327

39 You are waiting at a level crossing. A train has passed but the lights keep flashing. You must

mark one answer   🛈 p161

a carry on waiting
b phone the signal operator
c edge over the stop line and look for trains
d park and investigate

40 You park overnight on a road with a 40 mph speed limit. You should park

mark one answer   🛈 p179

a facing the traffic
b with parking lights on
c with dipped headlights on
d near a street light

41 The dual carriageway you are turning right onto has a very narrow central reservation. What should you do?

mark one answer   🛈 p95

a Proceed to the central reserve & wait
b Wait until the road is clear in both directions
c Stop in the first lane so that other vehicles give way
d Emerge slightly to show your intentions

42 At a crossroads there are no signs or road markings. Two vehicles approach. Which has priority?

mark one answer   🛈 p90

a Neither of the vehicles
b The vehicle travelling the fastest
c Oncoming vehicles turning right
d Vehicles approaching from the right

43 What does this sign tell you?

mark one answer   🛈 p181

a That it is a no-through road
b End of traffic calming zone
c Free parking zone ends
d No waiting zone ends

44 You are entering an area of roadworks. There is a temporary speed limit displayed. You should

mark one answer   🛈 p125

a not exceed the speed limit
b obey the limit only during rush hour
c ignore the displayed limit
d obey the limit except at night

45 You may drive over a footpath

mark one answer   🛈 p75

a to overtake slow-moving traffic
b when the pavement is very wide
c if no pedestrians are near
d to get into a property

46 A single carriageway road has this sign. What is the maximum permitted speed for a car towing a trailer?

mark one answer   🛈 p137

a 30 mph
b 40 mph
c 50 mph
d 60 mph

47 You are towing a small caravan on a du carriageway. You must not exceed

mark one answer   🛈 p137

a 50 mph
b 40 mph
c 70 mph
d 60 mph

48 You want to park and you see this sign. On the days and times shown you should

Meter **ZONE**

Mon - Fri
8.30 am - 6.30 pm
Saturday
8.30 am - 1.30 pm

mark one answer ℹ️ p181

a park in a bay and not pay
b park on yellow lines and pay
c park on yellow lines and not pay
d park in a bay and pay

49 As a car driver which THREE lanes are you NOT normally allowed to use?

mark three answers ℹ️ p75

a Crawler lane
b Bus lane
c Overtaking lane
d Acceleration lane
e Cycle lane
f Tram lane

50 You are driving along a road that has a cycle lane. The lane is marked by a solid white line. This means that during its period of operation

mark one answer ℹ️ p151

a the lane may be used for parking your car
b you may drive in that lane at any time
c the lane may be used when necessary
d you must not drive in that lane

51 A cycle lane is marked by a solid white line. You must not drive or park in it

mark one answer ℹ️ p151

a at any time
b during the rush hour
c if a cyclist is using it
d during its period of operation

52 While driving, you intend to turn left into a minor road. On the approach you should

mark one answer ℹ️ p97

a keep just left of the middle of the road
b keep in the middle of the road
c swing out wide just before turning
d keep well to the left of the road

53 You are waiting at a level crossing. The red warning lights continue to flash after a train has passed by. What should you do?

mark one answer ℹ️ p161

a Get out and investigate
b Telephone the signal operator
c Continue to wait
d Drive across carefully

54 You are driving over a level crossing. The warning lights come on and a bell rings. What should you do?

mark one answer ℹ️ p161

a Get everyone out of the vehicle immediately
b Stop and reverse back to clear the crossing
c Keep going and clear the crossing
d Stop immediately and use your hazard warning lights

55 You are on a busy main road and find that you are travelling in the wrong direction. What should you do?

mark one answer ℹ️ p167

a Turn into a side road on the right and reverse into the main road
b Make a U-turn in the main road
c Make a 'three-point' turn in the main road
d Turn round in a side road

56 You may remove your seat belt when carrying out a manoeuvre that involves

mark one answer ℹ️ p167

a reversing
b a hill start
c an emergency stop
d driving slowly

ANSWERS

39 a	44 a	49 b,e,f	54 c
40 b	45 d	50 d	55 d
41 b	46 c	51 d	56 a
42 a	47 d	52 d	
43 d	48 d	53 c	

57 You must not reverse

mark one answer 🛈 p167

- **a** for longer than necessary
- **b** for more than a car's length
- **c** into a side road
- **d** in a built-up area

58 You are parked in a busy high street. What is the safest way to turn your vehicle around so you can go the opposite way?

mark one answer 🛈 p167

- **a** Find a quiet side road to turn round in
- **b** Drive into a side road and reverse into the main road
- **c** Get someone to stop the traffic
- **d** Do a U-turn

59 When you are NOT sure that it is safe to reverse your vehicle you should

mark one answer 🛈 p168

- **a** use your horn
- **b** rev your engine
- **c** get out and check
- **d** reverse slowly

60 When may you reverse from a side road into a main road?

mark one answer 🛈 p169

- **a** Only if both roads are clear of traffic
- **b** Not at any time
- **c** At any time
- **d** Only if the main road is clear of traffic

61 You want to turn right at a box junction. There is oncoming traffic. You should

mark one answer 🛈 p90

- **a** wait in the box junction if your exit is clear
- **b** wait before the junction until it is clear of all traffic
- **c** drive on, you cannot turn right at a box junction
- **d** drive slowly into the box junction when signalled by oncoming traffic

62 You are reversing your vehicle into a side road. When would the greatest hazard to passing traffic occur?

mark one answer 🛈 p172

- **a** After you've completed the manoeuvre
- **b** Just before you actually begin to manoeuvre
- **c** After you've entered the side road
- **d** When the front of your vehicle swings out

63 You are driving on a road that has a cycle lane. The lane is marked by a broken white line. This means that

mark two answers 🛈 p151

- **a** you should not drive in the lane unless it is unavoidable
- **b** you should not park in the lane unless it is unavoidable
- **c** you can drive in the lane at any time
- **d** the lane must be used by motorcyclists in heavy traffic

64 Where is the safest place to park your vehicle at night?

mark one answer 🛈 p219

- **a** In a garage
- **b** On a busy road
- **c** In a quiet car park
- **d** Near a red route

65 To help keep your vehicle secure at night where should you park?

mark one answer 🛈 p219

- **a** Near a police station
- **b** In a quiet road
- **c** On a red route
- **d** In a well lit area

66 You are in the right-hand lane of a dual carriageway. You see signs showing that the right-hand lane is closed 800 yards ahead. You should

mark one answer 🛈 p125

- **a** keep in that lane until you reach the queue
- **b** move to the left immediately
- **c** wait and see which lane is moving faster
- **d** move to the left in good time

57 You are driving on an urban clearway. You may stop only to

mark one answer *i* p180

a set down and pick up passengers
b use a mobile telephone
c ask for directions
d load or unload goods

58 You are looking for somewhere to park your vehicle. The area is full EXCEPT for spaces marked 'disabled use'. You can

mark one answer *i* p180

a use these spaces when elsewhere is full
b park if you stay with your vehicle
c use these spaces, disabled or not
d not park there unless permitted

59 Your vehicle is parked on the road at night. When must you use sidelights?

mark one answer *i* p179

a Where there are continuous white lines in the middle of the road
b Where the speed limit exceeds 30 mph
c Where you are facing oncoming traffic
d Where you are near a bus stop

60 On which THREE occasions MUST you stop your vehicle?

mark three answers *i* p61

a When in an accident where damage or injury is caused *i* p68
b At a red traffic light
c When signalled to do so by a police officer *i* p239
d At a junction with double broken white lines
e At a pelican crossing when the amber light is flashing and no pedestrians are crossing

61 You are on a road that is only wide enough for one vehicle. There is a car coming towards you. What should you do?

mark one answer *i* p81

a Pull into a passing place on your right
b Force the other driver to reverse
c Pull into a passing place if your vehicle is wider
d Pull into a passing place on your left

72 What MUST you have to park in a disabled space?

mark one answer *i* p180

a An orange or blue badge
b A wheelchair
c An advanced driver certificate
d A modified vehicle

73 You are driving at night with full beam headlights on. A vehicle is overtaking you. You should dip your lights

mark one answer *i* p185

a some time after the vehicle has passed you
b before the vehicle starts to pass you
c only if the other driver dips their headlights
d as soon as the vehicle passes you

74 When may you drive a motor car in this bus lane?

mark one answer *i* p157

a Outside its hours of operation
b To get to the front of a traffic queue
c You may not use it at any time
d To overtake slow-moving traffic

75 Signals are normally given by direction indicators and

mark one answer *i* p58

a brake lights
b side lights
c fog lights
d interior lights

ANSWERS

57 a	62 d	67 a	72 a
58 a	63 a,b	68 d	73 d
59 c	64 a	69 b	74 a
60 b	65 d	70 a,b,c	75 a
61 a	66 d	71 d	

01 You MUST obey signs giving orders. These signs are mostly in

mark one answer **i** p63

a green rectangles
b red triangles
c blue rectangles
d red circles

02 Traffic signs giving orders are generally which shape?

mark one answer **i** p63

a   **b**

c   **d**

03 Which type of sign tells you NOT to do something?

mark one answer **i** p63

a   **b**

c   **d**

04 What does this sign mean?

mark one answer **i** p139

a Maximum speed limit with traffic calming
b Minimum speed limit with traffic calming
c '20 cars only' parking zone
d Only 20 cars allowed at any one time

05 Which sign means no motor vehicles are allowed?

mark one answer **i** p99

a   **b**

c   **d**

06 Which of these signs means no motor vehicles?

mark one answer **i** p99

a   **b**

c   **d**

07 What does this sign mean?

mark one answer **i** p333

a New speed limit 20 mph
b No vehicles over 30 tonnes
c Minimum speed limit 30 mph
d End of 20 mph zone

08 What does this sign mean?

mark one answer   p99

a No overtaking
b No motor vehicles
c Clearway (no stopping)
d Cars and motorcycles only

09 What does this sign mean?

mark one answer   p99

a No parking
b No road markings
c No through road
d No entry

10 What does this sign mean?

mark one answer   p99

a Bend to the right
b Road on the right closed
c No traffic from the right
d No right turn

11 Which sign means 'no entry'?

mark one answer   p99

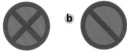

   b

   d

12 What does this sign mean?

mark one answer   p159

a Route for trams only
b Route for buses only
c Parking for buses only
d Parking for trams only

13 Which type of vehicle does this sign apply to?

mark one answer   p213

a Wide vehicles
b Long vehicles
c High vehicles
d Heavy vehicles

14 Which sign means NO motor vehicles allowed?

mark one answer   p99

ANSWERS			
01 d	05 b	09 d	13 c
02 d	06 a	10 d	14 b
03 a	07 d	11 d	
04 a	08 b	12 a	

15 What does this sign mean?

mark one answer ⓘ p85
- **a** You have priority
- **b** No motor vehicles
- **c** Two-way traffic
- **d** No overtaking

16 What does this sign mean?

mark one answer ⓘ p85
- **a** Keep in one lane
- **b** Give way to oncoming traffic
- **c** Do not overtake
- **d** Form two lanes

17 Which sign means no overtaking?

mark one answer ⓘ p85

18 What does this sign mean?

mark one answer ⓘ p181
- **a** Waiting restrictions apply
- **b** Waiting permitted
- **c** National speed limit applies
- **d** Clearway (no stopping)

19 What does this sign mean?

mark one answer ⓘ p181
- **a** End of restricted speed area
- **b** End of restricted parking area
- **c** End of clearway
- **d** End of cycle route

20 Which sign means 'no stopping'?

mark one answer ⓘ p181

21 What does this sign mean?

mark one answer ⓘ p181
- **a** Roundabout
- **b** Crossroads
- **c** No stopping
- **d** No entry

22 You see this sign ahead. It means

mark one answer ⓘ p181
- **a** national speed limit applies
- **b** waiting restrictions apply
- **c** no stopping
- **d** no entry

23 What does this sign mean?

mark one answer **ⓘ p181**
- **a** Distance to parking place ahead
- **b** Distance to public telephone ahead
- **c** Distance to public house ahead
- **d** Distance to passing place ahead

24 What does this sign mean?

mark one answer **ⓘ p181**
- **a** Vehicles may not park on the verge or footway
- **b** Vehicles may park on the left-hand side of the road only
- **c** Vehicles may park fully on the verge or footway
- **d** Vehicles may park on the right-hand side of the road only

25 What does this traffic sign mean?

mark one answer **ⓘ p81**
- **a** No overtaking allowed
- **b** Give priority to oncoming traffic
- **c** Two way traffic
- **d** One-way traffic only

26 What is the meaning of this traffic sign?

mark one answer **ⓘ p81**
- **a** End of two-way road
- **b** Give priority to vehicles coming towards you
- **c** You have priority over vehicles coming towards you
- **d** Bus lane ahead

27 What MUST you do when you see this sign?

mark one answer **ⓘ p89**
- **a** Stop, only if traffic is approaching
- **b** Stop, even if the road is clear
- **c** Stop, only if children are waiting to cross
- **d** Stop, only if a red light is showing

28 What does this sign mean?

mark one answer **ⓘ p81**
- **a** No overtaking No overtaking
- **b** You are entering a one-way street
- **c** Two-way traffic ahead
- **d** You have priority over vehicles from the opposite direction

ANSWERS			
15 d	19 b	23 a	27 b
16 c	20 b	24 c	28 d
17 b	21 c	25 b	
18 a	22 c	26 c	

29 What shape is a STOP sign at a junction?

mark one answer 🛈 p63

a ⬤   b △

c ▭   d ⬢

30 At a junction you see this sign partly covered by snow. What does it mean?

mark one answer 🛈 p63
- **a** Cross roads
- **b** Give way
- **c** Stop
- **d** Turn right

31 Which shape is used for a GIVE WAY sign?

mark one answer 🛈 p63

a △   b ◯

c ⬢   d ▽

32 What does this sign mean?

mark one answer 🛈 p139
- **a** Service area 30 miles ahead
- **b** Maximum speed 30 mph
- **c** Minimum speed 30 mph
- **d** Lay-by 30 miles ahead

33 Which of these signs means turn left ahead?

mark one answer 🛈 p75

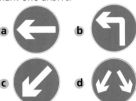

a ←   b ↰

c ↙   d

34 What does this sign mean?

mark one answer 🛈 p88
- **a** Buses turning
- **b** Ring road
- **c** Mini roundabout
- **d** Keep right

35 What does this sign mean?

mark one answer 🛈 p75
- **a** Give way to oncoming vehicles
- **b** Approaching traffic passes you on both sides
- **c** Turn off at the next available junction
- **d** Pass either side to get to the same destination

36 What does this sign mean?

mark one answer 🛈 p159
- **a** Route for trams
- **b** Give way to trams
- **c** Route for buses
- **d** Give way to buses

37 What does a circular traffic sign with a blue background do?

mark one answer p63

a Give warning of a motorway ahead
b Give directions to a car park
c Give motorway information
d Give an instruction

38 Which of these signs means that you are entering a one-way street?

mark one answer p75

 b

 d

39 Where would you see a contraflow bus and cycle lane?

mark one answer p75

a On a dual carriageway
b On a roundabout
c On an urban motorway
d On a one-way street

40 What does this sign mean?

mark one answer p156

a Bus station on the right
b Contraflow bus lane
c With-flow bus lane
d Give way to buses

41 What does this sign mean?

mark one answer p157

a With-flow bus and cycle lane
b Contraflow bus and cycle lane
c No buses and cycles allowed
d No waiting for buses and cycles

42 What does a sign with a brown background show?

mark one answer p65

a Tourist directions
b Primary roads
c Motorway routes
d Minor routes

43 This sign means

mark one answer p65

a tourist attraction
b beware of trains
c level crossing
d beware of trams

44 What are triangular signs for?

mark one answer ⓘ p63
- **a** To give warnings
- **b** To give information
- **c** To give orders
- **d** To give directions

45 What does this sign mean?

mark one answer ⓘ p89
- **a** Turn left ahead
- **b** T-junction
- **c** No through road
- **d** Give way

46 What does this sign mean?

mark one answer ⓘ p193
- **a** Multi-exit roundabout
- **b** Risk of ice
- **c** Six roads converge
- **d** Place of historical interest

47 What does this sign mean?

mark one answer ⓘ p89
- **a** Crossroads
- **b** Level crossing with gate
- **c** Level crossing without gate
- **d** Ahead only

48 What does this sign mean?

mark one answer ⓘ p89
- **a** Ring road
- **b** Mini-roundabout
- **c** No vehicles
- **d** Roundabout

49 Which FOUR of these would be indicated by a triangular road sign?

mark four answers ⓘ p63
- **a** Road narrows
- **b** Ahead only
- **c** Low bridge
- **d** Minimum speed
- **e** Children crossing
- **f** T-junction

50 What does this sign mean?

mark one answer ⓘ p151
- **a** Cyclists must dismount
- **b** Cycles are not allowed
- **c** Cycle route ahead
- **d** Cycle in single file

51 Which sign means that pedestrians may be walking along the road?

mark one answer ⓘ p145

a   **b**

c   **d**

52 Which of these signs warn you of a pedestrian crossing?

mark one answer ℹ️ p145

  b

 d

53 What does this sign mean?

mark one answer ℹ️ p145

- No footpath ahead
- Pedestrians only ahead
- Pedestrian crossing ahead
- School crossing ahead

54 What does this sign mean?

mark one answer ℹ️ p145

- School crossing patrol
- No pedestrians allowed
- Pedestrian zone – no vehicles
- Pedestrian crossing ahead

55 Which of these signs means there is a double bend ahead?

mark one answer ℹ️ p109

 b

 d

56 What does this sign mean?

mark one answer ℹ️ p159

- **a** Wait at the barriers
- **b** Wait at the crossroads
- **c** Give way to trams
- **d** Give way to farm vehicles

57 What does this sign mean?

mark one answer ℹ️ p113

- **a** Humpback bridge
- **b** Humps in the road
- **c** Entrance to tunnel
- **d** Soft verges

58 What does this sign mean?

mark one answer ℹ️ p237

- **a** Low bridge ahead
- **b** Tunnel ahead
- **c** Ancient monument ahead
- **d** Accident black spot ahead

ANSWERS

44 a	48 d	52 a	56 c
45 b	49 a,c,e,f	53 c	57 b
46 b	50 c	54 d	58 b
47 a	51 a	55 b	

59 What does this sign mean?

mark one answer ⓘ p75
- **a** Two-way traffic straight ahead
- **b** Two-way traffic crossing a one-way road
- **c** Two-way traffic over a bridge
- **d** Two-way traffic crosses a two-way road

60 Which sign means 'two-way traffic crosses a one-way road'?

mark one answer ⓘ p75

a **b**

c **d**

61 Which of these signs means the end of a dual carriageway?

mark one answer ⓘ p118

a **b**

c **d**

62 What does this sign mean?

mark one answer ⓘ p118
- **a** End of dual carriageway
- **b** Tall bridge
- **c** Road narrows
- **d** End of narrow bridge

63 What does this sign mean?

mark one answer ⓘ p75
- **a** Two-way traffic ahead across a one-way road
- **b** Traffic approaching you has priority
- **c** Two-way traffic straight ahead
- **d** Motorway contraflow system ahead

64 What does this sign mean?

mark one answer ⓘ p85
- **a** Crosswinds
- **b** Road noise
- **c** Airport
- **d** Adverse camber

65 What does this traffic sign mean?

mark one answer ⓘ p13:
- **a** Slippery road ahead
- **b** Tyres liable to punctures ahead
- **c** Danger ahead
- **d** Service area ahead

66 You are about to overtake when you se this sign. You should

Hidden dip

mark one answer ⓘ p85
- **a** overtake the other driver as quickly as possible
- **b** move to the right to get a better view
- **c** switch your headlights on before overtaking
- **d** hold back until you can see clearly ahead

7 What does this sign mean?

mark one answer **p161**

- Level crossing with gate or barrier
- Gated road ahead
- Level crossing without gate or barrier
- Cattle grid ahead

71 What does this sign mean?

mark one answer **p115**

- **a** Humpback bridge
- **b** Traffic calming hump
- **c** Low bridge
- **d** Uneven road

8 What does this sign mean?

mark one answer **p159**

- No trams ahead
- Oncoming trams
- Trams crossing ahead
- Trams only

72 What does this sign mean?

mark one answer **p168**

- **a** Turn left for parking area
- **b** No through road on the left
- **c** No entry for traffic turning left
- **d** Turn left for ferry terminal

9 What does this sign mean?

mark one answer **p111**

- Adverse camber
- Steep hill downwards
- Uneven road
- Steep hill upwards

73 What does this sign mean?

mark one answer **p168**

- **a** T-junction
- **b** No through road
- **c** Telephone box ahead
- **d** Toilet ahead

What does this sign mean?

mark one answer **p189**

- Uneven road surface
- Bridge over the road
- Road ahead ends
- Water across the road

74 Which sign means 'no through road'?

mark one answer **ⓘ p168**

a   b

c   d

75 Which of the following signs informs you that you are coming to a No Through Road?

mark one answer **ⓘ p168**

a   b

c   d

76 What does this sign mean?

mark one answer **ⓘ p181**
- a Direction to park and ride car park
- b No parking for buses or coaches
- c Directions to bus and coach park
- d Parking area for cars and coaches

77 You are driving through a tunnel and you see this sign. What does it mean?

mark one answer **ⓘ p111**
- a Direction to emergency pedestrian exit
- b Beware of pedestrians, no footpath ahead
- c No access for pedestrians
- d Beware of pedestrians crossing ahead

78 Which is the sign for a ring road?

mark one answer **ⓘ p65**

a   b

c   d

79 What does this sign mean?

mark one answer **ⓘ p65**
- a Route for lorries
- b Ring road
- c Rest area
- d Roundabout

80 What does this sign mean?

mark one answer **ⓘ p65**
- a Hilly road
- b Humps in road
- c Holiday route
- d Hospital route

81 What does this sign mean?

mark one answer **ⓘ p12**
- a The right-hand lane ahead is narrow
- b Right-hand lane for buses only
- c Right-hand lane for turning right
- d The right-hand lane is closed

2 What does this sign mean?

mark one answer   p125

- Change to the left lane
- Leave at the next exit
- Contraflow system
- One-way street

3 To avoid an accident when entering a contraflow system, you should

mark three answers   p125

- reduce speed in good time
- switch lanes anytime to make progress
- choose an appropriate lane early
- keep the correct separation distance
- increase speed to pass through quickly
- follow other motorists closely to avoid long queues

4 What does this sign mean?

rk one answer   p111

- Leave motorway at next exit
- Lane for heavy and slow vehicles
- All lorries use the hard shoulder
- Rest area for lorries

5 You are approaching a red traffic light. The signal will change from red to

rk one answer   p69

- red and amber, then green
- green, then amber
- amber, then green
- green and amber, then green

86 A red traffic light means

mark one answer   p69

- **a** you should stop unless turning left
- **b** stop, if you are able to brake safely
- **c** you must stop and wait behind the stop line
- **d** proceed with caution

87 At traffic lights, amber on its own means

mark one answer   p68

- **a** prepare to go
- **b** go if the way is clear
- **c** go if no pedestrians are crossing
- **d** stop at the stop line

88 You are approaching traffic lights. Red and amber are showing. This means

mark one answer   p68

- **a** pass the lights if the road is clear
- **b** there is a fault with the lights – take care
- **c** wait for the green light before you cross the stop line
- **d** the lights are about to change to red

343

89 You are at a junction controlled by traffic lights. When should you NOT proceed at

mark one answer   *i* p68

- **a** When pedestrians are waiting to cross
- **b** When your exit from the junction is blocked
- **c** When you think the lights may be about to change
- **d** When you intend to turn right

90 You are in the left-hand lane at traffic lights. You are waiting to turn left. At which of these traffic lights must you NOT move on?

mark one answer   *i* p68

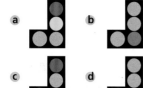

91 What does this sign mean?

mark one answer   *i* p68

- **a** Traffic lights out of order
- **b** Amber signal out of order
- **c** Temporary traffic lights ahead
- **d** New traffic lights ahead

92 When traffic lights are out of order, who has priority?

mark one answer   *i* p68

- **a** Traffic going straight on
- **b** Traffic turning right
- **c** Nobody
- **d** Traffic turning left

93 These flashing red lights mean STOP. In which THREE of the following places could you find them?

mark three answers   *i* p161

- **a** Pelican crossings
- **b** Lifting bridges
- **c** Zebra crossings
- **d** Level crossings
- **e** Motorway exits
- **f** Fire stations

94 What do these zigzag lines at pedestrian crossings mean?

mark one answer   *i* p143

- **a** No parking at any time
- **b** Parking allowed only for a short time
- **c** Slow down to 20 mph
- **d** Sounding horns is not allowed

95 When may you cross a double solid whi line in the middle of the road?

mark one answer   *i* p73

- **a** To pass traffic that is queuing back at a junction
- **b** To pass a car signalling to turn left ahead
- **c** To pass a road maintenance vehicle travelling 10 mph or less
- **d** To pass a vehicle that is towing a trailer

96 What does this road marking mean?

mark one answer ⓘ p73

- Do not cross the line
- No stopping allowed
- You are approaching a hazard
- No overtaking allowed

97 This marking appears on the road just before a

mark one answer ⓘ p90

- 'no entry' sign
- 'give way' sign
- 'stop' sign
- 'no through road' sign

98 Where would you see this road marking?

mark one answer ⓘ p112

- At traffic lights
- On road humps
- Near a level crossing
- At a box junction

99 Which is a hazard warning line?

mark one answer ⓘ p73

100 At this junction there is a stop sign with a solid white line on the road surface. Why is there a stop sign here?

mark one answer ⓘ p90

- **a** Speed on the major road is de-restricted
- **b** It is a busy junction
- **c** Visibility along the major road is restricted
- **d** There are hazard warning lines in the centre of the road

101 You see this line across the road at the entrance to a roundabout. What does it mean?

mark one answer ⓘ p90

- **a** Give way to traffic from the right
- **b** Traffic from the left has right of way
- **c** You have right of way
- **d** Stop at the line

102 Where would you find these road markings?

mark one answer ⓘ p102

- **a** At a railway crossing
- **b** At a junction
- **c** On a motorway
- **d** On a pedestrian crossing

103 How will a police officer in a patrol vehicle normally get you to stop?

mark one answer **ⓘ p163**
- **a** Flash the headlights, indicate left and point to the left
- **b** Wait until you stop, then approach you
- **c** Use the siren, overtake, cut in front and stop
- **d** Pull alongside you, use the siren and wave you to stop

104 There is a police car following you. The police officer flashes the headlights and points to the left. What should you do?

mark one answer **ⓘ p163**
- **a** Turn left at the next junction
- **b** Pull up on the left
- **c** Stop immediately
- **d** Move over to the left

105 You approach a junction. The traffic lights are not working. A police officer gives this signal. You should

mark one answer **ⓘ p61**
- **a** turn left only
- **b** turn right only
- **c** stop level with the officer's arm
- **d** stop at the stop line

106 The driver of the car in front is giving this arm signal. What does it mean?

mark one answer **ⓘ p60**
- **a** The driver is slowing down
- **b** The driver intends to turn right
- **c** The driver wishes to overtake
- **d** The driver intends to turn left

107 Where would you see these road markings?

mark one answer **ⓘ p122**
- **a** At a level crossing
- **b** On a motorway slip road
- **c** At a pedestrian crossing
- **d** On a single-track road

108 When may you NOT overtake on the left?

mark one answer **ⓘ p85**
- **a** On a free-flowing motorway or dual carriageway
- **b** When the traffic is moving slowly in queues
- **c** On a one-way street
- **d** When the car in front is signalling to turn righ

109 What does this motorway sign mean?

mark one answer **ⓘ p123**
- **a** Change to the lane on your left
- **b** Leave the motorway at the next exit
- **c** Change to the opposite carriageway
- **d** Pull up on the hard shoulder

110 What does this motorway sign mean?

mark one answer **ⓘ p123**
- **a** Temporary minimum speed 50 mph
- **b** No services for 50 miles
- **c** Obstruction 50 metres (164 feet) ahead
- **d** Temporary maximum speed 50 mph

11 What does this sign mean?

mark one answer **ⓘ p123**

Through traffic to use left lane
Right-hand lane T-junction only
Right-hand lane closed ahead
11 tonne weight limit

2 On a motorway this sign means

mark one answer **ⓘ p123**

move over onto the hard shoulder
overtaking on the left only
leave the motorway at the next exit
move to the lane on your left

3 What does '25' mean on this motorway sign?

mark one answer **ⓘ p64**

The distance to the nearest town
The route number of the road
The number of the next junction
The speed limit on the slip road

4 The right-hand lane of a three-lane motorway is

mark one answer **ⓘ p121**

for lorries only
an overtaking lane
the right-turn lane
an acceleration lane

115 Where can you find reflective amber studs on a motorway?

mark one answer **ⓘ p67**

a Separating the slip road from the motorway
b On the left-hand edge of the road
c On the right-hand edge of the road
d Separating the lanes

116 Where on a motorway would you find green reflective studs?

mark one answer **ⓘ p67**

a Separating driving lanes
b Between the hard shoulder and the carriageway
c At slip road entrances and exits
d Between the carriageway and the central reservation

117 You are travelling along a motorway. You see this sign. You should

mark one answer **ⓘ p123**

a leave the motorway at the next exit
b turn left immediately
c change lane
d move onto the hard shoulder

118 What does this sign mean?

mark one answer **ⓘ p123**

a No motor vehicles
b End of motorway
c No through road
d End of bus lane

ANSWERS

103 a	107 b	111 c	115 c
104 b	108 a	112 d	116 c
105 d	109 a	113 c	117 a
106 d	110 d	114 b	118 b

119 Which of these signs means that the national speed limit applies?

mark one answer p138

 a

 b

 c

 d

120 What is the maximum speed on a single carriageway road?

mark one answer p137
- **a** 50 mph
- **b** 60 mph
- **c** 40 mph
- **d** 70 mph

121 What does this sign mean?

mark one answer p123
- **a** End of motorway
- **b** End of restriction
- **c** Lane ends ahead
- **d** Free recovery ends

122 This sign is advising you to

mark one answer p65
- **a** follow the route diversion
- **b** follow the signs to the picnic area
- **c** give way to pedestrians
- **d** give way to cyclists

123 Why would this temporary speed limit sign be shown?

mark one answer p125
- **a** To warn of the end of the motorway
- **b** To warn you of a low bridge
- **c** To warn you of a junction ahead
- **d** To warn of road works ahead

124 This traffic sign means there is

mark one answer p125
- **a** a compulsory maximum speed limit
- **b** an advisory maximum speed limit
- **c** a compulsory minimum speed limit
- **d** an advised separation distance

125 You see this sign at a crossroads. You should

mark one answer p69
- **a** maintain the same speed
- **b** carry on with great care
- **c** find another route
- **d** telephone the police

26 You are signalling to turn right in busy traffic. How would you confirm your intention safely?

mark one answer　　　*i* p60

- Sound the horn
- Give an arm signal
- Flash your headlights
- Position over the centre line

27 What does this sign mean?

mark one answer　　　*i* p63

- Motorcycles only
- No cars
- Cars only
- No motorcycles

28 You are on a motorway. You see this sign on a lorry that has stopped in the right-hand lane. You should

mark one answer　　　*i* p125

- move into the right-hand lane
- stop behind the flashing lights
- pass the lorry on the left
- leave the motorway at the next exit

29 You are on a motorway. Red flashing lights appear above your lane only. What should you do?

mark one answer　　　*i* p123

- Continue in that lane and look for further information
- Move into another lane in good time
- Pull onto the hard shoulder
- Stop and wait for an instruction to proceed

130 A red traffic light means

mark one answer　　　*i* p69

- **a** you must stop behind the white stop line
- **b** you may go straight on if there is no other traffic
- **c** you may turn left if it is safe to do so
- **d** you must slow down and prepare to stop if traffic has started to cross

131 The driver of this car is giving an arm signal. What are they about to do?

mark one answer　　　*i* p60

- **a** Turn to the right
- **b** Turn to the left
- **c** Go straight ahead
- **d** Let pedestrians cross

132 Which arm signal tells you that the car you are following is going to turn left?

mark one answer　　　*i* p60

a 　 **b** 　 **c** 　 **d**

ANSWERS

119 d	123 d	127 d	131 b
120 b	124 a	128 c	132 a
121 b	125 b	129 b	
122 a	126 b	130 a	

133 When may you sound the horn?

mark one answer   *i* p59
- **a** To give you right of way
- **b** To attract a friend's attention
- **c** To warn others of your presence
- **d** To make slower drivers move over

134 You must not use your horn when you are stationary

mark one answer *i* p59
- **a** unless a moving vehicle may cause you danger
- **b** at any time whatsoever
- **c** unless it is used only briefly
- **d** except for signalling that you have just arrived

135 What does this sign mean?

mark one answer *i* p181
- **a** You can park on the days and times shown
- **b** No parking on the days and times shown
- **c** No parking at all from Monday to Friday
- **d** End of the urban clearway restrictions

136 What does this sign mean?

mark one answer *i* p115
- **a** Quayside or river bank
- **b** Steep hill downwards
- **c** Uneven road surface
- **d** Road liable to flooding

137 You see this amber traffic light ahead. Which light or lights will come on next?

mark one answer *i* p169
- **a** Red alone
- **b** Red and amber together
- **c** Green and amber together
- **d** Green alone

138 This broken white line painted in the centre of the road means

mark one answer *i* p73
- **a** oncoming vehicles have priority over you
- **b** you should give priority to oncoming vehicles
- **c** there is a hazard ahead of you
- **d** the area is a national speed limit zone

139 Which sign means you have priority over oncoming vehicles?

mark one answer *i* p81

 a   **b**

 c   **d**

140 You see this signal overhead on the motorway. What does it mean?

mark one answer   *i* p123

- Leave the motorway at the next exit
- All vehicles use the hard shoulder
- Sharp bend to the left ahead
- Stop, all lanes ahead closed

141 A white line like this along the centre of the road is a

mark one answer   *i* p73

- bus lane marking
- hazard warning
- give way marking
- lane marking

142 What is the purpose of these yellow criss-cross lines on the road?

mark one answer   *i* p90

- To make you more aware of the traffic lights
- To guide you into position as you turn
- To prevent the junction from becoming blocked
- To show you where to stop when the lights change

143 What is the reason for the yellow criss-cross lines painted on the road here?

mark one answer   *i* p90

- **a** To mark out an area for trams only
- **b** To prevent queuing traffic from blocking the junction on the left
- **c** To mark the entrance lane to a car park
- **d** To warn you of the tram lines crossing the road

144 What is the reason for the area marked in red and white along the centre of this road?

mark one answer   *i* p73

- **a** It is to separate traffic flowing in opposite directions
- **b** It marks an area to be used by overtaking motorcyclists
- **c** It is a temporary marking to warn of the roadworks
- **d** It is separating the two sides of the dual carriageway

ANSWERS

133 c	136 a	139 c	142 c
134 a	137 a	140 a	143 b
135 b	138 c	141 b	144 a

145 Other drivers may sometimes flash their headlights at you. In which situation are they allowed to do this?

mark one answer ❶ p58

- **a** To warn of a radar speed trap ahead
- **b** To show that they are giving way to you
- **c** To warn you of their presence
- **d** To let you know there is a fault with your vehicle

146 At roadworks which of the following can control traffic flow?

mark three answers ❶ p125

- **a** A STOP–GO board
- **b** Flashing amber lights
- **c** A police officer
- **d** Flashing red lights
- **e** Temporary traffic lights

147 You are approaching a zebra crossing where pedestrians are waiting. Which arm signal might you give?

mark one answer ❶ p60

148 The white line along the side of the road

mark one answer ❶ p73

- **a** shows the edge of the carriageway
- **b** shows the approach to a hazard
- **c** means no parking
- **d** means no overtaking

149 You see this white arrow on the road ahead. It means

mark one answer ❶ p84

- **a** entrance on the left
- **b** all vehicles turn left
- **c** keep left of the hatched markings
- **d** road bending to the left

150 How should you give an arm signal to turn left?

mark one answer ❶ p60

51 You are waiting at a T-junction. A vehicle is coming from the right with the left signal flashing. What should you do?

ark one answer *ⓘ* p59

Move out and accelerate hard
Wait until the vehicle starts to turn in
Pull out before the vehicle reaches the junction
Move out slowly

52 When may you use hazard warning lights when driving?

ark one answer *ⓘ* p58

Instead of sounding the horn in a built-up area between 11.30 pm and 7 am
On a motorway or unrestricted dual carriageway, to warn of a hazard ahead
On rural routes, after a warning sign of animals
On the approach to toucan crossings where cyclists are waiting to cross

53 You are driving on a motorway. There is a slow-moving vehicle ahead. On the back you see this sign. You should

rk one answer *ⓘ* p125

pass on the right
pass on the left
leave at the next exit
drive no further

154 You should NOT normally stop on these markings near schools

⋈ SCHOOL KEEP CLEAR ⋈

mark one answer *ⓘ* p113

a except when picking up children
b under any circumstances
c unless there is nowhere else available
d except to set down children

155 Why should you make sure that your indicators are cancelled after turning?

mark one answer *ⓘ* p57

a To avoid flattening the battery
b To avoid misleading other road users
c To avoid dazzling other road users
d To avoid damage to the indicator relay

156 You are driving in busy traffic. You want to pull up on the left just after a junction on the left. When should you signal?

mark one answer *ⓘ* p57

a As you are passing or just after the junction
b Just before you reach the junction
c Well before you reach the junction
d It would be better not to signal at all

ANSWERS			
145 c	148 a	151 b	154 b
146 a,c,e	149 c	152 b	155 b
147 a	150 c	153 b	156 a

DOCUMENTS

01 An MOT certificate is normally valid for

mark one answer   *i* p201

- **a** three years after the date it was issued
- **b** 10,000 miles
- **c** one year after the date it was issued
- **d** 30,000 miles

02 A cover note is a document issued before you receive your

mark one answer   *i* p200

- **a** driving licence
- **b** insurance certificate
- **c** registration document
- **d** MOT certificate

03 A police officer asks to see your documents. You do not have them with you. You may produce them at a police station within

mark one answer   *i* p198

- **a** 5 days
- **b** 7 days
- **c** 14 days
- **d** 21 days

04 You have just passed your practical test. You do not hold a full licence in another category. Within two years you get six penalty points on your licence. What will you have to do?

mark two answers   *i* p203

- **a** Retake only your theory test
- **b** Retake your theory and practical tests
- **c** Retake only your practical test
- **d** Reapply for your full licence immediately
- **e** Reapply for your provisional licence

05 To drive on the road learners MUST

mark one answer   *i* p11

- **a** have NO penalty points on their licence
- **b** have taken professional instruction
- **c** have a signed, valid provisional licence
- **d** apply for a driving test within 12 months

06 Before driving anyone else's motor vehicle you should make sure that

mark one answer   *i* p11

- **a** the vehicle owner has third party insurance cover
- **b** your own vehicle has insurance cover
- **c** the vehicle is insured for your use
- **d** the owner has left the insurance documents i the vehicle

07 Your car needs an MOT certificate. If you drive without one this could invalidate your

mark one answer   *i* p201

- **a** vehicle service record
- **b** insurance
- **c** road tax disc
- **d** vehicle registration document

08 When is it legal to drive a car over three years old without an MOT certificate?

mark one answer   *i* p201

- **a** Up to seven days after the old certificate has run out
- **b** When driving to an MOT centre to arrange a appointment
- **c** Just after buying a second-hand car with no MOT
- **d** When driving to an appointment at an MOT centre

09 To supervise a learner driver you must

mark two answers   *i* p13

- **a** have held a full licence for at least 3 years
- **b** be at least 21 years old
- **c** be an approved driving instructor
- **d** hold an advanced driving certificate

10 The cost of your insurance may be reduced if

mark one answer   *i* p20

- **a** your car is large and powerful
- **b** you are using the car for work purposes
- **c** you have penalty points on your licence
- **d** you are over 25 years old

1 How old must you be to supervise a learner driver?

mark one answer **ℹ** p13

- 18 years old
- 19 years old
- 20 years old
- 21 years old

2 A newly qualified driver must

mark one answer **ℹ** p200

- display green 'L' plates
- not exceed 40 mph for 12 months
- be accompanied on a motorway
- have valid motor insurance

3 What is the legal minimum insurance cover you must have to drive on public roads?

mark one answer **ℹ** p200

- Third party, fire and theft
- Fully comprehensive
- Third party only
- Personal injury cover

4 You have third party insurance. What does this cover?

mark three answers **ℹ** p200

- Damage to your own vehicle
- Damage to your vehicle by fire
- Injury to another person
- Damage to someone's property
- Damage to other vehicles
- Injury to yourself

5 For which TWO of these must you show your motor insurance certificate?

mark two answers **ℹ** p198 **ℹ** p201

- When you are taking your driving test
- When buying or selling a vehicle
- When a police officer asks you for it
- When you are taxing your vehicle
- When having an MOT inspection

16 Vehicle excise duty is often called 'Road Tax' or 'The Tax Disc'. You must

mark one answer **ℹ** p201

- **a** keep it with your registration document
- **b** display it clearly on your vehicle
- **c** keep it concealed safely in your vehicle
- **d** carry it on you at all times

17 Motor cars must FIRST have an MOT test certificate when they are

mark one answer **ℹ** p201

- **a** one year old
- **b** three years old
- **c** five years old
- **d** seven years old

18 Your vehicle needs a current MOT certificate. You do not have one. Until you do have one you will not be able to renew your

mark one answer **ℹ** p201

- **a** driving licence
- **b** vehicle insurance
- **c** road tax disc
- **d** vehicle registration document

19 Which THREE pieces of information are found on a vehicle registration document?

mark three answers **ℹ** p199

- **a** Registered keeper
- **b** Make of the vehicle
- **c** Service history details
- **d** Date of the MOT
- **e** Type of insurance cover
- **f** Engine size

20 You have a duty to contact the licensing authority when

mark three answers **ℹ** p199

- **a** you go abroad on holiday
- **b** you change your vehicle
- **c** you change your name
- **d** your job status is changed
- **e** your permanent address changes
- **f** your job involves travelling abroad

ANSWERS

01 c	06 c	11 d	16 b
02 b	07 b	12 d	17 b
03 b	08 d	13 c	18 c
04 b,e	09 a,b	14 c,d,e	19 a,b,f
05 c	10 d	15 c,d	20 b,c,e

21 You must notify the licensing authority when

mark three answers ⓘ p17
- **a** your health affects your driving
- **b** your eyesight does not meet a set ⓘ p199 standard
- **c** you intend lending your vehicle
- **d** your vehicle requires an MOT certificate
- **e** you change your vehicle

22 You have just bought a secondhand vehicle. When should you tell the licensing authority of change of ownership?

mark one answer ⓘ p199
- **a** Immediately
- **b** After 28 days
- **c** When an MOT is due
- **d** Only when you insure it

23 Your vehicle is insured third party only. This covers

mark two answers ⓘ p200
- **a** damage to your vehicle
- **b** damage to other vehicles
- **c** injury to yourself
- **d** injury to others
- **e** all damage and injury

24 Your motor insurance policy has an excess of £100. What does this mean?

mark one answer ⓘ p200
- **a** The insurance company will pay the first £100 of any claim
- **b** You will be paid £100 if you do not have an accident
- **c** Your vehicle is insured for a value of £100 if it is stolen
- **d** You will have to pay the first £100 of any claim

25 When you apply to renew your vehicle excise licence (tax disc) you must produce

mark one answer ⓘ p201
- **a** a valid insurance certificate
- **b** the old tax disc
- **c** the vehicle handbook
- **d** a valid driving licence

26 What is the legal minimum insurance cover you must have to drive on public roads?

mark one answer ⓘ p200
- **a** Fire and theft
- **b** Theft only
- **c** Third party
- **d** Fire only

27 Which THREE of the following do you need before you can drive legally?

mark three answers ⓘ p11
- **a** A valid driving licence with signature
- **b** A valid tax disc displayed on your vehicle
- **c** A vehicle service record
- **d** Proper insurance cover
- **e** Breakdown cover
- **f** A vehicle handbook

28 The cost of your insurance may reduce i̇ you

mark one answer ⓘ p200
- **a** are under 25 years old
- **b** do not wear glasses
- **c** pass the driving test first time
- **d** take the Pass Plus scheme

29 Which of the following may reduce the cost of your insurance?

mark one answer ⓘ p200
- **a** Having a valid MOT certificate
- **b** Taking a Pass Plus course
- **c** Driving a powerful car
- **d** Having penalty points on your licence

30 The Pass Plus scheme has been created fⲟ new drivers. What is its main purpose?

mark one answer ⓘ p253
- **a** To allow you to drive faster
- **b** To allow you to carry passengers
- **c** To improve your basic skills
- **d** To let you drive on motorways

ANSWERS

21 a,b,e	24 d	27 a,b,d	30 c
22 a	25 a	28 d	
23 b,d	26 c	29 b	

ACCIDENTS

1 At the scene of an accident you should

mark one answer **ⓘ p239**

- a not put yourself at risk
- b go to those casualties who are screaming
- c pull everybody out of their vehicles
- d leave vehicle engines switched on

2 You are the first to arrive at the scene of an accident. Which FOUR of these should you do?

mark four answers **ⓘ p239**

- a Leave as soon as another motorist arrives
- b Switch off the vehicle engine(s)
- c Move uninjured people away from the vehicle(s)
- d Call the emergency services
- e Warn other traffic

3 An accident has just happened. An injured person is lying in the busy road. What is the FIRST thing you should do to help?

mark one answer **ⓘ p239**

- a Treat the person for shock
- b Warn other traffic
- c Place them in the recovery position
- d Make sure the injured person is kept warm

4 You are the first person to arrive at an accident where people are badly injured. Which THREE should you do?

mark three answers **ⓘ p239**

- a Switch on your own hazard warning lights
- b Make sure that someone telephones for an ambulance
- c Try and get people who are injured to drink something
- d Move the people who are injured clear of their vehicles
- e Get people who are not injured clear of the scene

5 You arrive at the scene of a motorcycle accident. The rider is injured. When should the helmet be removed?

mark one answer **ⓘ p240**

- a Only when it is essential
- b Always straight away
- c Only when the motorcyclist asks
- d Always, unless they are in shock

6 You arrive at a serious motorcycle accident. The motorcyclist is unconscious and bleeding. Your main priorities should be to

mark three answers **ⓘ p240**

- a try to stop the bleeding
- b make a list of witnesses
- c check the casualty's breathing
- d take the numbers of the vehicles involved
- e sweep up any loose debris
- f check the casualty's airways

7 You arrive at an accident. A motorcyclist is unconscious. Your FIRST priority is the casualty's

mark one answer **ⓘ p240**

- a breathing
- b bleeding
- c broken bones
- d bruising

8 At an accident a casualty is unconscious. Which THREE of the following should you check urgently?

mark three answers **ⓘ p240**

- a Circulation
- b Airway
- c Shock
- d Breathing
- e Broken bones

ANSWERS

01 a	03 b	05 a	07 a
02 b,c,d,e	04 a,b,e	06 a,c,f	08 a,b,d

09 You arrive at the scene of an accident. It has just happened and someone is unconscious. Which of the following should be given urgent priority to help them?

mark three answers ⓘ p240

a Clear the airway and keep it open
b Try to get them to drink water
c Check that they are breathing
d Look for any witnesses
e Stop any heavy bleeding
f Take the numbers of vehicles involved

10 At an accident someone is unconscious. Your main priorities should be to

mark three answers ⓘ p240

a sweep up the broken glass
b take the names of witnesses
c count the number of vehicles involved
d check the airway is clear
e make sure they are breathing
f stop any heavy bleeding

11 You have stopped at the scene of an accident to give help. Which THREE things should you do?

mark three answers ⓘ p240

a Keep injured people warm and comfortable
b Keep injured people calm by talking to them reassuringly
c Keep injured people on the move by walking them around
d Give injured people a warm drink
e Make sure that injured people are not left alone

12 You arrive at the scene of an accident. It has just happened and someone is injured. Which THREE of the following should be given urgent priority?

mark three answers ⓘ p240

a Stop any severe bleeding
b Get them a warm drink
c Check that their breathing is OK
d Take numbers of vehicles involved
e Look for witnesses
f Clear their airway and keep it open

13 At an accident a casualty has stopped breathing. You should

mark two answers ⓘ p240

a remove anything that is blocking the mouth
b keep the head tilted forwards as far as possibl[e]
c raise the legs to help with circulation
d try to give the casualty something to drink
e tilt the head back gently to clear the airway

14 You are at the scene of an accident. Someone is suffering from shock. You should

mark four answers ⓘ p240

a reassure them constantly
b offer them a cigarette
c keep them warm
d avoid moving them if possible
e avoid leaving them alone
f give them a warm drink

15 Which of the following should you NOT do at the scene of an accident?

mark one answer ⓘ p240

a Warn other traffic by switching on your hazard warning lights
b Call the emergency services immediately
c Offer someone a cigarette to calm them dow[n]
d Ask drivers to switch off their engines

16 There has been an accident. The driver i[s] suffering from shock. You should

mark two answers ⓘ p240

a give them a drink
b reassure them
c not leave them alone
d offer them a cigarette
e ask who caused the accident

17 You are at the scene of an accident. Someone is suffering from shock. You should

mark three answers ⓘ p24[0]

a offer them a cigarette
b offer them a warm drink
c keep them warm
d loosen any tight clothing
e reassure them constantly

18 You have to treat someone for shock at the scene of an accident. You should

mark one answer ⓘ p240
a reassure them constantly
b walk them around to calm them down
c give them something cold to drink
d cool them down as soon as possible

19 You arrive at the scene of a motorcycle accident. No other vehicle is involved. The rider is unconscious, lying in the middle of the road. The first thing you should do is

mark one answer ⓘ p239
a move the rider out of the road
b warn other traffic
c clear the road of debris
d give the rider reassurance

20 At an accident a small child is not breathing. When giving mouth to mouth you should breathe

mark one answer ⓘ p240
a sharply
b gently
c heavily
d rapidly

21 To start mouth to mouth on a casualty you should

mark three answers ⓘ p240
a tilt their head forward
b clear the airway
c turn them on their side
d tilt their head back gently
e pinch the nostrils together
f put their arms across their chest

22 When you are giving mouth to mouth you should only stop when

mark one answer ⓘ p240
a you think the casualty is dead
b the casualty can breathe without help
c the casualty has turned blue
d you think the ambulance is coming

23 You arrive at the scene of an accident. There has been an engine fire and someone's hands and arms have been burnt. You should NOT

mark one answer ⓘ p240
a douse the burn thoroughly with cool liquid
b lay the casualty down
c remove anything sticking to the burn
d reassure them constantly

24 You arrive at an accident where someone is suffering from severe burns. You should

mark one answer ⓘ p240
a apply lotions to the injury
b burst any blisters
c remove anything stuck to the burns
d douse the burns with cool liquid

25 You arrive at the scene of an accident. A pedestrian has a severe bleeding wound on their leg, although it is not broken. What should you do?

mark two answers ⓘ p240
a Dab the wound to stop bleeding
b Keep both legs flat on the ground
c Apply firm pressure to the wound
d Raise the leg to lessen bleeding
e Fetch them a warm drink

26 You arrive at the scene of an accident. A passenger is bleeding badly from an arm wound. What should you do?

mark one answer ⓘ p240
a Apply pressure over the wound and keep the arm down
b Dab the wound
c Get them a drink
d Apply pressure over the wound and raise the arm

ANSWERS

09 a,c,e	14 a,c,d,e	19 b	24 d
10 d,e,f	15 c	20 b	25 c,d
11 a,b,e	16 b,c	21 b,d,e	26 d
12 a,c,f	17 c,d,e	22 b	
13 a,e	18 a	23 c	

27 You arrive at the scene of an accident. A pedestrian is bleeding heavily from a leg wound but the leg is not broken. What should you do?

mark one answer 🛈 p240

- **a** Dab the wound to stop the bleeding
- **b** Keep both legs flat on the ground
- **c** Apply firm pressure to the wound
- **d** Fetch them a warm drink

28 At an accident a casualty is unconscious but still breathing. You should only move them if

mark one answer 🛈 p240

- **a** an ambulance is on its way
- **b** bystanders advise you to
- **c** there is further danger
- **d** bystanders will help you to

29 At an accident you suspect a casualty has back injuries. The area is safe. You should

mark one answer 🛈 p240

- **a** offer them a drink
- **b** not move them
- **c** raise their legs
- **d** offer them a cigarette

30 At an accident it is important to look after the casualty. When the area is safe, you should

mark one answer 🛈 p240

- **a** get them out of the vehicle
- **b** give them a drink
- **c** give them something to eat
- **d** keep them in the vehicle

31 A tanker is involved in an accident. Which sign would show that the tanker is carrying dangerous goods?

mark one answer 🛈 p241

a   **b**

c   **d**

32 The police may ask you to produce which three of these documents following an accident?

mark three answers 🛈 p198

- **a** Vehicle registration document
- **b** Driving licence
- **c** Theory test certificate
- **d** Insurance certificate
- **e** MOT test certificate
- **f** Road tax disc

33 At a railway level crossing the red light signal continues to flash after a train has gone by. What should you do?

mark one answer 🛈 p161

- **a** Phone the signal operator
- **b** Alert drivers behind you
- **c** Wait
- **d** Proceed with caution

34 You see a car on the hard shoulder of a motorway with a HELP pennant displayed. This means the driver is most likely to be

mark one answer 🛈 p237

- **a** a disabled person
- **b** first aid trained
- **c** a foreign visitor
- **d** a rescue patrol person

35 On the motorway the hard shoulder should be used

mark one answer 🛈 p121

- **a** to answer a mobile phone
- **b** when an emergency arises
- **c** for a short rest when tired
- **d** to check a road atlas

36 For which TWO should you use hazard warning lights?

mark two answers 🛈 p58

- **a** When you slow down quickly on a motorway because of a hazard ahead
- **b** When you have broken down
- **c** When you wish to stop on double yellow line
- **d** When you need to park on the pavement

37 When are you allowed to use hazard warning lights?

mark one answer ⓘ p58

a When stopped and temporarily obstructing traffic

b When travelling during darkness without headlights

c When parked for shopping on double yellow lines

d When travelling slowly because you are lost

38 You are on a motorway. A large box falls onto the road from a lorry. The lorry does not stop. You should

mark one answer ⓘ p211

a go to the next emergency telephone and inform the police

b catch up with the lorry and try to get the driver's attention

c stop close to the box until the police arrive

d pull over to the hard shoulder, then remove the box

39 There has been an accident. A motorcyclist is lying injured and unconscious. Why should you usually not attempt to remove their helmet?

mark one answer ⓘ p240

a Because they may not want you to

b This could result in more serious injury

c They will get too cold if you do this

d Because you could scratch the helmet

40 After an accident, someone is unconscious in their vehicle. When should you call the emergency services?

mark one answer ⓘ p239

a Only as a last resort

b As soon as possible

c After you have woken them up

d After checking for broken bones

41 An accident casualty has an injured arm. They can move it freely, but it is bleeding. Why should you get them to keep it in a raised position?

mark one answer ⓘ p240

a Because it will ease the pain

b It will help them to be seen more easily

c To stop them touching other people

d It will help to reduce the bleeding

42 You are going through a congested tunnel and have to stop. What should you do?

mark one answer ⓘ p237

a Pull up very close to the vehicle in front to save space

b Ignore any message signs as they are never up to date

c Keep a safe distance from the vehicle in front

d Make a U-turn and find another route

43 You are going through a tunnel. What should you look out for that warns of accidents or congestion?

mark one answer ⓘ p237

a Hazard warning lines

b Other drivers flashing their lights

c Variable message signs

d Areas marked with hatch markings

44 You are going through a tunnel. What systems are provided to warn of any accidents or congestion?

mark one answer ⓘ p237

a Double white centre lines

b Variable message signs

c Chevron 'distance markers'

d Rumble strips

45 While driving, a warning light on your vehicle's instrument panel comes on. You should

mark one answer ⓘ p22

a continue if the engine sounds alright

b hope that it is just a temporary electrical fault

c deal with the problem when there is more time

d check out the problem quickly and safely

ANSWERS

27 c	32 b,d,e	37 a	42 c
28 c	33 c	38 a	43 c
29 b	34 a	39 b	44 b
30 d	35 b	40 b	45 d
31 b	36 a,b	41 d	

46 You have broken down on a two-way road. You have a warning triangle. You should place the warning triangle at least how far from your vehicle?

mark one answer *i* p235
- **a** 5 metres (16 feet)
- **b** 25 metres (82 feet)
- **c** 45 metres (147 feet)
- **d** 100 metres (328 feet)

47 You break down on a level crossing. The lights have not yet begun to flash. Which THREE things should you do?

mark three answers *i* p161
- **a** Telephone the signal operator
- **b** Leave your vehicle and get everyone clear
- **c** Walk down the track and signal the next train
- **d** Move the vehicle if a signal operator tells you to
- **e** Tell drivers behind what has happened

48 Your vehicle has broken down on an automatic railway level crossing. What should you do FIRST?

mark one answer *i* p161
- **a** Get everyone out of the vehicle and clear of the crossing
- **b** Phone the signal operator so that trains can be stopped
- **c** Walk along the track to give warning to any approaching trains
- **d** Try to push the vehicle clear of the crossing as soon as possible

49 Your tyre bursts while you are driving. Which TWO things should you do?

mark two answers *i* p235
- **a** Pull on the handbrake
- **b** Brake as quickly as possible
- **c** Pull up slowly at the side of the road
- **d** Hold the steering wheel firmly to keep control
- **e** Continue on at a normal speed

50 Which TWO things should you do when a front tyre bursts?

mark two answers *i* p235
- **a** Apply the handbrake to stop the vehicle
- **b** Brake firmly and quickly
- **c** Let the vehicle roll to a stop
- **d** Hold the steering wheel lightly
- **e** Grip the steering wheel firmly

51 Your vehicle has a puncture on a motorway. What should you do?

mark one answer *i* p236
- **a** Drive slowly to the next service area to get assistance
- **b** Pull up on the hard shoulder. Change the wheel as quickly as possible
- **c** Pull up on the hard shoulder. Use the emergency phone to get assistance
- **d** Switch on your hazard lights. Stop in your lane

52 Which of these items should you carry in your vehicle for use in the event of an accident?

mark three answers *i* p234 *i* p238
- **a** Road map
- **b** Can of petrol
- **c** Jump leads
- **d** Fire extinguisher
- **e** First Aid kit
- **f** Warning triangle

53 You are in an accident on a two way road. You have a warning triangle with you. At what distance before the obstruction should you place the warning triangle?

mark one answer *i* p235
- **a** 25 metres (82 feet)
- **b** 45 metres (147 feet)
- **c** 100 metres (328 feet)
- **d** 150 metres (492 feet)

54 You have broken down on a two way road. You have a warning triangle. It should be displayed

mark one answer **ⓘ p235**
a on the roof of your vehicle
b at least 150 metres (492 feet) behind your vehicle
c at least 45 metres (147 feet) behind your vehicle
d just behind your vehicle

55 You have stalled in the middle of a level crossing and cannot restart the engine. The warning bell starts to ring. You should

mark one answer **ⓘ p161**
a get out and clear of the crossing
b run down the track to warn the signal operator
c carry on trying to restart the engine
d push the vehicle clear of the crossing

56 You are on the motorway. Luggage falls from your vehicle. What should you do?

mark one answer **ⓘ p211**
a Stop at the next emergency telephone and contact the police
b Stop on the motorway and put on hazard lights whilst you pick it up
c Walk back up the motorway to pick it up
d Pull up on the hard shoulder and wave traffic down

57 You are on a motorway. When can you use hazard warning lights?

mark two answers **ⓘ p58**
a When a vehicle is following too closely
b When you slow down quickly because of danger ahead
c When you are towing another vehicle
d When driving on the hard shoulder
e When you have broken down on the hard shoulder

58 You are involved in an accident with another vehicle. Someone is injured. Your vehicle is damaged. Which FOUR of the following should you find out?

mark four answers **ⓘ p239**
a Whether the driver owns the other vehicle involved
b The other driver's name, address and telephone number
c The make and registration number of the other vehicle
d The occupation of the other driver
e The details of the other driver's vehicle insurance
f Whether the other driver is licensed to drive

59 You have broken down on a motorway. When you use the emergency telephone you will be asked

mark three answers **ⓘ p236**
a for the number on the telephone that you are using
b for your driving licence details
c for the name of your vehicle insurance company
d for details of yourself and your vehicle
e whether you belong to a motoring organisation

60 You lose control of your car and damage a garden wall. No one is around. What must you do?

mark one answer **ⓘ p239**
a Report the accident to the police within 24 hours
b Go back to tell the house owner the next day
c Report the accident to your insurance company when you get home
d Find someone in the area to tell them about it immediately

ANSWERS			
46 c	50 c,e	54 c	58 a,b,c,e
47 a,b,d	51 c	55 a	59 a,d,e
48 a	52 d,e,f	56 a	60 a
49 c,d	53 b	57 b,e	

61 Your engine catches fire. What should you do first?

mark one answer *ⓘ* p235

- **a** Lift the bonnet and disconnect the battery
- **b** Lift the bonnet and warn other traffic
- **c** Call the breakdown service
- **d** Call the fire brigade

62 Before driving through a tunnel what should you do?

mark one answer *ⓘ* p237

- **a** Switch your radio off
- **b** Remove any sunglasses
- **c** Close your sunroof
- **d** Switch on windscreen wipers

63 You are driving through a tunnel and the traffic is flowing normally. What should you do?

mark one answer *ⓘ* p237

- **a** Use parking lights
- **b** Use front spot lights
- **c** Use dipped headlights
- **d** Use rear fog lights

64 Before entering a tunnel it is good advice to

mark one answer *ⓘ* p237

- **a** put on your sunglasses
- **b** check tyre pressures
- **c** change to a lower gear
- **d** tune your radio to a local channel

65 You are driving through a tunnel. Your vehicle breaks down. What should you do?

mark one answer *ⓘ* p237

- **a** Switch on hazard warning lights
- **b** Remain in your vehicle
- **c** Wait for the police to find you
- **d** Rely on CCTV cameras seeing you

66 Your vehicle breaks down in a tunnel. What should you do?

mark one answer *ⓘ* p237

- **a** Stay in your vehicle and wait for the Police
- **b** Stand in the lane behind your vehicle to warn others
- **c** Stand in front of your vehicle to warn oncoming drivers
- **d** Switch on hazard lights then go and call for help immediately

67 You have an accident while driving through a tunnel. You are not injured but your vehicle cannot be driven. What should you do first?

mark one answer *ⓘ* p237

- **a** Rely on other drivers phoning for the Police
- **b** Switch off the engine and switch on hazard lights
- **c** Take the names of witnesses and other drivers
- **d** Sweep up any debris that is in the road

68 When driving through a tunnel you should

mark one answer *ⓘ* p237

- **a** Look out for variable message signs
- **b** Use your air conditioning system
- **c** Switch on your rear fog lights
- **d** Always use your windscreen wipers

69 What TWO safeguards could you take against fire risk to your vehicle?

mark two answers *ⓘ* p235

- **a** Keep water levels above maximum
- **b** Carry a fire extinguisher
- **c** Avoid driving with a full tank of petrol
- **d** Use unleaded petrol
- **e** Check out any strong smell of petrol
- **f** Use low octane fuel

ANSWERS

61 d	64 d	67 b
62 b	65 a	68 a
63 c	66 d	69 b,e

15

VEHICLE LOADING

01 You are towing a small trailer on a busy three-lane motorway. All the lanes are open. You must

mark two answers   *ⓘ* p213

- **a** not exceed 60 mph
- **b** not overtake
- **c** have a stabiliser fitted
- **d** use only the left and centre lanes

02 Any load that is carried on a roof rack MUST be

mark one answer   *ⓘ* p211

- **a** securely fastened when driving
- **b** carried only when strictly necessary
- **c** as light as possible
- **d** covered with plastic sheeting

03 You are planning to tow a caravan. Which of these will mostly help to aid the vehicle handling?

mark one answer   *ⓘ* p213

- **a** A jockey-wheel fitted to the towbar
- **b** Power steering fitted to the towing vehicle
- **c** Anti-lock brakes fitted to the towing vehicle
- **d** A stabiliser fitted to the towbar

04 If a trailer swerves or snakes when you are towing it you should

mark one answer   *ⓘ* p213

- **a** ease off the accelerator and reduce your speed
- **b** let go of the steering wheel and let it correct itself
- **c** brake hard and hold the pedal down
- **d** increase your speed as quickly as possible

05 How can you stop a caravan snaking from side to side?

mark one answer   *ⓘ* p213

- **a** Turn the steering wheel slowly to each side
- **b** Accelerate to increase your speed
- **c** Stop as quickly as you can
- **d** Slow down very gradually

06 On which TWO occasions might you inflate your tyres to more than the recommended normal pressure?

mark two answers   *ⓘ* p211

- **a** When the roads are slippery
- **b** When driving fast for a long distance
- **c** When the tyre tread is worn below 2mm
- **d** When carrying a heavy load
- **e** When the weather is cold
- **f** When the vehicle is fitted with anti-lock brakes

07 A heavy load on your roof rack will

mark one answer   *ⓘ* p211

- **a** improve the road holding
- **b** reduce the stopping distance
- **c** make the steering lighter
- **d** reduce stability

08 Are passengers allowed to ride in a caravan that is being towed?

mark one answer   *ⓘ* p213

- **a** Yes, if they are over fourteen
- **b** No, not at any time
- **c** Only if all the seats in the towing vehicle are full
- **d** Only if a stabiliser is fitted

09 You are towing a caravan along a motorway. The caravan begins to swerve from side to side. What should you do?

mark one answer   *ⓘ* p213

- **a** Ease off the accelerator slowly
- **b** Steer sharply from side to side
- **c** Do an emergency stop
- **d** Speed up very quickly

ANSWERS

01 a,d	04 a	07 d
02 a	05 d	08 b
03 d	06 b,d	09 a

10 A trailer must stay securely hitched-up to the towing vehicle. What additional safety device can be fitted to the trailer braking system?

mark one answer   **ⓘ p212**

a Stabiliser
b Jockey wheel
c Corner steadies
d Breakaway cable

11 Overloading your vehicle can seriously affect the

mark two answers   **ⓘ p211**

a gearbox
b steering
c handling
d battery life
e journey time

12 Who is responsible for making sure that a vehicle is not overloaded?

mark one answer   **ⓘ p211**

a The driver of the vehicle
b The owner of the items being carried
c The person who loaded the vehicle
d The licensing authority

13 Which of these is a suitable restraint for a child under three years?

mark one answer   **ⓘ p233**

a A child seat
b An adult holding a child
c An adult seat belt
d A lap belt

14 A child under three years is being carried in your vehicle. They should be secured in a restraint. Which of these is suitable?

mark one answer   **ⓘ p233**

a An adult holding a child
b A lap belt
c A baby carrier
d An adult seat belt

ANSWERS

10 d	12 a	14 c
11 b,c	13 a	

R

S

LEARN TO DRIVE

ACKNOWLEDGEMENTS

Author	Robert Davies
Project Manager	Louise McIntyre
Design	Simon Larkin
Technical Advisors	John Farlam
	Jason Youé
Photographer	Simon Clay
Learner Driver	Gillian Franks

Photo credits:

Alvey & Towers	p23, 152
Robert Davies	p15 (top right)
	p17 (top left)
	p61 (bottom right)
	p124, 220
Freefoto.com	p162, 187, 224, 241
Getty Images	p238
Bob Langrish	p146, 147
Richard Sowersby	p240
Neil Atkinson	
Tramlink Croydon Ltd	p158, 159

The author and publishers would like to thank the Gryphon School in Sherborne for their help with market research for this title.